PHENOMENOLOGY AND PSYCHOLOGICAL RESEARCH

Phenomenology and Psychological Research

Edited and with an introduction by Amedeo Giorgi

Essays by Christopher Aanstoos, William F. Fischer, Amedeo Giorgi, and Frederick J. Wertz.

DUQUESNE UNIVERSITY PRESS
PITTSBURGH, PA

Published by:
Duquesne University Press
600 Forbes Ave.
Pittsburgh, PA 15282

Library of Congress Cataloging in Publication Data
Main entry under title:
Phenomenology and psychological research.

Bibliography: p.
Contents: Sketch of a psychological phenomenological method / Amedeo Giorgi—The phenomenological psychology of learning and the verbal learning tradition / Amedeo Giorgi—The structure of thinking in chess playing / Christopher M. Aanstoos—[etc.]
1. Phenomenological psychology—Addresses, essays, lectures. 2. Psychology—Research—Addresses, essays, lectures. I. Giorgi, Amedeo, 1931-
BF204.5.P49 1985 150.19'2 84-21168
ISBN 0-8207-0174-2

Printed in the United States of America

Eighth Printing - December 1999

CONTENTS

Editor's Preface

IT would be realistic to assume that the expression "scientific research" would quickly bring the association "incontrovertible fact" to the minds of members of a scientific community. Indeed, science's main claim to fame is that it has the means to establish irrefutable facts, and it has a rich and successful tradition of establishing and building upon such solid facts. It is well known, however, that this tradition began and continues to be most successful with the phenomena of nature, but the application of the same procedures and mentality to human phenomena has met with only partial success. Some take this partial success to be a sign that more of the same, with proper modifications, will lead to the same success as the natural sciences enjoy. Others note the same partial success and interpret it to mean that a radical shift of perspective is necessary to do justice to human phenomena. The research findings presented in this book are inspired by the latter attitude.

The articles in this volume exemplify primarily a phenomenological psychological method for doing research on human phenomena as lived and experienced. As such they exemplify what is often taken to be paradoxical: a rigorous attitude toward soft phenomena. On the surface, it would seem that the acceptance of descriptions as raw data would have to exclude a scientific analysis—at any rate, this reaction is typical of one trained in the scientific tradition, and it was certainly my first reaction as well. Descriptions seem to be propaedeutic or auxiliary to science, not the very stuff of science. But once one goes beyond the surface and begins to probe more deeply, it is no longer so obvious that one cannot work with descriptions rigorously and systematically, especially if one operates within a phenomenological theory of science. My own change of attitude on this issue occurred as follows.

My attraction to the study of psychology was always along the lines of theory and research. I was trained as an experimental psychologist specializing in psychophysics. This training is an important part of my background and was valuable in many respects, but was disappointing in one major way: Where rigor and precision were best, the phenomena seemed to be on the fringe of psychology, and where interest in psychological matters was strongest, especially when dealing with human phenomena, rigor and precision seemed weakest. I began to concern myself with this state of affairs even as a graduate student and gradually came to the conclusion that psychologists would have to find another way of being rigorous and precise with more complex human phenomena. That is, the general ideals of percision and rigor were affirmed, but wholly new definitions of them would have to come about in order to deal with human phenomena adequately, and this led to the conviction that the best way to approach this problem was to examine very carefully the complex human phenomena themselves.

I was in this open-ended state of search and expectancy for about five years when I became aware of phenomenology. After questioning, probing, reading, and testing I began to sense a way out of the difficulties. Perhaps in phenomenological thought, and its existential variations, one could find the foundational framework that would enable psychologists to study in a genuinely scientific way the complex processes of human psychological phenomena. The major philosophers of this movement have always respected the complexity and richness of human reality, and they developed concepts and categories that tried to describe that complexity in the most penetrating way. Perhaps situating oneself within that framework could be the answer to the difficulties I perceived with the theoretical and research tradition in psychology.

After arriving at Duquesne University in September 1962, I sat in numerous courses on philosophical phenomenology, participated in many seminars and discussions concerning the fine points of phenomenological interpretation with my departmental colleagues as well as with philosophers and scientists from the United States and Europe. I satisfied myself that the development of this line of reasoning could indeed make a significant contribution to psychology without having to posit that phenomenology had to or could do everything. What it promised was an access to human phenomena that led to findings and discoveries that were not captured by other approaches. At the very least, then, a phenomenological psychology could offer complementary insights and perhaps even more, once the full impact of its promissory but undeveloped potential was elaborated.

After having shown, at least to myself, why psychology might be better off conceived as a human science (Giorgi, 1970), I took on the problem of the research praxis. In September 1970 I offered for the first time a course in Qualitative Research in the psychology department at Duquesne University. There was no text, and the only guidelines the students and I had was Husserl's dictum, "Back to the things themselves." The "things" the students elected to investigate that year were feelings and emotions. We obtained descriptions from various friends and neighbors, and we proceeded to try to analyze them qualitatively, systematically, and rigorously. The method presented here is what emerged from that and subsequent courses.

Since that time colleagues and students at Duquesne as well as visitors and colleagues at other institutions have all applied the basic strategy with many variations, and it seems to me that the basic method is sound. I can still affirm that it would be good for psychology as a whole to have such a method available in its storehouse of scientific methods. However, it should be noted that much more work, both theoretical and practical, will have to be done before I feel fully satisfied that all problems and complications have been worked out. Indeed, my own estimation is that only about one-tenth, at best, of what has to be achieved has been achieved. The rest still has to be worked through. I can honestly state that there has been a radical transformation on my understanding between 1970 and today, and I have to assume that an equally radical change may ensue between today and, say, 1990, but I know of no way of getting there other than by working at it.

A major difficulty, of course, is that the living work and thinking is ahead of what has been published. Indeed, only one minor publication has appeared thus far (Giorgi, 1975), and that was merely a brief example reflecting a mode of research that is no longer practiced exactly as presented. Thus, this work will fill in an important gap, but it is still an intermediate step. Not all theoretical and practical problems have been answered although what is presented here is a big step over what was available before. Primarily this work demonstrates how the method can be applied to several different content areas. A book explaining the various steps in detail along with extended theoretical justifications, however, is in progress.

When Ebbinghaus (1964/1885) first published the method of memory investigation he employed, as well as the results of his investigations on memory, he wrote in preface (p.xiii):

> The author will be pardoned the publication or preliminary results in view of the difficulty of the subject investigated and the time-consuming character of the tests. Justice demands that the many defects due to incompleteness shall not be raised as objections against such results.

I can only share and echo Ebbinghaus's statements. Certainly criticism should be leveled where warranted, but what is incomplete should not be made into "in principle" objections to the method itself.

A.G.

References

Ebbinghaus, H. (1964/1885). *Memory* (Trans. H. Ruger and C. Bussenius) N.Y., Dover. (German original, 1885).

Giorgi, A. (1970). *Psychology as a human science* New York: Harper & Row.

Giorgi, A. (1975). An application of the phenomenological method in psychology. In A. Giorgi, C. Fischer, & E. Murray (Eds.) *Duquesne studies in phenomenological psychology II*. Pittsburgh, PA: Duquesne University Press. 82–103.

Introduction

WHAT is being attempted in the following pages is a direct analysis of the psychological meaning of naive descriptions of personal experiences provided by individuals from all walks of life in situations that are easily recognizable as belonging to everyday life. Since all psychologists, at least chronologically, were or are first and foremost human beings living the everyday world, they are not foreign to the kind of experiences being provided by the subjects, granted relative social and cultural stability. Such things as jealousy, depression, learning, thinking, anger, attending, aggression, dishonesty, hostility, caring, and others are phenomena both individually experienced and perceived in others at one time or another. In everyday life, of course, certain sedimented and practical ways of perceiving, understanding, and dealing with such phenomena are developed, but these pragmatic modes of coping do not have the clarity, precision, or systematization that one expects of a scientific perspective. Nor are they necessarily completely nor exclusively psychological as they are lived although psychological aspects are almost always included. Hence, it is not unreasonable to assume that the science of psychology would want to understand these everyday phenomena in its own terms and in a more precise way. Since its commitment to become a natural science, psychology has primarily (obviously, with historical exceptions) attempted to gain this precision and systematization with either a laboratory setting or one type of quantitative measurement or another. In doing so, we believe that many important aspects of these phenomena *as lived and experienced* were either overlooked or severely distorted because the methods of the natural sciences were invented primarily to deal with phenomena of nature and not experienced phenomena. Consequently, the purpose of the method being developed and exemplified here is to do justice to the lived aspects of human phenomena, and to do so, one first has to know how someone actually experienced what has been lived. This means that a description becomes necessary when it is possible to get one. (Without descriptions of experiences, one has to turn to indirect methods, but these cannot be pursued here.)

As such, the efforts presented in this volume are best interpreted or understood as belonging to the tradition of "Descriptive Psychology". Again, we cannot present the history of this tradition here, but we can point out that the idea of descriptive psychology goes at least as far back as Dilthey (1977/1894) and that it was mentioned and spoken for by Brentano (1973/1874), Husserl (1970/1900), Ladd (1894), Wundt (1973/1911), Thorndike (1907), and Titchener (1912), among others. Prior to this explicit late nineteenth century articulation, almost all of the work done under the heading of "philosophical psychology" (for example, Aristotle, Descartes, Christian Wolff, Immanuel Kant, and others) was also descriptive in nature. Somewhere in the early part of this century it seems that descriptive psychology became identified with introspectionism, and when the latter went out of vogue, descriptive approaches seemed to phase out as well. At least they seemed to disappear under that name but as Boring (1953) suggested, it may be that the contributions of introspectionism, or even of descriptive psychology, have continued as "verbal reports." In any event, the awareness that at least a descriptive phase of research, if not an explicit recognition that the role of descriptive psychology should be made explicit and thematized, seems to be coming to the fore again (for example, Torbert (1972); Ericsson & Simon (1980); Moustgaard (1981; 1982)). Thus, even though the specific orientation of the articles contained in this volume is phenomenological, the overall perspective is descriptive psychology, and it is with such trends as those mentioned above that it seeks to place itself. Phenomenology is but one theory of treating descriptions.

While there are still many unsolved problems surrounding the use of descriptions in psychological research, the overall assumption of this volume, supported somewhat by about a dozen years' experience, is that a qualitative analysis of descriptions can yield psychological insight of a value at least equal to what quantitative approaches yield, although different in character and style. The major difficulty in its acceptance seems to be the fact that it seems to be too straightforward, too facile. A description seems to be such a flimsy thing upon which to base a science. But if one reflects for a moment, it can be seen that descriptions actually pervade science. Articles containing verbal descriptive results pervade the major psychological journals in the early part of this century (check for example, the first twenty volumes of the *American Journal of Psychology*), interpretation and discussion sections of scientific articles communicate their ideas through written langauge and the apparatus and method sections of all scientific reports are descriptions intended to be so precise that anyone reading them is meant to be able to replicate the experiment. Instructions are given to subjects through language, whether written or oral, and very frequently pilot studies are conducted prior to experimentation in which postpiloting interviews are conducted that are critical for setting up the actual experiment. All of these interviews presuppose information that is communicated linguistically. Moreover, other aspects of psychology are even more dependent upon descriptions. For example, most therapies consist basically of descriptions: Clients talk about their worlds, their problems, their relationships with others, their dreams, their hopes, anxieties, and so on. Questionnaires and surveys, even if they only require a check mark, are entirely dependent upon linguistic communication. Thus, descriptions have pervaded, and continue to pervade, psychology. But it seems that when they are brought to the fore and explicitly acknowledged as raw data, or especially as the primary findings, objections abound. Moreover, so disparate and numerous are the objections that to try to handle them all within a single work is like trying to slay the Hydra—for every question answered, two or more arise. Obviously, one has to go about this task one step at a time.

Consequently, this work is not an *ultimate* justification for a descriptive psychology. Actually, it primarily speaks to those who already are convinced that there is some value in descriptions. Surely, one can lie or even honestly distort in a descriptive communication, but one can also lie behaviorally or else perform in a lackadaisical way; yet these objections are not brought against behaviorists. Thus, the assumption is that, even if there are some problems with descriptions (and there can be!), they can be corrected with other descriptions. In other words, just as poor or false perceptions can be corrected by better or true perceptions, so too can inadequate descriptions be replaced by more adequate ones. Thus, the real question is what makes an adequate description as opposed to an inadequate one. But, if this is the case, it means that the issue is an *intra-descriptive one* and not a matter of turning away from descriptions for something better. That descriptions can work at least part of the time is attested to by everyday life as well as by science itself as we have already indicated.

Thus, in attempting to come back to the frame of reference of descriptive psychology, the primary issue did not so much seem to be the fruitfulness of descriptions (whatever the problems) as what one does after the descriptions are obtained. The major obstacle seemed to be the post-descriptive analysis, especially from a qualitative perspective. Consequently, if a procedure could not be worked out, it initially would not be necessary to worry about good or bad descriptions. The next chapter in this volume specifies the procedure arrived at and the subsequent chapters, in varying ways, indicate the types of findings that can be expected from the application of a qualitative method to descriptions. It should be emphasized, however, that this is only one way, out of many possible ways, depending especially upon the type of phenomenon being researched and the interests of the investigator, that a qualitative analysis can be done. Even then, as the subsequent chapters show, many variations within a fundamental methodical concept are possible.

We mentioned above that this fits primarily within the context of descriptive psychology, and that is true, but we also said that its specific orientation was phenomenological. This point is important because the concept of descriptive psychology is much broader than that of phenomenological psychology, and it is the criteria of the latter that we are trying to meet. Thus the method being developed is meeting more severe criteria than merely scientific criteria: It is trying to approach psychological subject matter with the criteria of science in a phenomenological way. This particular aim, at the concrete level at which it is being done, is what makes the effort unique. Certainly, philosophical phenomenological analyses, even on traditional psychological content—such as Sartre (1962/1936; 1962/1939; 1966/1940) on emotions and imagination—have been done, but these efforts are usually very foundational and in the service of a philosophical project rather than a psychological one. The results of such analyses are usually highly universal essences or structures that are presupposed by psychologists rather than thematized by them. Psychological analyses explore and probe the same phenomena at a more concrete level even while trying to remain faithful to phenomenological criteria. There are no universally accepted models for such analyses and that is why the difficulties in communication are so numerous, both with philosophers and scientists.

With hindsight, it is possible to mention at least three general problem areas that make communication with those unfamiliar with scientific, phenomenological qualitative methods difficult. These difficulties are: (1) problems arising because of a lack of history, (2) problems due to the lack of a clear sense of psychological phenomenology as opposed to philosophical phenomenology, and (3) problems relating to the question of "face validity."

The major difficulty with beginning the development of a method without historical precedent is that every problem becomes a foundational one that has to be worked through from scratch. Very few precedents have been established and there is a tendency to make every step a model when in fact it is merely a probe. The problems of premature codification are as large as those of inventing strategies that are fruitful. Equally problematic when operating within a new vision is that all phases of the research presuppose each other, and yet one can only work on one at a time. Thus, one should be able to speak, first, to all of the factors involved in getting a description; second, what one has to do to go beyond the description; and third, how to do subsequent research. Our emphasis thus far has been merely on the middle phase (the most crucial one in our view), but clearly much detailed work has to be done in the other two phases as well. Of course, such work is contemplated, but it will take much effort on the part of a community of scholars to accomplish all that has to be done.

We have been emphasizing a lack of history, but of course this has to be clearly understood. Phenomenology, as a movement, has been in existence since at least 1900, and psychology since 1879, but they haven't really ever gotten together in a proper way before. Phenomenology has been a philosophy and psychology a natural science. This is what we mean by our second difficulty. Psychological phenomenology will probably have to break away from philosophical phenomenology in the same way as psychology differentiated itself from philosophy in general. I would say that a genuine phenomenological psychology does not yet exist in the sense of a community of psychological scholars who share research interests and strategies with a tradition in the same sense as, say, the verbal learning tradition or the psychoanalytic movement despite their controversies and heresies. Just why this does not yet exist is hard to say in full, but in my opinion, a large part of it results from the fact that phenomenology is understood primarily as a philosophy (which it is) which has *implications for psychology* rather than actually developing into a phenomenological psychology. Only the latter development will be able to make the impact on psychology that we are seeking. A genuine phenomenological psychology will have to be defined along with the development of a phenomenological psychological research practice.

The last difficulty we mentioned was that of face validity which relates to psychology as a natural science. A major obstacle in the communication of this method to psychological colleagues is that it does not appear to be scientific. After all, no measurement is used, no computers or other apparatus are employed, one deals only with meanings, and aren't they always subjective? At best, the method may be useful for some preparatory work, but surely it cannot pass for actual science. Well, in our opinion it does represent an example of the practice of human science, if not natural science.

One cannot help but notice that there is a lopsided development in the realm of psychological methods. Psychology is ultra-sophisticated with respect to progress in quantitative methods. But the best options we have for qualitative penetration of phenomena is to transform the qualitative question into a quantitative scale. Certainly this approach enjoys a limited success, but aren't other procedures available? If not, why not? Before accepting the position that no other options were possible, it was important to see whether such a decision was indeed the only possible one. The critical question is the following one: Does it ever make sense in psychology to pose a qualitative question? For example, is it meaningful to ask *why* a person is anxious as well as how often or how intensely? Is it meaningful to ask *why* learning took place and how as well as how much more quickly? Is it important to know how suspicion is *qualitatively different* from paranoia so that we can distinguish the two? It seems to me that these questions make sense and that psychology could only be improved if there were a way to answer these questions systematically and rigorously. Some qualitative procedure that could answer such questions in depth was necessary because transformation into quantitative scales could not do it. Now phenomenology is precisely the discipline that tries to discover and account for the presence of meanings in the stream of consciousness. It is the discipline that tries to sort out and systematize meanings and if a way could be found to do qualitative research perhaps it would be by exploring the phenomenological approach.

Thus, it is important to emphasize again the self-imposed limits accepted in trying to develop the method presented in this work. The guiding idea was not a broadly based integration of all that one could possibly do with a description from within a phenomenological frame of reference. The aim was far more narrow than that. It had to do with the consistent development of an explicitly qualitative method in order to see just what would come out of it and how far one could go. It was to see what kinds of findings the method could yield and whether or not they were worth pursuing. Even the possibility of abandoning the project because of a lack of fruitfulness was a viable option. However, an affirmative decision was made—and thus this work—but operating within that frame placed many restrictions on the development that are contingent and might not have been present had a different set of assumptions been the guide. For example, since phenomenology is obviously descriptive and since all science admits some role of description, the conditions necessary for adequate description were bypassed in order to concentrate on the procedures to be followed after descriptions were obtained. Grant a different set of assumptions and a different looking method may have ensued. That is why we keep emphasizing that the method being developed here is neither exclusive nor exhaustive but merely one way in which phenomenological psychological research can be practiced.

Still, there is enough generality to the method (as opposed to the specific procedures) so as to be applicable to a wide variety of phenomena. The chapters of this volume give some indication of this potentiality. It was developed largely in dialog with the phenomenon of learning and that is what the first content chapter deals with. Chris Aanstoos applies it to another cognitive process, thinking while playing chess. William Fischer uses it to explore a phenomenon that seems to run through much of clinical literature, namely, self-deception. Finally, Fred Wertz employs the method in the area of social psychology, specifically, to the phenomenon of being criminally victimized. None of the authors believes that the research presented is the final word, nor that the method can do everything, but they all do believe that something worthwhile can be achieved by means of it.

References

Boring, E. G. (1953). A history of introspection. *Psychological Bulletin, 50,* 169–189.

Brentano, F. (1973/1874). *Psychology from an empirical standpoint* (A. Rancurello, D. B. Terrell, L. L. McAlister, Trans.). New York: Humanities Press (German original, 1874).

Dilthey, W. (1977/1894). Ideas concerning a descriptive and analytic psychology. In W. Dilthey (Ed.), *Descriptive psychology and historical understanding* (R. Zaner and K. Heiges, Trans.). The Hague: Nijhoff, 1977 (German original, 1894).

Ericsson, K. A. & Simon, H. (1980). Verbal reports as data. *Psychological Review, 87,* 215–251.

Husserl, E. (1970/1900). *Logical investigations* (Vols. 1 and 2). (J. N. Findlay, Trans.). New York: Humanities Press (German original, 1900).

Ladd, G. T. (1894). *Psychology, descriptive and explanatory.* New York: C. Scribner's Sons.

Moustgaard, I. (1981). *Beskvivelse og kommunication.* Copenhagen: Munksgaard.

———. (1982). *Descriptive psychology: The psychology of description.* Copenhagen: Private Printing.

Sartre, J. P. (1962/1936). *Imagination.* (F. William, Trans.). Ann Arbor, MI: University of Michigan Press (French original, 1936).

———. (1962/1939). *Sketch for a theory of the emotions.* (P. Mairet, Trans.). London: Methuen (French original, 1939).

———. (1966/1940). *The psychology of imagination.* New York: Citadel Press (French original, 1940).

Thorndike, E. L. (1907). *The elements of psychology* (2nd ed.). New York: A. G. Seiler.

Titchener, E. B. (1912). The schema of introspection. *American Journal of Psychology, 23,* 485–508.

Torbert, W. R. (1972). *Learning from experience toward consciousness.* New York: Columbia University press.

Wundt, W. (1973/1911). *An introduction to psychology.* New York: Arno Press (German original, 1911).

1/Sketch of a Psychological Phenomenological Method

Amedeo Giorgi

As indicated in the Introduction, it is beyond the scope of this section to give either a detailed breakdown or full theoretical justification of the psychological phenomenological method that is in the process of being developed. That will be presented in a future work. Here only a sketch will be provided so that the reader can understand the reasons for the major steps of the method (and its variations). This background, in turn, should make the investigations included in this work more intelligible because they have all assumed the presence of this section and thus did not emphasize method. The fact that this method is both phenomenological and scientific will be argued in the next chapter; here it will be merely presented.

The guiding theme of phenomenology is to go "back to the 'things themselves' " (Husserl, 1970/1900, p. 252) and for a phenomenological psychologist one interpretation of that expression means to go to the everyday world where people are living through various phenomena in actual situations. Since we are researching the phenomenon of learning, we are interested in obtaining descriptions of learning. On the pragmatic level, this does not seem to be difficult. When subjects, after a brief introduction concerning my interest in the psychology of learning, are confronted with the statement: "Please describe for me a situation in which you have learned," there inevitably follows a concrete description of a learning experience. It seems best to present the method in conjunction with a concrete description, so that first a description will be presented and then comments will be added. Here is one response to the request "Please describe for me as concretely as you can a situation in which you have learned".

Some time ago I gave my oldest son a chess set which had been in my possession for a number of years. For a variety of sentimental reasons I considered this chess set to be a possession of rare personal significance. In other words, its value, to me, could in no way be equated with its market price. Consequently, the decision to pass this treasure on to my oldest son was arrived at with all due consideration; and the actual "passing on" had, for me, all the significance of a sacramental act—a deeply intimate encounter between a father and his son.

My son was quite excited about the gift and seemed, to me, to sense its symbolic value. Indeed, during the weeks that followed he was rarely seen without the chess set in his possession. Following the initial period, however, the appearance of the chess set steadily diminished to the point of being rarely seen. My occasional queries concerning the chess set were met with reassuring answers. Recently, however, the issue of the chess set once more became central, in a dramatic fashion.

During a game of chess with my youngest son, he asked why the pieces made "that sound" when moved from one square to another. I explained that most "good" chess pieces were weighted for stability, and that often the weights became loose through use and made a strange rattling sound when moved. He looked at me for a moment, and said "Oh yeah, I know what you mean. Tommy has a whole bunch of them."

"Of what?" I asked.

"A whole bunch of weights."

"Where did he get them?"

"Out of the chess men you gave him; that's why he wanted them."

I was crushed, and then angry. Tommy was in the next room playing with a cat—he was startled when I shouted his name.

"Do you know what you've done?" I asked.

"No," he said.

"Why did you tear your chess men apart?"

"For the lead weights; why are you so mad Daddy?"

Tommy's face was a mask of puzzlement. He had no idea what I was talking about.

By now I was feeling ashamed, but wasn't sure why. I hugged my son, told him that I was wrong, and assured him that the value he placed on his chess men was up to him. Later that day it was clear to me what I had learned.

Aquinas once wrote that "the quality of a gift is determined not by the giver's ability to give, but by the receiver's ability to receive." I learned that day what that meant.

I had given my son a gift, which was not merely the chess set, but all the value, meaning, and sentiment which I attached to it. For

> me, the chess set was a symbol of what a father desires to give his son; for my son, the chess set was a source of lead weights. I had offered him a gift that he was not able to receive, either as a symbol, or as a chess set—since he was not able to perceive my values, my meanings, or my sentiments. Consequently, the quality of my gift was determined by the chess-set-as-source-of-lead-weights, the gift my son was able to receive.
>
> "The quality of a gift is determined not by the giver's ability to give but by the receiver's ability to receive." I first read this sentence years ago; I learned its painful lesson only recently.

Again, it would take us too far afield in this article to attempt a justification of the use of description in psychological research. While a preliminary expression of a theoretical justification is given by Giorgi (1982), the method we wish to employ begins *after* the description has been obtained. Moustgaard (1981) delineates some of the conditions for a descriptive psychology, and Ericsson and Simon (1980) describe the prevalence, types, and value of verbal reports in research. In sum, our position is that caution must be exercised in the use of descriptions, but also that these cautions are no worse than with any other form of expression of psychological reality and certainly far from vitiating the whole project.

The method contains four essential steps; expressed most generally, they are as follows: (1) One reads the entire description in order to get a general sense of the whole statement. (2) Once the sense of the whole has been grasped, the researcher goes back to the beginning and reads through the text once more with the specific aim of discriminating "meaning units" from within a psychological perspective and with a focus on the phenomenon being researched. (3) Once "meaning units" have been delineated, the researcher then goes through all of the meaning units and expresses the psychological insight contained in them more directly. This is especially true of the "meaning units" most revelatory of the phenomenon under consideration. (4) Finally, the researcher synthesizes all of the transformed meaning units into a consistent statement regarding the subject's experience. This is usually referred to as the structure of the experience and can be expressed at a number of levels. Now, let's examine these steps a little more closely.

(1) *Sense of the Whole.*–Little has to be said about this step, since nothing more is involved than a simple reading of the text and the ability to understand the language of the describer. Of course, the researcher should feel free to read the text as often as is necessary to get a good grasp of the whole. For a description of one or two pages, such as the above, a simple reading should suffice, but descriptions (or transcribed interviews) of 15 to 20 pages may take multiple readings. The general

sense grasped after the reading of the text is not interrogated nor made explicit in any way. Primarily, it serves as a ground for the next step, the discrimination of meaning units.

(2) *Discrimination of Meaning Units Within a Psychological Perspective and Focused on the Phenomenon Being Researched.*–Since one cannot analyze a whole text simultaneously, one has to break it down into manageable units. Since it is a psychological analysis that we are interested in, it seems logical that the units should be made with psychological criteria in mind. Thus, the meaning units that emerge as a consequence of the analysis are spontaneously perceived discriminations within the subject's description arrived at when the researcher assumes a psychological attitude toward the concrete description, and along with it, the set that the text is an example of the phenomenon of learning (in this case).

Some brief elaborations concerning the attitude adopted toward the description can be enumerated. The meaning unit discriminations are noted directly on the description whenever the researcher, upon rereading the text, becomes aware of a change of meaning of the situation for the subject that appears to be psychologically sensitive. Thus, if one consults the meaning units determined for the example description under consideration as presented below (pp. 00–00), one can see that changes or transitions in meanings are noted when the narrator shifts from the value of the chess set for himself to his son's excitement about the gift and again from his son's excitement to the lack of appearance of the gift to the narrator's awareness of the real meaning of the gift to his son, and so on. It should be noted that in this step the subject's language is not changed in any way. It is essential for the method that the discriminations take place first, before being interrogated further (which is the next step) and that they be done spontaneously, although within the attitude and set described above, (that is, within a psychological attitude and the set that the description is to be taken as an example of learning).

To say that a psychological attitude and special set toward the description must be adopted means that we operate within the assumption that psychological reality is not ready-made in the world and simply seen and dealt with but rather that it has to be constituted by the psychologist. Of course, this observation has been made throughout the history of psychology (e.g., James, 1950/1890, I, pp. 183–185; Politzer, 1968/1928, pp. 239–262; Linschoten, 1968, pp. 36–40; Danziger, 1981) and is what James meant by the "psychologist's reality." Being unmindful of the fact that a certain perspective toward reality is necessary in order to constitute psychological reality has led to the "psychologist's fallacy" and to the excesses of psychologism. In our view, the everyday world is richer and more complex than the psychological perspective (however complex it may be itself) and thus this description could just as easily lend itself to a sociological or anthropological analysis depending upon the interests of the researcher and the perspective toward the concrete description that is adopted. Similarly, within the psychological attitude, one could adopt the set that one would do an analysis of the "perceptions" or of the "emotions" expressed by the description and come up with some findings. Thus, to adopt a set means to set some limits or controls on the analysis and to thematize only a particular aspect of a more complex reality. But, of course, traditional psychology does the same thing. The difference between memory and learning in an experimental situation involving nonsense syllables is usually the difference in perspective introduced by the experimenter.

Just how one gets into a psychological attitude or a specific set is one of those difficult questions that are successfully lived more facilely than theoretically articulated. What is time? What is the meaning of existence? Millennia of philosophical thought have not satisfactorily answered these questions although anyone who is alive has a concrete lived sense of both terms. What is the meaning of psychology? What is learning? The same thing applies. A comprehensive yet precise meaning of both terms is lacking despite the effort of hundreds of people over many years. But we all carry a lived sense of both terms because we live them as well as try to study them. Thus, the method allows the lived sense of these terms to operate spontaneously first and later tries to assess more precisely the meaning of the key terms by analyzing the attitudes and set actually adopted. In other words, while the researcher may not be able to articulate the precise meaning of psychology that he lives, or that of learning, his spontaneous discriminations and the manner in which he transforms the everyday language of the subject into more precise psychological terminology will express more concretely than he can say the meaning of psychology that he adopts or of the set toward learning. An analysis of the steps of the method following the application of the method can help articulate (although still incompletely) the meaning of psychology or of learning for the researcher.

Of course, this doesn't mean that one should not try to make the meaning of psychology or of learning more clear, and we have made such attempts ourselves (for example, Chapter 3), but only that the expectation of total clarity on this point may be misleading. Minimally however, one can say that a psychological analysis would involve the individual way in which a subject lives—that is, behaves and experiences—situations. Learning, in a minimal sense, would mean the way in which a subject appropriates new repertoires of behavior or experience as a consequence of specific situations. But these are only general descriptions that in no way do justice to the vivid and concrete modes of presence that actually working through the method provides.

While these theoretical problems are weighty, on a practical level many individuals can apply the method after instruction and some training rather well and very frequently with essential intersubjective agreement. Consensus concerning disagreements can also be arrived at frequently by probing and clarifying researchers' assumptions. However, consensus among researchers is not an intrinsic demand of the method. Sometimes researchers disagree even though they are making statements about the same set of data. Thus, the lack of theoretical clarity concerning the adoption of the psychological attitude or the specific set a phenomenon demands are indeed concerns that call for further developments but these lacks do not exceed the "state of the art" of psychology in other areas. For example, a consensual, comprehensive, and precise understanding of intelligence and therapy is also lacking, but the practice of both intelligence testing and therapy is well entrenched. The recourse to operational definitions seems to us to be a rather transparent *ad hoc* solution, and we prefer to live with the tensions created by a relatively successful praxis and less successful theoretical clarification. Granted that more can be done, it is nevertheless our assumption that this praxis will never be completely codified.

From another perspective one could describe the attitude adopted in making the meaning unit discrimination as one of "circumscribed indeterminateness" or "empty determinateness." This means that certain circumscription, a certain general expectation is established (a psychological analysis clarifying how learning is lived is being sought) but on the other hand, a certain open-endedness is also maintained so that genuine discoveries may ensue. To help understand this attitude two contrasting ones will be mentioned. A logical-empirical approach would first posit the criteria for learning and then note those places in the description that matched the criteria (or where the criterion failed) and draw out the implications. A more radical empirical approach would emphasize the performance itself and then try to relate performance change (for example, response rate) to environmental changes. In the former case one always knows what one is looking for; it's just a matter of detecting when the subject displays it. While the latter perspective initially produced a genuine discovery (response rate is a measure of learning), it now too knows what it is looking for. Having been successful, each situation is now seen in the light of the one successful index without realizing that it may be only one measure. The phenomenological approach being described here tries to make genuine discoveries concerning what is important about learning. The fact that the researcher's perspective is circumscribed means that not any fact will be deemed worthy of consideration, but rather, the fact would have to be a psychological one and relevant to learning. On the other hand, while there are presuppositions and a general precomprehension, these are not specific enough to delineate the relevant categories in an exclusionary way and thus, genuine discoveries can be made with respect to specific facts and very frequently categories as well. What differentiates the phenomenologically inspired method is the fact that a disciplined spontaneity is allowed to function whereby one first discovers the relevant meaning unit, or its category, and only later, based upon a subsequent analysis, explicates its actual full import.

In a certain sense the procedure being outlined here is the practice of science within the "context of discovery" rather than in the "context of verification." The usual attitude is that anything can take place in the phase of discovery just so it is strictly verified because science is defined by verification. Verification is important for science, but it does not exhaust the definition of scientific practice because nobody just verifies. A complete understanding of science depends upon the total activity of the scientist, and this includes many activities that do not fall under the heading of verification. Moreover, it is far from logically certain that the criteria for verification should be the standards against which the activities that take place in the context of discovery should be measured. In the terms of this argument, we are trying to systematize scientific activity within the context of discovery and it is being done independently of the criteria of verification.

The meaning units that are constituted by this procedure are understood to be constituents and not elements, following the terminology of Gurwitsch (1964/1957). A constituent is a part determined in such a way that it is context-laden. An element is a part determined in such a way that its meaning is as much as possible independent of context. Thus, the letter "l" as the 12th letter of the alphabet means the same regardless of where it is found, whereas the specific concrete meaning of a word more often than not depends upon the whole sentence or even the paragraph. The former would be an element, the latter a constituent. The meaning units discriminated in this method are understood to be constituents.

The above distinction also helps us to understand why the qualitative method being described here is not identical to traditional content analysis. In its classic sense, traditional content analysis is best defined by Berelson (1952 p. 18) in the following way: "*Content analysis is a research technique for the objective, systematic and quantitative description of the manifest content of communication.*" As a contrast, we would not consider our method to be a technique, but precisely a *method* (it is not static or mechanical enough to be a technique), nor is our analysis primarily quantitative (although quantification is not in principle excluded), nor do we limit ourselves to manifest content (genuine meaning can only be apprehended in depth). Unfortunately, we see in the definition of content analysis the same constraints that operate in psychology as a whole, that is, the a priori adoption of natural scientific criteria as final arbiters of a phenomenon. However, as with psychology as a whole, reactions to these constraints have also developed in that arguments have been proposed for the necessity of a qualitative analysis as well (e.g., George, 1959; Anderson, 1974), but full-fledged methods of qualitative analysis have not been proposed, or else they have been used as adjuncts to making better quantitative analyses (e.g., Pool, 1959). In other words, the qualitative aspects we are arguing for here are, in the area of content analysis, still, at best, merely adjuncts to the dominant, established quantitative approaches rather than equal alternatives.

One last point concerning the constitution of the meaning units: It is important to note that we are not saying that the meaning units exist in the text *as such*. They exist only in relation to the attitude and set of the researcher. For example, if one were to do a grammatical analysis of the description, one would look at the text differently than if one were to do a stylistic analysis. In changing from one purpose to the other, one can feel the gestalt of the text shift. The same is true when one shifts from an everyday attitude to a psychological one or from an interest in emotions to learning. What stands out depends very much upon the researcher's perspective. In practice this often means that the meaning units established are neither univocal nor arbitrary and the very effort of clarifying them often leads to self-correction. To discuss this further, however, would lead us into a detailed discussion of the specific steps of the procedure, and we are reserving that discussion for another work.

Before introducing the next step, we shall present the meaning units we determined for the exemplar description we introduced above. The left-hand column represents the first spontaneous discrimination, expressed entirely in the subject's language, and the right-hand column represents the meaning units transformed into psychological language, more directly revealing the phenomenon of learning. The right-hand column presents the results of Step 3, which is discussed below.

(A)	(B)
All Constituents Present in S's Description.	*Constituents of Description Expressed More Directly in Terms Revelatory of Learning.*
(1) S gave his oldest son a chess set which had been in his possession for a number of years. For a variety of sentimental reasons S considered the chess set to be a possession of rare personal significance. Its value to S could not be equated with its market price. Consequently the decision to pass this treasure on to his oldest son was arrived at with all due consideration; and the actual passing on had for S all the signifi-	(1) S presents a gift that had deep personal significance for him, after considerable deliberation, to his son in an encounter that S perceived to be intimate and highly significant.

cance of a sacramental act—a deeply intimate encounter between a father and son.

(2) S's son was excited about the gift and seemed to S to sense its symbolic value. Indeed, during the weeks that followed S's son was rarely seen without the chess set in his possession.

(2) S perceives his son as apparently receiving and using the gift as intended by S.

(3) Following the initial period, however, the appearances of the chess set steadily diminished to the point of rarely being seen. S's occasional queries concerning the chess set were met with reassuring answers.

(3) With time, the presence of the gift was not as pronounced, but S's queries concerning it were met with reassurance in terms of S's intentions and values with respect to the gift, or at least that is how S heard his son's replies.

(4) Recently, the issue of the chess set once more became central in a dramatic fashion for S. During a game of chess with his youngest son. S was asked why the chess pieces made "that sound" when moved from one square to another. S explained that most "good" chess pieces were weighted for stability and that often the weights became loose through use and made a strange rattling sound when moved. S's youngest son looked at S for a moment, and said, "Oh yeah, I know what you mean. Tommy has a whole bunch of them." "Of what?" S asked. "A whole bunch of weights." "Where did he get them?" "Out of the chess men you gave him; that's why he wanted them."

(4) The real meaning with which S's son received the gift became central again when S accidently discovered through another son that a behavior with respect to the gift on the part of his son (dismantling pieces to get weights) was not in line with his intention when he gave the gift.

(5) S was crushed and then angry. Tommy was in the next room playing with the cat—he was startled when S shouted his name. "Do you know what you've done?" S asked. "No," S's oldest son said. "Why did you tear your chess men apart?" "For the lead weight; why are you so mad, Daddy?"

(5) S was hurt, then angry and he confronted his son in an ugly mood and in such a way that the son was puzzled that S should be upset with him because he used the gift the way he did, i.e., according to his own intentions.

(6) S's oldest son's face was a mask of puzzlement. He had no idea of what S was talking about.

(6) S could see that his son was puzzled and had no idea why S was angry.

(7) By now S was feeling ashamed, but wasn't sure why. S hugged his son,

(7) S felt ashamed and responded to the immediate situation by reassuring

told him that he (S) was wrong, and assured him that the value he placed in his chess men was up to him.	his son that he (S) was in error and that the gift could be used in any way that his son wanted it to be used.
(8) Later that day it was clear to S what he had learned. Aquinas once wrote, "The quality of a gift is determined not by the giver's ability to give, but by the receiver's ability to receive." S learned that day what that meant.	(8) Later reflection clarified for S what had happened when he related the experience to a philosophical sentence concerning giving and receiving that he had read.
(9) S had given his son a gift, which was not merely the chess set, but also all the value, meaning, and sentiment which S had attached to it. For S, the chess set was a symbol of what a father desires to give his son; for S's son, the chess set was a source of lead weights. S had offered his son a gift that he was not able to receive, either as a symbol or as a chess set, since he was not able to perceive S's values, meanings, or sentiments. Consequently, the quality of S's gift was determined by the "chess-set-as-source-of-lead-weights," the gift S's son was able to receive.	(9) S realized later that his son could not receive the gift with the full depth and intensity with which it was offered (chess-set-as-rare,-meaningful-symbolic exchange-between-father-son); he could only receive it at his own level (chess-set-as-source-of-lead-weights). Awareness of this discrepancy makes the situation intelligible for S. S's son could behave differently with respect to the gift because he was incapable of comprehending S's full intention—and on the other hand, S's different behavior could even be understood to be meaningful or valuable at another level.
(10) "The quality of a gift is determined not by the giver's ability to give, but by the receiver's ability to receive." S first read that sentence years ago, but learned its painful lesson only recently.	(10) S's experience clarifies, as well in an experiential or existential way, the saying of a philosopher that he had read long ago.

(3) *Transformation of Subject's Everyday Expressions into Psychological Language with Emphasis on the Phenomenon Being Investigated.*- The transformations presented above take place basically through a process of reflection and imaginative variation. This is another one of those instances where achievement—even consistent intersubjective achievement—is ahead of comprehension. Undoubtedly there is a tension between the specifics of the concrete situation and the more general psychological categories evoked by the description. The intent of the method, however, is to arrive at the general category by *going through* the concrete expressions and not by abstraction or formalization, which are selective according to the criteria accepted.

These transformations are necessary, we said, because the descriptions by the naive subjects express in a cryptic way multiple realities, and we want to elucidate the psychological aspects in a depth appropriate for the understanding of the events. We do so by reflection and imaginative variation.

Let us take the second meaning unit as an example. The subject describes his son's excitement about the gift and how he seems to sense the importance it has for the father; the father receives support for that interpretation because the chess set was constantly with the son. Now, what is truly essential, psychologically speaking vis-à-vis learning, about this meaning unit? Thus, the researcher begins to reflect on possibilities and discards those that do not withstand criticism. For example, does one have to mention each time that it was a chess set? Surely it is apparent that the subject valued chess, and this tells us something about the subject, but is chess as such absolutely essential to understand the dynamics of learning as presented here? One tests this thought in terms of imaginative variation. Should one say "game" instead of chess? Perhaps one can just say "gift." Will that hold up? How does one tell? Drawing from the knowledge of the whole, one tries to estimate how the learning develops. What is the central issue that the learning revolves around? It has to do with the fact that the son did not use the chess set as the father intended. With respect to that criterion, then, it seems that simply stating that the father gave his son a gift is sufficient, since knowledge of all of the complexities of chess are not necessary to understand the learning dynamics except in the most incidental way. Thus, we come to understand that it is the manner in which the chess set is received by the son and given by the father that matters and not the rules of the game of chess, so we can concentrate on the "gift" qualities rather than "chess" or "game" aspects. This is already a transformation in the direction of "psychological reality," since we realize that our analysis will have to explore further the qualities of the "gift transaction."

The necessity for the transformation can be seen as well in the way we expressed this second unit in Column B. We said that "the subject perceived" his son using the gift "as intended by the subject." But the subject himself did not use these words himself although he expressed them indirectly when he spoke about his "son's excitement" and his apparently "sensing the symbolic value" of the gift. Similarly, the entire second sentence indicates that the subject was sensitive to *how* his son was relating to the chess set, and it seemed to him to be fully in line with the way he (the subject) intended. Thus we were able to make thematic the subject's perceptions and intentions at this stage of the analysis which are important to understand how this description can evolve into an example of the phenomenon of learning.

This analysis could be repeated for each meaning unit, but we hope that one example is sufficient to clarify how reflection and imaginative variation play a role in the transformation from everyday language by the subject to psychological language by the experimenter. Of course, a major obstacle for this process is the fact that there is no already established consensual psychological language. The language of psychology is currently tied to psychological perspectives (behaviorism, psychoanalysis, and so on). In the face of this dispersion our only alternative is to state our own perspective: We use the language of common sense enlightened by a phenomenological perspective. Obviously this is not the most desirable solution, but the only practical one short of taking on the whole question of psychological language in a thematic way.

(4) *Synthesis of Transformed Meaning Units into a Consistent Statement of the Structure of Learning*: First of all it should be mentioned that one would rarely conduct research of this type with only one subject. It is important to realize this because it is most difficult to write an essential general structure with only one instance. The more subjects there are, the greater the variations, and hence the better the ability to see what is essential. On the other hand, specific situated structures might still be desired, and these could be based on only one subject.

In any event, the last step of the analysis is for the researcher to synthesize and integrate the insights contained in the transformed meaning units into a consistent description of the psychological structure of the event. In this synthesis all transformed meaning units must be taken into account. The criterion would be that all of the meanings of the transformed meaning units are at least implicitly contained in the general description. The structure is then communicated to other researchers for the purposes of confirmation or criticism. The structures for this example are as follows:

Specific Description of Situated Structure of Learning

In a significant encounter S presents his son a gift with the intention that it be received with the historically laden symbolic value that the gift had for S. Early experiences with his son with respect to the gift gave every indication that it had been received with S's intention. Accidently, S became aware through another son of certain behavior with respect to the gift that was clearly out of line with his intentions and interpretation. When S confronted his son regarding the behavior, his son was obviously confused. S responded to the confusion by ameliorating it in the immediate situation, but he was also aware that something was wrong, but he was not sure what it was. Later reflection clarified the meaning of the situation for S. He realized finally that his son could not receive the gift with the depth and intensity he intended, and therefore, he (the son) inevitably had to place his own value on the gift. S accepted this state of affairs. S related the situation to a philosophical statement he had read long ago, and mutual clarification of the statement and the situation ensued.

General Description of Situated Structure of Learning

Learning, for S, consisted in the clarification of a situation rendered ambiguous because a false assumption did not allow S to see the same situation in terms of different perspectives for different persons. This experience also enabled S to learn a deeper meaning of the philosophical saying he had previously read, but the saying also helped him interpret the situation he had ambiguously lived through.

The specific description of the situated structure remains more faithful to the concrete subject and specific situation whereas the general description of the situated structure tries as much as possible to depart from the specifics to communicate the most general meaning of the phenomenon. We have retained the term "situated" here because only one subject is the base, but for multiple subjects the term could be dropped if all subjects can be subsumed under one typology.

This last step is a difficult one because more so than with traditional research, where conventions are already established, one has the freedom to express findings in multiple ways. To a large extent how the findings are presented very much upon the audience with whom one is communicating. If I were speaking to a group of phenomenologists obviously familiar with phenomenology but unfamiliar with the psychology of learning, I would speak one way, whereas if I were writing for psychologists knowledgeable in the traditional psychology of learning but unfamiliar with phenomenology, I would write up results differently. Similarly, if I wanted to give feedback to this particular subject about how he learns, I would write the results differently than if I wanted to speak about what a phenomenological approach could contribute to the psychology of learning. In each case, the same essential findings would be differently expressed. The problem of how to write up the results is most difficult when the audience is wholly unknown or is highly diversified.

Some cautionary comments about the above exposition of the method are in order. My experience suggests that there is a great risk of misunderstanding in presenting the method in such a schematic fashion. Thus far it seems that workshop contexts have been best mostly because there is a concrete working through of the issue for a longer period of time. Without a concrete "working through" of the method it seems that one can imagine many difficulties, whereas the very "working through" solves many of them before they become problems. What is schematically given above, therefore, is generally encompassing, but very incomplete with respect to the horizon of possible questions one can imagine.

Another important caution is to state that what has been developed and presented thus far, in my opinion, is only the tip of the iceberg. More concrete experience with the method across a greater range of phenomena and more theoretical reflection and clarification will undoubtedly deepen our understanding in ways that are not predictable from where we now stand. In other words, more remains to be developed than has been achieved, but the point here is merely to demonstrate that the qualitative method being developed can, in principle, meet both scientific and phenomenological criteria based merely upon what has been achieved thus far.

The last word of caution refers to the findings. While findings concerning learning are included, no claim is made that what is presented represents the best that the method can yield. These early studies are directed as much to the problems of method as they are to questions of content. Nevertheless, given this historical context we would still argue that some important findings regarding learning emerge.

References

Anderson, B. (1974). *The quantifier as qualifier: Some notes on qualitative elements in quantitative research analysis. Department of History Publications: Research Section Post War History*, Goteborg, Sweden: University of Goteborg.

Berelson, B. (1952). *Content analysis in communication research. Glencoe, IL: Free Press.*

Danziger, K. (1981, June). *An approach to a critical history of psychology.* Paper presented at the meeting of Cheiron, River Falls, WI.

Ericsson, K. A., & Simon, H. (1980). Verbal reports as data. *Psychological Review, 87*, 215–251.

George, A. L. (1959). Quantitative and qualitative approaches to content analysis. In I. de S. Poll (Ed.), *Trends in content analysis* (pp. 7–33). Urbana, IL: University of Illinois Press.

Giorgi, A. (1982, August). *Theoretical justification for the use of descriptions in psychological research.* Paper presented at symposium entitled "The Value of a Descriptive Method for Psychology" meeting of the American Psychological Association, Washington, DC.

Gurwitsch, A. (1964/1957). *The field of consciousness.* Pittsburgh, PA: Duquesne University Press (French original, 1957).

Husserl, E. (1970/1900). *Logical investigations* (vol. 1), (J. N. Finley, Trans.)

New York: Humanities Press (German original, 1900).

James, W. (1950/1890). *The principles of psychology*. New York: Dover Publications (original publication, 1890).

Linschoten, H. (1968). *On the way towards a phenomenological psychology: The psychology of William James*. Pittsburgh, PA: Duquesne University Press,

Moustgaard, I. (1981). Beskrivelse og kommunication. Copenhaven: Munhsgaard, (See also: *Descriptive psychology: The psychology of description*, Personal publication, 1982).

Politzer, G. (1968/1928), Critiques des fondements de la psychologie. Paris: Presses Universitaires de France (1st edition, 1928).

Pool, I. de S. (1959). Trends in content analysis today: A summary. In I. de S. Pool (Ed.), *Trends in content analysis* (pp. 189-233). Urbana, IL: University of Illinois Press.

2/The Phenomenological Psychology of Learning and the Verbal Learning Tradition*

Amedeo Giorgi

ONE of the most difficult problems concerning phenomenological thought is the communication of it. There are numerous reasons for this difficulty, and without trying to be exhaustive, I shall try to mention some of the more important ones: (1) Phenomenological thinking is intrinsically difficult, since it goes against the natural tendency of consciousness to go toward things rather than its own processes and it attempts to analyze these spontaneous processes that present themselves as already formed unities even though they are in constant flux: (2) The work of Husserl, phenomenology's founder, which spans almost a half century from his first publication in 1890 until his death in 1938, kept evolving and changing. Indeed, even at this date, not all of his manuscripts have been posthumously published. (3) Not only did Husserl's thought and language develop, but very few of his disciples developed consistent interpretations of phenomenology. Indeed, among his followers there were as many "deviants" as "true followers." Even when attempts are made to be explicit about criteria, there are differences. For example Schmitt (1961-1962) defines thinkers as belonging to the phenomenological movement in terms of recognizing the same problem as the starting point of contemporary philosophy, but Spiegelberg (1960) and Merleau-Ponty (1962) define it in terms of the phenomenological method, but then their interpretation of the method differs. A consen-

* A good part of this article was prepared while the author was a fellow at the Netherlands Institute for Advanced Study in the Humanities and Social Sciences in Wassenaar, Holland, and grateful acknowledgment is hereby made to the institute. A shorter and modified version of this paper was presented at Duquesne University's special Centennial Symposium on Phenomenology and Psychology, November 19, 1978 at Pittsburgh, PA.

sual, univocal interpretation of phenomenology is hard to find.

These difficulties exist at the strictly philosophical level, and when one moves on to the relationship between phenomenology and psychology, especially with the research interests of the latter, then the difficulties are compounded because one enters into an additional context of scholarship, namely, science, and its problems of self-understanding. Without getting into all of the problems of a precise definition of science, we do know that science can be defined as broadly as "systematic knowledge" and as narrowly as the specific procedures and criteria of the hypothetical-deductive method. Of course, we know that psychology's history shows that its relationship to science is even more complicated insofar as it has been conceived of as belonging within the context of the human sciences as well as the natural sciences (Giorgi, 1970). In other words, in dealing with the meaning of psychology as a science, one is dealing with just as unstable a context as with philosophical phenomenology, and the meeting of the two contexts only enhances the volatility of the mixture with respect to the problem of precise communication.

As if the mixture of phenomenology and psychology were not difficult enough, there is the further problem of levels of understanding, which one can refer to as conventional or radical. At a conventional level, we all know what philosophy is and what science is, but at a more radical level, that is, at a level where we want to express meanings precisely, the conventional meanings become problematic. Fortunately or unfortunately, phenomenological thought also seeks to understand things at the radical level, and therefore it always speaks at a level where problems exist and the sailing is not smooth.

All of this is prologue for introducing the relationship between phenomenology and psychological research in an as problem-free a manner as possible, for experience has shown that the relationship inevitably presents difficulties: It immediately sets up two sets of conventional expectations that must be resisted. On the one hand, those who are versed in philosophical phenomenology and know the field well have certain definite ideas concerning phenomenology and wonder about how the transcendental reduction can be applied at the level of concrete psychological research. Or they are experts in Husserl; they know his writings concerning phenomenological psychology[1] and are curious to see if all the steps of the procedure as they understand them will be carried out properly, and so on. The difficulty here is that all of these expectations issue from philosophical phenomenology and may or may not be legitimate concerns at the level of psychological phenomenology. I will come

1. In my interpretation, what Husserl called phenomenological psychology is really philosophical psychology and neither psychological phenomenology nor a phenomenologically grounded concrete psychology. See also John Scanlon, Translator's Introduction, *Phenomenological Psychology* (The Hague: Nijhoff, 1977), p. xi.

back to this in a moment. Scientific psychologists, on the other hand, certainly know what science is, and while many will readily admit that they know little about phenomenology, what they have heard about it in a conventional sense is that it deals with feelings, experience, consciousness—in short, with subjectivity in general, and they wonder how one can be genuinely rigorous with subjective—an age-old problem for the science of psychology. But what has to be fought here are not the expectations concerning phenomenology that psychologists hold, which are generally flexible because they are vague and not well formulated, but precisely those of science, which are more deeply rooted. Hence, the preconceptions concerning science are what must be radicalized. Thus, the problem of communication concerning the relationship between phenomenology and psychological research has now been made more precise. The difficulty is that the expression "Phenomenology and Psychological Research" creates a double set of expectations that are only generally and conventionally legitimate but not precisely so for the proximate context of the discussion: The term phenomenology creates a set based upon philosophical phenomenology whereas the discussion proceeds at the level of psychological phenomenology. Science, in general, creates expectations based upon the natural scientific understanding of science whereas psychology as a human science is intended. Moreover, again, difficulties are compounded because neither psychological phenomenology nor psychology as a human science is as yet a well-founded, fully mature discipline; both are only in the process of coming into being. In brief, the thesis of this essay is that there is a void or gap where a frame of reference for a genuine psychology should be; this gap is filled in by philosophy or natural science and neither is appropriate.

Allow me, momentarily, to leap to the positive articulation of the frame of reference that would be most suitable for what is to follow. The fundamental assumption is that an originary perspective—one that has not as yet been successfully articulated, although often implicitly and intuitively assumed—is necessary to be present to the psychological dimensions of human beings. Moreover, this writer's biases are that a phenomenological frame of reference and psychology conceived as a human science are more likely to achieve the articulation of the originary psychological perspective for humans, although it is granted beforehand that this is not the only access to the problem. However, the important point for this paper is that the conventional understandings of both phenomenology and science must be bracketed in order to allow for the possibility of the more radical understandings to emerge. Since the understanding of phenomenology is so heavily weighted by the articulations of philosophical phenomenology and since the meaning of science is so dominated by the natural scientific understanding of science, these understandings must be bracketed so that the differences that psychological phenomenology and human scientific psychology introduce can be given room to appear. In other words, both phenomenological psychology as a psychological theory and human scientific psychology are programs, not achievements, and thus they should not be judged by the achievements of natural scientific psychology or philosophical phenomenology. Another way of saying this is to say that I do accept the demands to be "scientific" and "phenomenological" in general, but the ways in which these demands are to be translated into criteria and courses of action are still to be worked out. The only thing of which one can be sure is that the already worked out criteria and achievements cannot be blindly applied precisely because they were not sensitive to the originary perspective that the presence to the psychological demands.

The above description of my own perspective presents two problems: (1) in what sense can I still be guided by phenomenology and science while I still bracket them? and (2) is it possible to do more than merely assert my perspective—that is, is it possible to demonstrate it? The answer to the first question is that I accept the demand to be phenomenological and scientific, in general, but not in the specific sense that I accept beforehand articulated, known, concrete criteria. The specific criteria that have yet to emerge might be identical to or different from others used in the past, but they will have emerged as a result of a concrete demand rather than a priori. To be phenomenological, in general, means to return to the phenomena themselves, to obtain a description of those phenomena, to submit them to imaginative variation, and then obtain an eidetic intuition of their structures. For phenomenological *psychology*, however, the difference is that phenomena are selected for their relevance to psychology, the initial description is naive and does not imply the reduction (although the analysis of it does, and the descriptions of structures do), and the structures (or essences) sought are psychological and may be typical or general rather than universal. In other words, a minimum number of *general* phenomenological criteria are still adhered to (what may be described as the "phenomenological as such") but not necessarily specific, already achieved criteria. The same holds true for science. To accept the demand to be scientific means that one wants to approach the phenomenon one is interested in investigating in a methodical, systematic, and rigorous way, each defined according to how the very appearance of the phenomenon invites the researcher to be methodical, systematic, and rigorous. Again, the difference from traditional science is that with the latter the specific criteria are known and announced beforehand whereas with me only the general demand to be scientific is accepted initially and the concrete steps are specified and worked out in dialog with the phenomenon, rather than beforehand. This is simply applying the phenomenological procedure of bracketing to the question of method. The motivation for this step is the one mentioned before, that is, that in the history of psychology, the radical originary perspective that is necessary in order to be psychological was never fully articulated, and therefore all prior methodical achievements with respect to the psychological are either dogmatic, naive, or only pragmatically correct, but not articulated and understood as genuinely human scientific in relation to human phenomena. In brief, I accept the *general demand* to be both phenomenological and scientific, but no historical criteria are accepted, only those specific ones emerging from my concrete analysis and praxis.

I will try to demonstrate how the perspective assumed in this paper speaks to a gap by the following procedure. First, I will describe an experiment on learning where a first attempt to integrate phenomenology and traditional scientific research took place. Secondly, I will present an interpretation of phenomenological philosophy and show how, as articulated, it does not meet the needs of psychologists—even those who are sympathetic to phenomenology. Thirdly, I will present a brief historical and systematic account of a concrete area of psychological research, that of verbal learning, and show how it falls short of capturing in a rigorous way the phenomenon of learning as it is lived. Last, I will present a second attempt at integrating phenomenology and scientific research, showing how both phenomenological and scientific criteria are met in a more adequate way. My point is that this gap between beginning from phenomenology as understood philosophically and trying to help with concrete psychological research, on one hand, and beginning with natural scientific psychology and trying to capture the phenomenon as it is lived, on the other, must exist given the historical phase of development that psychology is presently in because neither framework was meant to be applied to the psychological as such. Moreover, these approaches could not be applied to the psychological without radical modification of the respective frameworks, and this radical modification was resisted, in one case, in the name of "pure phenomenology" and in the other in the name of "real science." I would now like to proceed to the issues.

A First Attempt at Synthesizing Phenomenology and Natural Scientific Psychological Research in the Field of Verbal Learning

By traditional or natural scientific psychology is meant that psychology that accepts and operates within a natural scientific interpretation of science. Although some exceptions can be documented, mainstream psychology has developed principally within that context and almost all research in psychology is guided by criteria emerging from that frame of reference. It is generally known that the natural sciences flourished within the framework of empirical and logical-positivistic philosophies. Since phenomenology does not share many values with those philosophies, the question of how to do phenomenologically inspired research and what makes it different constantly arise. Early in the phenomenological phase of my career I made an attempt to answer these questions by designing an experiment that first met all of the criteria of traditional psychology and then adding a noninterfering modification inspired by phenomenological thought (Giorgi, 1971).

I situated myself within the subfield known as verbal learning and designed the following traditional experiment. I was interested in exploring the role of meaning in learning, and so I wanted subjects to learn both meaningful and nonmeaningful items. Consequently, I planned to use nonsense syllables of 0% association value as meaningless material and monosyllabic words as meaningful material. This problem had been researched many times before (e.g., Lyon, 1914; McGeogh, 1930; Noble, 1963), but since I was adding the phenomenological modification, I wanted a well-researched problem for comparison purposes. However, precisely because of my phenomenological interest, my pilot work indicated a problem with respect to the 0% association value syllables. Since the association value of these syllables is low, they are difficult to pronounce, and in attempting to learn these syllables (or trigrams), subjects reported that they had to break them up into their single constituent letters in order to learn them. That meant, in effect, that the list consisted of a possible maximum of 30 items (10 syllables × 3 letters each) if each syllable had to be broken down instead of the 10 the experimenter thought he had constructed. Consequently, this meant that a list of nonpronounceable nonsense syllables is not experientially equal to a list of pronounceable syllables or to a list of words, although both lists apparently contain the same number of items as determined by other criteria. I then decided to use letters, which were highly familiar but not meaningful in the dictionary sense, and contrast the learning of a list of ten letters with monosyllabic words which were not only familiar but meaningful as well. In order to match for familiarity with letters, all words were chosen from the highest frequency list of words as determined by Thorndike and Lorge (1944). The actual randomly selected letters and words employed and their order are as follows: *Letters*: A, F, G, W, C, V, H, E, Q, M; *Words*: did, path, hand, same, lead, else, chair, bird, make, taste.

The phenomenological modification consisted in asking the subjects to respond to two questions after the performance phase of the experiment was over. The questions were: (1) You have just learned a list of letters and a list of words. Was one of these lists easier to learn? (2) If you have answered that one list was easier to learn, please explain why. The answers to these questions were analyzed qualitatively.

The performance results of the experiment were as follows. The mean number of trials to learn the letters was 8.22 with a standard deviation of 3.75, and the mean number of trials to learn the words was 11.67 with a standard deviation of 5.51. While the letters, nonmeaningful in a dictionary sense, were learned a little more quickly, the difference was not large enough to be statistically significant. Consequently, either the letters and words were basically equally easy to learn or there were just as many subjects that found the letters easier to learn as there were subjects who found the words easier to learn.

According to the descriptive results, however, only one subject of the 27 reported that the two lists were equally easy to learn; 15 said the letters were easier and 11 said that the words were. Thus, the descriptive results tend to indicate that there was an experiential preference for the ease with which either list was learned, but there was almost an even division between words and letters. This experiential preference, of course, could only be ascertained by means of subjects' descriptions.

The answers to the second question revealed the role of meaning in the study. My original intention in the qualitative analysis of the second question was to place the reasons that letters were easier to learn on one side and the reasons for words on the other in order to contrast them. However, I soon discovered that the same reasons were being given for both items. For example, some subjects said that letters were easier to learn because they were easier to relate, order, or associate; others said that letters were more difficult to learn because they were harder to relate or associate; some subjects said words were easier to learn because they had meanings; others said words were more difficult to learn because they had meanings; and so on. What sense could be made out of this? Sometimes meaning aided and sometimes it hindered the learning process.

What it means, essentially, is that what the experimenter defines as a stimulus object may not be the stimulus object for the subject. In other words, there is no stimulus object "in itself"; there is only a stimulus object "for the experimenter" and then a stimulus object "for the subject," and whether or not the two match is something that has to be ascertained rather than assumed. This distinction helps us because unless one introduces it, one cannot make sense of the fact that the same reasons for ease or difficulty of learning can be ascribed to the different materials.

Whether letters were easier or harder or whether meaning helped or hindered depended upon the strategy that the subject adopted with respect to the material. For example, a subject who stated that letters were easier to learn wrote as follows: "I am used to working with number series such as six-number prescription numbers and eight-number serial numbers. By grouping the given letters into groups of three or four, no special problem was involved in learning them. The words were not familiar in this manner." A subject who said that words were easier stated: "With words, once you went through a few trials the preceding word would help you anticipate the next word. Especially if you could group three or four words together and learn them in groups of sequences. Letters seemed confusing and had no connections." Thus, in one case, one was able to group items because of the lack of meaning, and in the other case, one grouped items together by using the meanings. Thus, whether or not meaning aids the learning process is very much dependent upon the strategy the subject adopts, and the strategy in turn co-determines what aspect of the stimulus object is perceived.

There is one other implication emerging from the descriptive data to which I will address myself, and it relates to the term "meaning." I started out to see if meaning in the dictionary sense of the term would make a difference in either the experience or performance of learning. The performance data showed that the presence of meaning did not have a significant effect, and the descriptive data showed that while dictionary meanings could be used, they were not essential for learning. Other features of the stimulus object could serve just as well because what mattered was the relationship between the strategy adopted by the subject and whatever aspect of the stimulus object could serve the needs of the strategy. In other words, there is a distinction between meaning in the dictionary sense and meaning in the psychological sense, and psychologically the letters and words were equally meaningful. In the dictionary sense only words were meaningful, but the fact that they were was neutral with respect to the learning process in general. Although meaning was highly relevant for specific subjects, it was not consistently so across all subjects.

Did the phenomenologically inspired modification[2] contribute anything to the understanding of the study? It enabled us to equate the stimulus objects in an experientially equal way (letters versus words instead of trigrams versus words); it enabled us to understand that there is no stimulus "in itself" but only "for the subject" or "for the experimenter"; it enabled us to distinguish between psychological meaning and dictionary meaning; and it helped us to understand the priority of the former in psychological situations. These interpretations were easily picked up by the simple expedient of adding descriptions that were analyzed phenomenologically. One cannot help but wonder why the inclusion of descriptions is not an integral part of all psychological research,[3] except that we know

2. It should be noted that the phenomenologically inspired modification cannot be reduced to the sheer presence of subject descriptions. What is necessary is descriptions, by subjects or experimenters, plus a qualitative analysis of their meaning within phenomenological attitude. Note also that phenomenological research is not necessarily dependent upon subject reports. An experimenter could design a series of experiments in which he might be able to discover indirectly that certain subjects prefer letters to words, but only if he also, at least implicitly, described the behavior in the situation. Of course, it would also take much longer.

3. Subject descriptions are still obtained haphazardly by a minority of psychologists, but usually they are used as inputs for better control rather than as data in their own right. One spot check (Giorgi, 1971) showed that only 12% of the experiments performed in-

that as a historical fact introspection as a method failed. The issue, of course, is whether or not introspectionism was an adequate theory of description, but in psychology, a generalization took place which simply interpreted introspection as *the* method of description. Thus when it failed, descriptions officially disappeared from the stock of desirable data in psychology.

In any event, while the descriptions included in this study reveal some significant additional information, one is also aware that there is something nonharmonious about the whole study—and indeed there is. It is inevitably so, given the way in which the study was designed. The deliberate intention was to accept all standard natural scientific criteria in the design of the study *first*, and then to add noninterfering phenomenological modifications. However, this results in a certain "side-by-sideness," a kind of bad eclecticism that would never sustain a research program because as soon as one began to explore the research problems further, a conflict of criteria would ensue. In other words, the research can clearly pass for good science—and perhaps with sympathetic interpretation, one may even see it as quasi-phenomenological—but it could never pass for an integration of phenomenology and science, which is our goal. The reason it cannot serve as a good model for integrating the two, and that one can doubt the genuine presence of phenomenological features, is that preference was deliberately given to natural science and thus the phenomenological perspective was truncated. An attempt to do justice to both would have simply revealed the contradictions we are trying to overcome. A deeper analysis of the problem would be necessary.

But before we move on to what we consider to be a better example of integration of science and phenomenology, we should inquire into the conditions and reasons that formed the traditional experimental program in verbal learning. How did the nonsense syllable come to be? Why did verbal learning research take on the form it did? What are some of the consequences of this type of research for the understanding of the psychological human? Our point is to show the inadequacy of the theory behind this tradition of research for a genuine understanding of the human person who is the subject of a psychological experiment.

The Verbal Learning Tradition Within the Context of Natural Scientific Psychology

One of the most succinct phrases ever coined to describe the difficulties of the natural scientific approach to psychology is the sentence written

---

cluded subjects' descriptions. However, arguments for more systematic use of verbal reports are being made once again (Ericsson & Simon, 1980).

by Sigmund Koch (1959, p. 783) when he said: "But, at the time of *its* inception, psychology was unique in the extent to which its institutionalization preceded its content and its method preceded its problems" (italics in original). That precisely this process took place with respect to verbal learning is easy to demonstrate. I have described this as briefly as possible elsewhere (Giorgi, 1976, pp. 300–301), so I will repeat it here for the sake of convenience:

> All psychologists agree that the experimental investigation of memory began in 1885 with the publication of *Memory* by Ebbinghaus. If we look at the attitude which he approached the phenomenon, we can detect an obvious natural scientific bias. Ebbinghaus (1964, p.7) writes as follows:
>
> "The method of obtaining exact measurements—i.e. numerically exact ones—of the inner structure of causal relations is, by virtue of its nature, of general validity. This method, indeed, has been so exclusively used and so fully worked out by the natural sciences that, as a rule, it is defined as something peculiar to them, as *the* method of natural science. To repeat, however, its logical nature makes it generally applicable to all spheres of existence and phenomena. Moreover, the possibility of defining accurately and exactly the actual behavior of any process whatever, and thereby of giving a reliable basis for the direct comprehension of it depends above all upon the possibility of applying this method.
>
> We all know of what this method consists: an attempt is made to keep constant the mass of conditions which have proven themselves causally connected with the a certain result; one of these conditions is isolated from the rest and varied in a way that can be numerically described; then the accompanying change on the side of the effect is ascertained by measurement or computation."
>
> Ebbinghaus then goes on to describe the difficulties encountered in applying the natural scientific method to memory processes and how to surmount them. Unwittingly, Ebbinghaus demonstrates exactly how method preceded content in psychology since he can describe the scientific method fully but has to argue for the application of this method in psychology.

The above text clearly establishes the role of the natural sciences in initiating the verbal learning tradition. Some of the consequences of this step will be spoken to shortly, but first we want to indicate the vitality of the tradition that Ebbinghaus began. The history of this subfield can be traced in broad strokes from Ebbinghaus's first work in 1885 to that of his German colleague, G. E. Müller (1911, 1913, 1917), who almost immediately picked up Ebbinghaus's work (see Boring, 1950, p. 375) and published research first with students (Müller & Schumann, 1893; Müller & Pilzecker, 1900) and then later summarized most of his findings in three separate volumes entitled *Zur Analyse der Gedächtnistätigkeit und des Vorstellungsverlaufes*, published between 1911 and 1917; to McGeoch's (1942) summary of the literature and experiments published in 1942, down through the edited volumes by Cofer (1961) and Cofer and Musgrave (1963) and the founding of the *Journal of Verbal Learning and Verbal Behavior* (1962); to the most contemporary syntheses of the field by Jung (1968) and Harcum (1975). While some of the terminology and acronyms might appear puzzling to him, Ebbinghaus could read the latest works and recognize many of the parameters that he introduced back in 1885. Indeed, Ebbinghaus was frequently praised for his ingenuity and for being ahead of his time, and no praise can be better than that provided by Hilgard when he wrote the introduction to the Dover edition of the translation of Ebbinghaus's book, and which at the same time, indicates that the values that Ebbinghaus implemented are still shared by experimental psychologists today. Hilgard (1964, p. vii) writes:

> In this very first experimental study of learning and memory Ebbinghaus did at least four things, all ahead of his times, and valid today: (1) He abandoned reliance upon the testimony of introspection in favor of objective evidence of memory. . . . (2) He invented a calibrated material (nonsense syllables) to provide a new substance to be memorized. (3) He criticized the established laws of association, particularly those of contiguity and immediate succession, by introducing a quantitative study of remote associations. (4) He made use of statistical and mathematical notions to test the significance of his findings and to formulate his results in accordance with a mathematical model. For the beginner in a new field to have done all of these things—and more—is so surprising as to baffle our understanding of how it could have happened.

Thus, Hilgard, is praising Ebbinghaus for being objective, quantitative, and inventing the nonsense syllable, a standardized and calibrated material. All these features are characteristics of natural scientific psychology, which in our judgment is the primary reason that verbal learning studies took the form they did, so let us explore their implications a little more.

We will begin with Ebbinghaus's most famous invention—the nonsense syllable. The primary motivation for inventing the nonsense syllable was to provide as homogeneous a material as possible, and Ebbinghaus, since he could not control language or the past history of the subject, introduced material as devoid of meaning as possible. In his own words Ebbinghaus (1964/1913/1885, p. 23) states: "The nonsense material, just described, offers many advantages, in part because of this very lack of meaning." Another advantage of the meaninglessness of the material is that the subject's history is neutral with respect to it. Thus, it should be equally new to everyone. In addition, in his attempt to keep all conditions constant, Ebbinghaus tried to assume as passive an attitude as possible. Again, he (Ebbinghaus, 1964/1913/1885, p. 25) writes: "There was no attempt to connect the nonsense syllables by the invention of special associations of the nmemotechnik type: learning was carried on solely by the influence of the mere repetitions upon the natural memory." It should be noted that Ebbinghaus was conducting his study within the context of association theory, thus the lack of activity on the part of the subject was for him a way of insuring that the mechanisms of association could operate more purely. Lastly, Ebbinghaus did all his work and published all the results of only one subject—himself. He was aware that this was a limitation of his study, but he also was convinced that some general findings were produced in addition to whatever idiosyncracies may have been present.

The point that I would like to raise about this study is its context. If one looks at the contextual implications of the Ebbinghaus model of learning research, a striking thing emerges: It presupposes a subject that is ahistorical, asocial, and without meaning-giving attributes. The subject is ahistorical in being deliberately confronted with material that is ideally nonsensical and which should be entirely new; meaning-giving attributes are lacking because the subject is meant to be passive in attitude and function in a merely rote manner; and the subject is asocial not only in working alone but also in the passive attitude, which minimized the use of language and relations with others. It should be noted that this context is a direct consequence of attempting to apply the method of the natural sciences to the problem of learning and memory. It is also an amazing contrast to the attitude of the subjects who performed in the experiment I described earlier, who were highly active and groping for meanings and connections.

But of course, what I have just described took place back in 1885, and Ebbinghaus was only the first to start such research. Despite Hilgard's praise, one does not expect an originator to solve all the problems his research initiates. What has happened since 1885? To avoid all suspense, let me say at the outset that within the Ebbinghaus tradition there are parallel discoveries to all of the points that I introduced by means of the phenomenological analysis of descriptive material. Let me briefly review how these discoveries surfaced.

When presenting the findings from my own study, I indicated that I decided not to use nonsense syllables because pilot research had indicated that not all of the syllables were of equal value with respect to pronounceability, nor for that matter, in certain other respects. Ebbinghaus had already noted this fact himself, and G. E. Müller improved the situation somewhat by specifying more rigorous rules for the production of nonsense syllables (Boring, 1950). Finally, psychologists saw the need to calibrate more precisely the association value or meaning of the alleged nonsense syllables, and Glaze (1928) did a systematic study of over 2,000 consonant-vowel-consonant nonsense syllables rating them from 0% to 100% association value, Witmer (1935) rated over 4,000 consonant-consonant-consonant syllables according to their ability to elicit associations, and Noble (1952) determined the meaningfulness of verbal units that included nonsense syllables, bisyllabic nonsense syllables, and some words with a low frequency of use index as determined by Thorndike and Lorge (1944). The point that the tradition is attempting to establish here is that a more precise calibration of the meaningfulness, meaning, or association value of the syllables is necessary in order to do more precise research because nonsense material is never uniformly nonsensical, and so more precise expressions are called for. However, for us, the lack of uniformity with respect to nonsense material also implies that what is "equal" to the learner cannot be defined by the characteristics of the stimulus object "in itself" but only in relation to the learner.

Related to the question of the actual meaninglessness of the syllables is the question of what the real stimulus object is—the one intended by the experimenter or the one experienced by the subject. In our study we saw that it was necessary to determine the convergence and not assume it. For example, the stimulus object QIR might be a 0% association value stimulus for the experimenter, but it might be experienced as immediately recognizable by a subject because by chance it matches his initials; or an experimenter might expect a subject to pronounce the syllable TAK in order to learn it, but the subject spells it instead and uses the first letter as a mnemonic for learning the other two. In the early 1960s Underwood (1963) wrote a paper entitled "Stimulus Selection in Verbal Learning" in which he distinguished between a nominal stimulus, the stimulus for the experimenter, and a functional stimulus, the characteristics of the stimulus which the subject actually uses to cue a response, and spoke of the potential theoretical difficulties involved if there were a discrepancy between them. Of course, this is precisely the distinction we introduced earlier. Underwood noted that the distinction did exist in conditioning studies with animals, but he was unaware of any systematic use of the distinction in the verbal learning area until he raised the issue.

Our third finding related to the fact that the same reasons were given by subjects for learning either letters or words, and this led us to uncover the role of the subject's strategy in learning and the fact that the subject selected aspects of the stimulus in terms of strategy. In other words, subjects organize the lists in various ways, including the "distorting" of items in psychologically meaningful ways. Ebbinghaus himself chose not to include mnemonics or memory aids and stressed rote memory and a passive attitude. However, it did not take long to break that precedent, since his contemporary G. E. Müller uncovered the large number of strategies and devices spontaneously adopted by the subjects, including rhythmical organization as well as reading into the material (Murphy, 1949). Since the mid 1950s investigators have been working with the situations described as free recall or free learning, which refers to the fact that subjects may learn or recall items in any order, which in turn allows the subject's organizational processes to become much more manifest than possible in more constrained situations. What this line of research has established is that the subject's output has systematic features not present in the input, which can only mean that the subject has put them there. It has also emphasized the preexperimental habits and experiences that the subject had as relevant factors in the experimental situation. In brief, the subject is anything but passive when not constrained to be passive.

The last finding we emphasized was that we could distinguish between the dictionary meaning of a word and its psychological meaning. The latter was understood in a functional significance sense, so that what was meaningful about the stimulus object was any aspect that allowed itself to be discriminated in such a way that the unit it represented and its place in the sequence could be known and repeated by the subject. For example, one subject transformed the sequence "else-chair" into "easy-chair," so that he could remember it more easily, but always spoke it correctly as "else-chair." The transformation of "else" into "easy" only made sense within the context that he had to repeat the items verbatim in correct sequence, and hence it is a manifestation of the psychological meaning that the items had for the subject. Ebbinghaus himself did not pick up this aspect, but his followers did without ever calling it psychological meaning. What has happened is that psychological meaning is spoken to in terms of variables, and one such example is a task variable.

For example, a task variable difference that is relevant to this point is the difference between learning with the intention of repeating items in order and learning in terms of free learning. Even though the same items are used, the psychological meaning of the items differs. Another example is the strategy adopted by the subject. Our own study showed that dictionary meaning could be a help or a hindrance depending upon the strategy adopted—help or hindrance indirectly referring to the psychological meaning. Thus, what we call the psychological meaning involved in learning is being tapped by traditional experimenters and is increasingly being seen as important. Jung (1968, pp. 8–9) has summarized the recent trends in the following way: "An implicit assumption in much verbal learning research is that 'raw' learning is being observed. However, recent evidence and formulations emphasize the interaction or transfer between preexperimental verbal habits and the acquisition and retention of laboratory associations. At the same time, greater interest in the role of cognitive processes is developing."

Thus subsequent developments within the Ebbinghaus tradition of research on verbal learning have yielded findings and expressions that parallel those emerging from the qualitative analysis of descriptive data that we analyzed under the banner of phenomenology. What that indicates to us is that historicity, sociality, and meaning-giving attributes are being returned to the subject despite the ideals of the paradigm. To be interested in preexperimental verbal habits and the acquisition of verbal learning is to recognize the subject as historical, to understand the distinction between the nominal stimulus and the functional stimulus, or the stimulus as it is for the subject versus the stimulus as it is for the experimenter is to understand the experimental situation as a potentially dialectical one, or at least as a social situation; and finally, to understand that the subject employs strategies and organizes the material on his own is to say that he has meaning-giving characteristics. If this is true, and we believe it is, it means that traditional research, while using a different language, basically converges with the phenomenological approach, and if so, why then do we need a phenomenological approach?

The question is a legitimate one, and we shall try to answer it by considering the following three points. First, there is an intrinsic tension between the organization and criteria of science as practiced by traditional psychology and human phenomena as they are lived. Second, more positively stated, a phenomenologically grounded theory of science is more faithful to the total phenomenon. Third, a better understanding of the subject-experimenter relationship is necessary, and a phenomenological analysis of that relationship can be enlightening for psychological science.

We will deal with the tensions between human phenomena as lived and the criteria of traditional psychology first. There are a number of ways that this issue can be discussed, but it seems that we can make our point by discussing two distinctions: (1) that between the external viewpoint and the internal viewpoint, and (2) the difference between the assumed independence of variables as opposed to the idea of already-related discriminations of a whole situation. The natural sciences have developed by assuming the external viewpoint and independence of variables prior to experimentation, and psychology began by attempting to impose the same criteria on its phenomena. Externality was desirable in order to avoid subjectivity and independence of variables was a way of applying the twin features of isolation and analysis. Thus, in the verbal learning tradition, nonsense syllables were invented as a means of establishing independence between the learner and the material, and of course, the syllables are discrete items to be learned; they can be easily manipulated so that they can be given many desirable characteristics.

The difficulty is that while these criteria are valid for the natural sciences, they are not theoretically defensible when transposed to psychological scientific practice with human subjects. The practice of psychological science always exceeds the constraints of these criteria in a significant way and it undoubtedly would help psychology's scientific self-understanding if it invented modes of praxis more consonant with the givens of its research situation as revealed by more open-ended and precise descriptions. Our first point is simply that sustaining an external attitude and assumed independence of variables cannot most adequately make sense of the verbal learning studies; rather, one has at least to assume implicitly an internal relation and understand the total situation as a complex gestalt. For example, there is no way in which a subject can learn a syllable without relating to it internally. Even under the strict conditions that Ebbinghaus set up—a passive, rote learner—the learner at least has to set up the correct relationship among the items and to do that, to see them as "items to be learned in correct sequence" is already a transformation of the material that can be descriptively shown to be different from ten discrete items on a memory drum (Colaizzi, 1971). Even to establish the association value or meaningfulness (*m*) of a syllable requires a relationship to a subject—they are not characteristics that syllables have "in themselves"—but the tradition establishes these characteristics in relation to a group of subjects who are not subjects of the specific experiment. But that simply means that the syllables acquire certain characteristics in relation to a certain task, but thought is never given as to whether the *tasks themselves* are identical or similar. For example, Glaze (1928) determined his association value of syllables by exposing one syllable at a time to each of 15 subjects and allowing 3 seconds for the arousal of an association, if any. The syllables were then classified according to the percentage of subjects who had an association. Noble determined meaningfulness by having subjects write all the different words they could to a given stimulus word within a 60-second period. Undoubtedly these tasks indicate something about the stimulus words or syllables, but they do not necessarily tell us very much about how the syllable may be used in a task where each of them has to be learned in correct order in relation to each other. The tradition itself has already established that task is a variable and much depends upon the strategy that a subject uses. The tasks and strategies establishing association value or meaningfulness are highly dissimilar from the task used in serial learning. What is really being established is a relationship that could be described somewhat as follows (for the case of Glaze): "What is the relationship between syllables that evoke a single association differentially among a large group of subjects and the ability to memorize in correct sequential order a list of syllables grouped either according to their ability to provoke few or very many such single associations?" Could it not be, as in the case with words, that the many associations could be either a help or a hindrance, depending upon the strategy the subject adopts? And how can that be ascertained unless the internal relation between the subject and the material was established and understood in context? This also means that an internal viewpoint and a holistic, contextual situational approach would be called for—which is our point. In other words, until the item is assumed under the perspective of "item-to-be-reorganized-so-that-it-can-be-learned," no internal relation is established, and how the item is reorganized depends very much upon the method (for example, paired-associate versus free learning), the material (nonsense syllables or letters) and the task, and these factors are interdependent.

The same reasoning would apply to the distinction between "nominal stimulus" and "functional stimulus"—or we could say that the discovery of the distinction is itself a recognition of the internal relation between the subject and the material. To say that there is a functional stimulus is to assert that what counts is how a subject relates to stimulus material, and that is what we mean by an internal relation. A nominal stimulus is the way the experimenter intends the stimulus object to be perceived or related to, that is, the way the experimenter hopes the subject will establish an internal relation with it. At the beginning of the experiment there is only the experimenter's relation to the stimulus material, that is, specially constructed or selected material that the experimenter hopes will be responded to precisely in terms of the special construction or selection. The relationship between the special construction or selectivity of the material and the experimenter is for us also an internal relation. The very fact that stimulus material has so often to be specially constructed also demonstrates that there is no totally independent stimulus. Either it reflects characteristics that are designed by the experimenter, and hopefully responded to, or else it reflects characteristics in part determined in more unknown ways by others in the everyday world. It would be more precise in the long run to acknowledge this fact than to assume an alleged independent stimulus.

Finally, the studies of free learning situations, demonstrate that an internal relation is once again presupposed. If one asks free learning of *what*, or subjective organization of *what*, the answer is of the nonsense material or other stimulus items. And what happens in such situations? Subjects recall the items in any order and are able to impose meanings and organizational factors on them, that is, they use their meaning-giving capacities and set up an internal relation with the items. What counts ultimately are not the characteristics that the stimulus objects had prior to their experimental role, but precisely the aspects that the subjects respond to. The former designations have merely a provisional role in research.

But what does all this imply? It means that researchers who use the Ebbinghaus model in a way pretend that the human characteristics of the subject are not there and then grudgingly admit them. When they surface, however, the experimental situations and language being used are not geared to those human characteristics, and thus they have to be admitted through the back door. Another way of saying this is to say that since the 1950s the researchers in this tradition (Müller and his co-workers were a prior exception) have finally explicitly broken from the constraints of association theory but not from the natural scientific paradigm itself. In order to do the latter, one must surrender the privilege granted to the external viewpoint and the assumed independence of variables, since both assumptions block one from being faithful to features of a learning situation as experienced in everyday life that naive descriptions introduce. The last point we have already demonstrated with the analysis of the descriptive material of our experiment. In our view, consequently, the only way to overcome the conflict between the characteristics of human phenomena and the criteria of traditional psychology is to change the framework within which traditional psychology developed and works. This leads to the second reason for the necessity of a phenomenological approach.

The second point, that the phenomenological view is more faithful to the total phenomenon, is really the obverse of the critique offered above, and we shall limit ourselves to a theoretical argument that hopefully will show why a consistent descriptive approach is more faithful to the total phenomenon and therefore necessary for the proper development of psychology. Merleau-Ponty (1962) has written that the real is not to be constructed or explained but described. Yet, almost all verbal learning research is based upon situations constructed, implicitly or explicitly, by the experimenter, and an ideal experiment is one in which everything is "explained" in terms of the major variables identified by the experimenter. First there is analysis—for example, all verbal learning situations must consist of a stimulus, some mediating activities, and a response. Then variables are introduced for one or two (or sometimes all) analytic terms. For example, an experimenter might divide the stimulus into 0% and 100% association value items, he might assume that response variability will be greater with 100% association value items (a mediating factor) plus the fact that both remote and proximate forward and backward associations will be more pronounced with 0% association value items (other mediating factors) and hence will observe what effect these stimulus object characteristics combined with those mediating factors will have on the responses in terms of number correct or incorrect or in terms of number of trials with 100% correct responses in order. If the experiment runs true to form, the experimenter can then explain the (presumed) better performance with 100% association value items in terms of the stimulus characteristics and the mediating factors.

But it should be noted that all of these exist for the consciousness of the researcher. They are conceptualizations (constructions) that he has either brought into being directly (nonsense syllables) or allows to take place by experimental constructions (forward and backward associations because items must be learned in order). What is not known is what the experience of the subject is in the face of these "constructions." Clearly, the subject does not experience what the experimenter "constructs" *as* he constructs it, and yet one has to admit that the constructions make a difference for the performance, and one can in part "explain" performance in terms of the "constructions." So there is a relationship between the "constructed manipulations" of the experimenter (which, ironically, are based upon insights into meaningful aspects of the totality) and the experience and/or performance of the subjects, but again this relationship is understood externally—precisely because the variables are understood to be neutral with respect to each other at the start, and only come into relationship with each other after the experiment begins. Yet, one knows that the 0% association value syllables are never purely so, and one also knows that more mediating processes other than response availability and forward and backward associations are taking place. Still, the researcher limits himself to first analyzing his data in terms of his constructions and then to seeing what other factors might have influenced the outcome. This demonstrates the "functional formalism," based upon abstraction, that Politzer (1968/1928) has so effectively criticized with respect to psychology in his argument for a concrete psychology. The basic problem is that the products of the researcher's analysis are placed "realistically" into the situation and are presumed to operate precisely as he conceives of them. Thus, the real is first constructed, and then these same "constructs" are used as explanations for the "real" performance data, yet we never actually know what "really" happened because the subject's entire perspective and the experimenter's total presence to the situation are not brought in as legitimate data.

Thus, description is necessary, so that we know what actually happened concretely before analysis of some type can begin, and the subject's perspective and what he lives (experiences and behaves and knows) must be kept separate from the experimenter's perspective and what he lives (observes and behaves) as well as from what he knows. If traditional psychology proceeds the way it does, it is not only because of the influence of the natural sciences but also because of the acceptance of mixed realistic and idealistic philosophical postulates, which is beyond the scope of this paper to analyze, but we will simply state that we accept phenomenological philosophical guidelines, choose to begin descriptively, and proceed from there. But if such is the case, why do we have to remain tied to the situation begun by Ebbinghaus, which was inspired by so many assumptions that are alien to what phenomenological philosophy would want to assume? The answer is that we do not have to remain so tied, and thus we seek a new starting point for research in the psychology of learning.

Thus, a phenomenological psychology is still desirable despite the advances of traditional psychological research because a more positive articulation of a scientific framework which takes into account in a serious way obvious human characteristics is still sorely needed. The fact that a human subject is historical and social and dwells in a world of meanings, whether actively constituted or passively assumed, are three paramount characteristics that should not be grudgingly admitted and backed into, but rather directly seized, spoken to, and taken advantage of. But to do so means that the traditional psychological framework must be broken, and that is why a totally different self-understanding of psychological science is necessary. Of course, it does not mean that traditional researchers do not perceive this need (indeed, the evidence is to the contrary, e.g., Mandler, 1967) nor that many findings cannot be incorporated in the new perspective (many clearly can) but only that a new theoretical perspective is necessary to bring greater clarity to this area of psychology, and the only way to do so is to use the peculiarly human characteristics when they are available rather than to ignore them.

The third point, the need for a deeper understanding of the relationship between the experimenter and the subject, will be discussed after the presentation of the alternative model for psychology.

Having shown that the traditional psychological paradigm cannot speak to human characteristics without a radical change, we have demonstrated the lack that exists by trying to begin with traditional psychology and approaching human phenomena. We will now leap to the perspective of phenomenological philosophy and try to work down to human psychological analysis.

Phenomenological Philosophy

I have already indicated the problems involved in attempting to give an unambiguous, succinct presentation of phenomenology, but fortunately, for this context, another option is possible. Rather than a presentation of the common denominator of a broad range of phenomenological philosophers' expressions of the meaning of phenomenology, I shall situate myself within the perspective of one philosopher, Merleau-Ponty, whom, no one ever took to be nonphenomenological no matter how much one may question his reading or interpretation of Husserl. Merleau-Ponty's own clearest statement in defense of phenomenology appears in the preface of *The Phenomenology of Perception* (1962), and I will use that as the basis for the meaning of philosophical phenomenology. I might also add that in selecting Merleau-Ponty as the representative of phenomenological philosophy, I am also selecting a philosopher who knew psychology as well as any phenomenological philosopher with whom I am acquainted, and hence I am in no way biasing the case of the inadequacy of philosophical phenomenology for direct relevance to psychology. Indeed, one could argue the opposite.

In any event, for Merleau-Ponty, phenomenology can be best understood in terms of the phenomenological method, and it has four characteristics. First of all, it is descriptive, and the return to description "excludes equally the procedure of analytical reflection . . . and that of scientific explanation" (Merleau-Ponty, 1962, p. ix). It is not that analysis or explanation of some sort does not go on, but simply that the analysis should follow naive description, and one has to be sure that the categories of analysis or explanation do not enter the initial descriptions.

The second characteristic of the phenomenological method is the reduction. Not only must we be sure that our theoretical prejudices in terms of analytic or explanatory categories do not enter our initial descriptions—and therefore we bracket them—but we also want to be sure that we do not even naively prejudge the nature of our experiences, so we describe them simply as they present themselves and precisely as meanings for us without taking the further step of stating that they *are* what they present themselves to be, or that they *are* what they mean to us. That is the meaning of reduction, and it is a necessary attitude for phenomenological analysis or description, for it is one of the best ways of revealing our spontaneous, prereflective ways of dealing with world. Reflective modes of describing are too much in the service of an implicit or explicit posited goal, and nonreduced, natural descriptions tend to cover up the experienced moments and race on to the realness of the thing.

The third characteristic of the method is the search for essences. Once one is in the presence of descriptions revealing how subjects prereflectively actually relate to the world, the phenomenologist tries to comprehend the essence, or structure, of those lived relations. He does this by employing the process of free imaginative variation in order to discover what meanings must necessarily belong to the phenomenon in order for it to be a phenomenon of a certain type, for example, the essence of perception or anger, and so on. Merleau-Ponty (1962, p. xv) takes great pains to point out that the achievement of the essence is not the end of phenomenological analysis, but only a means of bringing to light all of the actual "living relationships of experience."

The last characteristic is intentionality, which means that consciousness is always directed or oriented toward something that is not consciousness itself. But for Merleau-Ponty the major significance of intentionality is the distinction that Husserl introduced between intentionality of act and operative intentionality. The former refers to the reflective level and it indicates a voluntary taking up of a position or attitude toward an object, whereas the latter refers to a certain manner of taking a stand with respect to a human situation or real event that is discoverable only in being lived since it manifests a pre-predicative unity of our life and world. The uncovering of operative intentionality requires description from within the reduction in order to be made manifest, and consequently, understood.

If the phenomenological method can be understood in the way I have just described, what is its value for psychology as a science? Before we proceed to a direct answer to that question, perhaps we should examine the concrete ways in which philosophical phenomenologists believe that they already have helped psychology.

Philosophical phenomenologists see in their field a means of aiding the science of psychology's theoretical problem, its foundational issues, its problems with clarification of concepts, and finally, as a way of opening up new possibilities for psychological research (Husserl, 1977; Sartre, 1962a, 1962b; Spiegelberg, 1972; Kockelmans, 1971; Gurwitsch, 1974). However, these values are almost always merely spoken to, sketched, adumbrated, or argued for logically rather than actually worked through, demonstrated, or implemented. In short, they are proposals that include arguments or examples in order to demonstrate the necessity and value of the proposal, but they are not achievements. The second way in which philosophical phenomenologists have helped the science of psychology is by critiquing specific psychological studies or experiments, usually emphasizing how some preconception or implicit philosophical assumption somehow limited the interpretation of the studies (e.g., Sartre, 1962b; Merleau-Ponty, 1963; Strasser, 1957). Undoubtedly these critiques contain many good insights and provide a valuable critical perspective on how psychological science is practiced. Moreover, I agree with most of the critiques. The major problem is that the constructive alternative implied by the critique is never spoken to concretely, at the level of praxis. Only the theoretical, foundational, and conceptual implications are developed. How these revised conceptions and theories can be the basis for a different practice in psychology is left to be worked out if it is referred to at all. In brief, we could say that philosophical phenomenology has contributed to the development of psychological theory, and to a clarification of the foundations of psychology as a science, but it has not developed the implications of these contributions in a positive and concrete way.

With that point established, we can return to our question: How can the phenomenological method as articulated above be of help for psychology as a science? The answer is not clear. We are told that if we want to be considered phenomenologists, we should use the phenomenological method, and that means that we should describe our phenomenon from within a reduced attitude and then seek the essence of the phenomenon by means of free imaginative variation while respecting the fact that consciousness is intentional. However clear this may be at the philosophical level of discourse (and it is clear), it is ambiguous with respect to how to go about doing concrete research in psychology. Certainly, we know what descriptions are, but still, numerous questions arise: What is a good description as opposed to a bad one? Is psychological description the same as or different from everyday descriptions? When is a description finished? What is the relationship between the question posed and the answer given in a description? With respect to the reduction, the following questions quickly present themselves: Are there any checks or guarantees that one has assumed the reductive attitude, or is it simply assumed that one can execute it if one understands what Merleau-Ponty means? What are the concrete consequences of the fact that one cannot achieve a complete reduction (Merleau-Ponty, 1962, p. xiv)? What is the relationship between the reduced description and a contrasting nonreduced description of the same situation? What about the intention to seek essences? That, too, raises questions. Does psychological research seek its own essences or merely imply philosophical ones? Must essences always be ascertained first, before we go to the facts, or is the procedure reversible? If the former, then how can one have experience as a ground for eidetic analysis? It is one of phenomenology's claims always to be a contact with experience. If the latter, on what basis are the facts selected. How are relevant and irrelevant facts discerned? Finally, what are the implications of intentionality for psychological analysis? Certainly, man and world, subject and object, are now to be understood as intrinsically related, but how is that meaning to be translated into concrete praxis? Intentional analysis means an analysis of meanings in terms of the correlation between subjective acts (noeses) and the objects of those acts (noemata). Yet, Merleau-Ponty, whose thought is to be our guide, hardly ever uses the terms and yet performs many analyses that are unquestionably phenomenological. Moreover, how does one discriminate the effects of operative intentionality in a description?

Such are the questions awaiting a psychologist who, even if he understands the phenomenological method as explicated by Merleau-Ponty and is totally sympathetic to it, wishes to translate the fundamental and valuable insights of phenomenology into a concrete program of psychological scientific research. We have elaborated all this primarily to show that there are difficulties involved and to give some examples of the nature of the difficulties. The point here is not that the philosophers have failed to do something that they should have done it is that very expectation that has to be challenged. It is not a philosophical project that has to be accomplished—it is a scientific one and a specifically psychological one at that. We come back to the key assumption of this paper: A psychological perspective is an originary one, and it cannot be reduced to other perspectives. It must discover its own methods, procedures, rules of interpretation, and so on by a direct contact with its own phenomena of interest and by working through whatever is necessary to achieve stable and significant psychological findings.

However, psychology does not and cannot operate in a vacuum—there are social and historical factors that constantly influence it and have preceded it. Thus, historically speaking, since it became an independent discipline in the late nineteenth century, it was greatly influenced by the prevalent philosophy of that period and it achieved its independence by identification with the natural sciences (Giorgi, 1970). However, the internal development of psychology has placed great pressure on its presuppositions and self-understanding as it tries to achieve greater clarity concerning its unique contribution to knowledge. Different philosophical methods and different conceptions of science have been proposed as more attune to the intrinsic demands of psychology. Among the suggested alternatives for psychology is philosophical phenomenology, a suggestion that has been made by both philosophers and psychologists. But the point here is that the philosophy to be adopted, however helpful, cannot be handed over ready-made. It has to be mediated. The very way in which philosophy introduces its concepts or languages its problems, or poses its questions is influenced by the fundamental philosophical nature of the project. Thus, the articulation of a phenomenological method for philosophy, as such, may or may not be helpful for science. Nevertheless, the fundamental philosophical orientation and manner of conceiving reality may be helpful to the scientist. Thus, perhaps a scientist wants to be inspired by a particular philosophy and even wants to situate himself within its general frame of reference and work within it, but at the same time he desires to meet the exigencies of his scientific discipline at the level of science. Such is precisely the case with many psychologists who seek help from phenomenological philosophy for the science of psychology. That is why so many questions can arise for the psychologist despite Merleau-Ponty's incisive description and analysis of the phenomenological method. That is also one reason for the confusion in understanding phenomenology—the level at which one is speaking is often not clarified. It is also a reason for the fitful and constantly unsuccessful attempts of the genuine development of a phenomenological psychology. Those who really understand phenomenology are philosophers, and as they articulate the genuine meaning of phenomenology they do it *as a philosophy*. The psychologists who attempt to use it often "discover" that either they are misunderstanding phenomenology, and therefore allegedly define themselves outside the perspective, or else they see no relevance of such an exposition for their science and dismiss it. Thus, phenomenology, to be helpful to psychology, *must not remain just a philosophy*; it must be expressed in a way that makes it proximately helpful to psychological praxis, and that would be the meaning of phenomenological psychology as a human science rather than phenomenological psychology as a subfield of philosophy.[4] I shall provide one example of how such a mediation can take place by adapting Merleau-Ponty's description of the phenomenological method in a way that could make it more directly applicable to psychological research praxis. By mediation I mean that the general criteria of the phenomenological method can be accepted, but only with modification.

The first criterion that Merleau-Ponty mentions is that the phenomenological method must be descriptive because we want to avoid premature analytic or explanatory constructs. The major modification that we would introduce here is that the original naive descriptions come from another person—the subject of the research. If phenomenology is interpreted strictly, this could be considered a nonphenomenological step because the instructions are that one is to bring to "self-evidence" whatever intuitions one is to describe. Thus, if I have another subject describe a learning situation for me, he is the direct experiencer of the situation, and I am present to it only through his description and therefore, in a sense, once removed.

A number of points can be made about this objection. First of all, one wonders whether the self-descriptive emphasis belongs specifically to phenomenology or to philosophy as a whole. That is, the self-descriptive or self-experiential mode is such an integral part of the philosophical project and style of thinking that it may simply be taken for granted despite phenomenology's sensitivity to implicit presuppositions. Moreover, there is a sense in which the researcher is directly present to a description and the task is to come up with a meaning that objectively belongs to the state of affairs contained in the description. If a phenomenological psychologist cannot do this, how can a phenomenological philosopher grasp the meanings contained in the texts of dead philosophers? Thus, descriptions of experienced situations by others could be considered an example of the "phenomenology of reading a text," which, presumably, phenomenologists would find acceptable. Lastly, without presenting all of the arguments here, one could say that a description of an experience is an analog or variation of the behavior of another in one's presence, and if one can ascertain the meaning of another's behavior in a situation by observation, then one can obtain the meaning of a description of that same situation.

Coming from the other side, the reason that descriptions of experienced situations by others are so critical, on a pragmatic level, is that the climate of self-understanding in psychological science is still such that a description of an experience and the analysis of it by the same person (the researcher) is simply not acceptable because of the fear of "subjective

4. A work spelling out this distinction in a more elaborate way is currently in the planning phase.

bias." The core of truth in such a fear, of course, is the concern that the description may directly or unconsciously be in the service of the theory of the researcher, and thus he proves his own biases. While it is true that with a well-developed theory of the meaning of objectivity and with sufficient checks and balances one can presumably overcome the objection, the effort is so great compared to the simple expedient of getting a description from naive others who know nothing about the prejudices of the researcher, that the latter alternative seems eminently commendable.

The second criterion of the phenomenological method is the reduction. From the viewpoint of strict phenomenological interpretation, the reduction is a stumbling block because all science operates within the natural attitude, and only phenomenology practices the phenomenological reduction which breaks from that attitude. We would argue, however, that such a stumbling block is more apparent than real, at least where research with human subjects is concerned. Now, it is generally known that Husserl's comments regarding the reduction are difficult to interpret consistently (Schmitt, 1967), and there is even question concerning the number he ultimately came to decide upon, but the fundamental notion guiding the introduction of the reduction is clear: Whatever presents itself to consciousness should be taken precisely with the meaning with which it presents itself, and one should refrain from affirming that it is what it presents itself to be, even if that particular existential characteristic belongs to the presentation. The point is that such an attitude is implicitly present in most psychological praxis with respect to the noemata of the subject's experience, although not with respect to his acts of consciousness. Let me demonstrate that point with a number of examples. A subject in a visual threshold experiment reports that a barely visible light is white although from the wavelength characteristics the experimenter knows that it has to be blue, but he records the subject's judgment as presented; a subject in a recognition threshold experiment does not report recognizing tachistoscopically presented taboo words although he does report the recognition of "neutral" words which have shorter exposure times, but the experimenter records the results; a subject in a perceptual experiment goes along with the suggestiveness of the conditions and gives an accurate description of an illusion, which the experimenter knows is an illusion, and therefore not corresponding to the reality, but he accepts and records the result; a client in a therapist's office describes an early memory, which from other sources the therapist knows to be false, but he lets the client continue his elaboration of the memory. In each case, while the subject of the experiment lived in the natural attitude and was affirming what he experienced to be the way he experienced it (often helped along by the very conditions of the experiment, when it was an experiment), the experimenter or therapist merely accepted that what the subject reported was the way he reported it to be even though the experimenter or therapist knew differently. But this is precisely a reduction: the difference between the way in which a situation is and the way it is experienced. The subject lives in the situation, but the psychologist understands it as "being for the subject." Thus, for the psychologist, the object pole is reduced, but the subject pole is not. That is, in each case, the experimenter or therapist still understands that the actual conscious processes are taking place in real time for the subjects or clients. Thus, the psychological phenomenological reduction is a mixed one; the objects of the experience are understood to be within the reduction, that is, taken merely as they present themselves, but the stream of consciousness of the subject is understood as a real process because it is the specifically human mode of organization of consciousness in which the psychologist is interested (Giorgi, 1981). The above characterization of the implicit use of the reduction on the part of psychology requires some clarification, for not all psychologists would interpret it the way we have, nor would all experiments necessarily permit such an analysis. It would only be true if we understood psychology as a human science, that is, a discipline wherein certain characteristics of the human mode of existence itself could emerge and be emphasized.

In a way, the presence and extensiveness of the reduction can serve the function of distinguishing among different interpretations of psychology. Psychology conceived as a natural science accepts both the object of the subject's experience and the processes (or acts) to be in the natural attitude and thus tries to understand the subject-object relation strictly in terms of cause-effect relationships. For philosophical phenomenology, which operates within the transcendetal reduction, both the object of the experience and the acts of experience are reduced. With a phenomenologically inspired psychology, we have the mixed case, a partial reduction—objects of consciousness are reduced but the acts are not—but the fact that psychology in this interpretation does not make the total transcendental move should not eliminate it from the phenomenological movement altogether. Again it is a compromise between the criteria for being phenomenological, which is seen to be desirable, and the exigencies of meeting human scientific psychological criteria.

But this very possibility for distinguishing between the living of the situation by the subject and the understanding of it in terms of a reduction could not come about if one did not first accept the possibility of another's description for phenomenological analysis, and this leads to another difference with philosophical phenomenology. Usually, one first assumes the attitude of the reduction and then one describes. When the procedure is used with other subjects in a psychological context, one can accept naive descriptions within the natural attitude, but they are analyzed within the reduction. Thus, even though a subject is describing an hallucination while very much believing in it and believing to be affected by it, a phenomenological analysis within the reduction can be performed on the material because the psychologist need only understand that the description simply reveals how the situation was presented to the subject. In other words, while it may be the subject's role to believe in what he experiences, it is the psychologist's role to understand the subject, and that requires the reduction.

The third characteristic of the method was the search for essences. Usually, the phenomenologist first situates himself at the universal level of analysis and then proceeds, by way of imaginative variation, to uncover the invariants of the phenomenon. A description of the invariants constitutes their essence. The procedure at the psychological level is similar, but not identical. The major difference is that what is usually sought is a level of analysis that is neither universal nor particular but general. Psychologists are more interested in essences or structures that are context related, or relevant for typical situations or typical personalities, and so on, rather than the universal as such. Nevertheless, even though stopping short of complete universality, the procedure can still claim to be phenomenological because the method of free variation is employed in obtaining the typical essence. One consequence of stopping short of universality is that the meanings arrived at are subject to change more than universal essences because the very relationship to contexts or situations that limits the range of generality introduces a dependency on contingencies that universal essences do not have. Nevertheless, this dependency is understood as a price the psychologist has to pay in order to arrive at structures that are responsive to his interests. Yet, the modification introduced still stays within the phenomenological framework because free variation is employed and also because regardless of the fact that the essences are limited, they still transcend the facts upon which they are based—just as universal structures do.

The last feature of the phenomenological method as described by Merleau-Ponty was the notion of intentionality. The intentional relation was discovered within the context of consciousness, and it refers to the fact that consciousness is always consciousness of something and the object of awareness transcends the act in which it appears. Merleau-Ponty added that Husserl's genuine innovation with respect to intentionality was the idea of an operative intentionality that operated below the level of the intentionality of act and this made possible a "phenomenological comprehension" which is distinguished from traditional "intellection" which is confined to "true and immutable natures" (Merleau-Ponty, 1962, p. xviii). While these expressions are significant and accurate, they are of little help, as they stand, for psychology.

The significance of "operative intentionality" for psychology can be expressed in a psychologically more relevant way by saying that behavior is intentional. That is, behavior is always directed to something that is not behavior itself, which we can best characterize by saying that it is directed toward a situation. Such a description immediately breaks from all naturalistic attempts to understand behavior and at the same time involves the body as a subject in all analyses because unlike as with pure consciousness, there can be no behavioral description without implicating the body. Moreover, to deal with intentionality at the level of behavior is to get involved with something that is both more and less precise than intentionality at the level of reflective consciousness. It is less precise because it is more difficult to know the exact thematized object of behavior because behavior is far more responsive to the totality of the situation, and its adaptability to the totality exceeds direct apprehension by both the actor and observer. On the other hand, precisely because of its sensitivity to the totality, one could say that behavior is ultimately and effectively much more precise even though knowing the meaning of the precision can be difficult. The emphasis on behavior also converges with the need for descriptions from others for phenomenological psychology, since one of the poorest perspectives for accurate *behavioral* description is the perspective of self-description.

The above analyses are simply one example, however extended, of how a psychologist interested in grounding psychology in phenomenological thought in general, is forced to mediate between the valuable insights of phenomenological philosophy and the kinds of problems he encounters in trying to work out a concrete program of psychological praxis. Many problems unforeseen from a philosophical phenomenological perspective present themselves and can only be dealt with from a genuinely psychological perspective. In each of the above examples we have tried to emphasize the intrinsic logic of the situation, showing that an elaboration of strict phenomenological understanding could be achieved in such a way that phenomenological thought in a large sense was deepened and extended. However, we can also support our own modifications by showing that the very moves we have advocated are already present in philosophical phenomenological thought. For example, Spiegelberg (1964) has argued for an expansion of phenomenology in the direction of others in terms of "vicarious experience," which implies accepting the descriptions of experiences by others; Schütz (1962, p. 132) has already argued for a "true descriptive psychology within the natural attitude"; Merleau-Ponty (1962) has already introduced the notion of a concrete essence, which attempts to express the generality of a phenomenon as well as its particularity, and he speaks of an ambiguous essence that is differentiable but still not totally clear, as well as of the fact that essences, while having a different temporality, are not outside time, and all these expressions are indications that many types of essences are possible. Lastly, Mohanty (1972) has delineated an existentialist conception of intentionality based upon the writings of Heidegger, Sartre, Merleau-Ponty, and Ricoeur. Thus, while our psychological project necessitated the introduction of modifications to a strict understanding of phenomenology, they turn out to be no more radical than similar distinctions introduced in the unfolding of phenomenological movement itself, and thus, there is further evidence that one does not have to move outside the framework of phenomenology in order to meet the exigencies of sound psychological praxis. But it should also be clear that the types of modifications that psychologists introduce may be very different from philosophical developments of phenomenological thought.

Let us try to summarize what we believe to have accomplished thus far. As psychological scientists we see value in phenomenological philosophy, especially with respect to clarifying the foundations of psychology as a human science. Many phenomenological philosophers have also noted this possibility and many have explicitly and directly spoken to the issue, including Husserl himself. However, all of the philosophical literature on the question of psychology stop short of setting up specific suggestions for a concrete program in phenomenological psychology, let alone initiating such a program. The suggestions offered are so foundational (even if valuable) as to be considered contributions to philosophical psychology rather than scientific psychology. Other philosophical contributions have been in the nature of a critique of traditional praxis without elaborating the constructive alternative implied by such a critique. Finally, most exemplars of good phenomenological psychological analysis have been based upon self-descriptive efforts, which while theoretically legitimate, are often too embedded in a philosophical style of scholarship to make a genuine impact upon scientific psychology. The whole style, even at this late date, is still too close to the "armchair philosophizing" that psychology broke away from. The most significant consequence of these limitations is the profound fact that an adequate phenomenological psychology simply does not as yet exist.

This last point has to be correctly understood. It does not mean that there are not genuine phenomenological psychological descriptions and insights in the writings of phenomenological philosophers or that in the writings of traditional psychology one cannot discover findings that would be consistent with phenomenological psychology. There are, but they are scattered throughout authors and even then appear only sporadically within a given author. Rather, saying that an adequate phenomenological psychology does not yet exist means that an acceptable, generally agreed upon manner of conceptualizing phenomenological psychology and conducting phenomenological psychological research, so that psychologists aspiring to think along the same lines or to perform such research know precisely what to do or whom to use as a model, simply is not available. In brief, phenomenological psychology has not been sufficiently developed to be institutionalized in the same sense as, say, behaviorism or psychoanalysis. This end is what we wish to achieve, and it cannot be done by remaining within a phenomenological philosophical perspective.

Thus, mediation of the philosophical phenomenological perspective is inevitable. What philosophical phenomenology provides is good as far as it goes, but it does not go far enough. We shall now proceed to our own integrated attempt to mediate these two traditions.

Psychological Phenomenological Findings Regarding Learning

In the first chapter we outlined our method and gave one example of a learning description. Since multiple examples usually help, we will present two more descriptions with the method of analysis and two descriptions with the results only.

Example I: Naive Description

In a health food store in downtown Pittsburgh a friend and I asked the clerk if she knew how to make yogurt. She said yes and proceeded to give us the recipe. This is what I thought she said: "To a half-gallon of milk, add 1/4 cup of plain Dannon yogurt, to serve as the culture. Keep this mixture at a temperature between 90° and 110° for five hours. Then chill the yogurt in order to make it firmer." Because of its simplicity, I did not write down the recipe but assumed that I could remember it. I tried the recipe about 10 days later. I added 1/4 cup of plain Dannon yogurt to a half-gallon of milk. Then I put the mixture in our oven at 110° and made a mental note as to when five hours would be up. I checked the mixture four or five times during the five hour period. I noted some thickening in the beginning but it did not get past a soupy consistency even after it had been in the oven for five hours. Unsure as to whether it was progressing properly, but wishing to follow the directions and impatient for the yogurt to be finished, I took the bowl out of the oven and put it in the refrigerator thinking that perhaps it would firm when chilled. I checked it in the refrigerator once after two hours and again after four, and all that had occurred was the chilling of the soupy mixture. Then I decided that something had gone wrong, and I tried to think of what it was. I immediately considered the period when I kept the mixture in the oven because I was uncertain about it when I took it out. Perhaps I hadn't given it enough time. . . but the recipe said five hours. Aha! Although I had kept the bowl in the oven for five hours, the recipe called for keeping the mixture at 90° to 110° for five hours and the mixture started out quite cold. I added another 1/4 cup of yogurt in case I had killed the first yogurt culture by the temperature changes it went through in the first unsuccessful run. I put the bowl in the oven and left it in for 10 hours (overnight). When I got up the next morning, I checked it, and the mixture had become yogurt. I took it out of the oven and put it in the refrigerator, where it got thicker.

The next day I described the experience to the friend who had also heard the instructions given by the clerk in the health food store. I described my mistake in keeping the mixture in the oven for 5 hours where the instructions called for keeping the mixture at the high temperature for

5 hours. I was at her apartment a few days later when she was preparing to make yogurt. She had borrowed a bowl from a neighbor to make the yogurt in because she didn't have any large glass bowls. She took the bowl in her hand and asked me if it would be big enough. I looked at it and estimated that it was only one half the size of the bowl that I had used, and my bowl could hold 1/2 gallon of milk. She looked at me in a puzzled way and told me that the recipe called for a 1/4 cup of yogurt per quart of milk. On hearing this, I stopped for a moment and wondered how mine could have worked, since I had not followed these instructions. Aha! I had added the extra 1/4 cup of yogurt in case I had killed the first culture. Evidently I hadn't killed the first culture, and the two portions together were enough to turn the mixture into yogurt the second time around. So in spite of the fact that I had successfully made yogurt, it was only after my friend had corrected my misconception that I knew how to make yogurt.

Example II: Qualitative Analysis

Discriminated meaning units expressed as much as possible in S's language based upon perspective that description was an example of learning.	*Discriminated meaning units expressed more directly in psychological language and with respect to relevancy for the phenomenon of learning.*
1. In health food store, S and friend get recipe for yogurt	1. S gets instructions she desires from "expert other."
2. S remembers recipe as "1/2 gallon milk and 1/4 cup yogurt—keep mixture at 90°–110°for 5 hours—chill to make firmer	2. Instructions consist of step procedures wherein subsequent phases presuppose correctness of earlier phases. Three essential steps are given.
3. Because of recipe's simplicity, S assumed she could remember recipe—tried it 10 days later	3. Instructions seem simple to S; therefore she committed them to memory and attempted to execute procedure 10 days later
4. S adds 1/4 cup to 1/2 gallon milk—put in oven at 110°—made mental note for end of 5 hours	4. S begins to follow procedure, executes first step, and proceeds to second step.
5. S checks mixture occasionally, but does not get past soupy mixture even after 5 hours	5. Second step of process does not meet S's expectations
6. S impatient and unsure—therefore decided on next step—mixture only chilled but did not thicken	6. Second step still does not meet S's expectations, S then moves on the third step hoping that it may come out correctly anyway

7. S decides something is wrong	7. Third step of process seems not to help, thus S continues to have doubts about correctness of procedure and decides that there is a "error somewhere"
8. S searches for possible error: distinguishes between 5 hours in oven and 5 hours heating at 90°-110° plus notes fact that mixture starts cold	8. Reflection on procedures uncovers "a lived ambiguity"—S now realizes a crucial distinction where previously she assumed a univocal meaning. S specifically aims for more fitting interpretation ("high temperature" for 5 hours rather than merely "in oven" 5 hours) in procedure
9. S adds another 1/4 cup of yogurt in case old culture died and puts mixture in oven for 10 hours	9. Because of error S spontaneously modified procedure "to be sure" and follows clarified second step
10. Mixture becomes yogurt and then thickened in refrigerator	10. Process is successful
11. S describes experiences to same friend who heard recipe the first time with S	11. S described experience of successful application to the same friend who heard instructions originally with S
12. S explains error and distinction between oven and high temperature	12. S communicates error and the clarified meaning that resulted in success to a friend.
13. S at friend's apartment when latter borrowed bowl to make yogurt with same recipe and asked S about adequacy of bowl's size	13. S with friend when latter is about to execute same instructions and asks S's judgment about what appears to be a simple procedural matter
14. S said it was only 1/2 her size that held 1/2 gallon milk—friend said recipe called for quart of milk—S then puzzles at success	14. Through friend's question S discovers a second error in her procedure and that makes her ponder the reason for her success
15. S remembers that she added extra 1/4 cup as correction	15. Reflection shows that spontaneously modified step (second 1/4 cup) based upon wrong assumption, was precisely right for reason that only now becomes apparent
16. S then convinced she knows *how to* make yogurt as opposed to making yogurt successfully	16. Therefore S knows she executed procedure successfully and why—i.e. she learned

Example II. Specific Description of Situated Structure of Learning

A learning situation begins when S, attempting to follow a procedure involving steps never before carried out by her, discovers that the execution of the steps does not meet her expectations. S decides therefore that an error was made and reflection on her procedure shows that the second step, apparently clear, involved a "lived ambiguity." Her reflection distinguishes two meanings of the lived ambiguity, and proceeding according to what S believed to be a clarified, proper interpretation of the second step enables S to achieve her intention. Later dialog with a significant other presents S with another ambiguous situation when S discovers an implicit error in her procedure, but also with successful achievement. However, a second reflection shows S that a correctional procedure she introduced to rectify the first error was dependent on an assumption that was erroneous, but was precisely adequate to counteract the error in her procedure. Thus, learning for S was the achievement of a successful application of the procedure and the knowledge gained through the clarification of the ambiguities assures S that she could perform the procedure on demand.

Example II: General Description of Situated Structure of Learning

Learning is the acquisition of knowledge concerning, and the actual execution of, as well as the belief in one's ability to execute on one's own, on demand, a progressive steplike procedure which initially involved the clarification through the mediation of others, of ambiguously lived-through moments on account of lack of knowledge or wrongly posited assumptions.

Example III: Naive Description

Subject:–You know I left my restaurant downtown to come here. All I wanted was a little delicatessen. Just what I needed for my restaurant, and I thought I was rid of all the problems. Now, after last night I wonder if I can keep it up.

Researcher:–What happened? I thought things were going well for you here.

Subject:–They were. That is I thought they were until last night. I learned so much last night and now I don't know what I should do.

Researcher:–What did you find out?

Subject:–I learned about these girls (waitresses). Last night with the snow and all, the young crowd came here. This place was packed and business was great. Then I realized the girls were cheating. We must have cooked hundreds of hamburgers, but when I went over the slips only a few people had paid for hamburgers. The girls gave their friends all this food and only wrote them a slip for a coke or a cup of coffee. This has been going on for months. Last night I caught them. I really didn't know what to do. I felt like I wanted to hit them; then I felt like crying because of all my hard work trying to make a go if it here. I learned that after all these months these girls don't have any respect for me. . . . I also found out that they don't give a damn about their jobs. So I fire them, what do they care! All they are concerned about is getting a date for Friday night and giving away my food.

In my restaurant downtown it was different. The girls wanted to work; they needed to jobs to keep their families. These kids today don't give a damn about anything. I don't know how much money I've lost. What a fool I have been! I've really been stupid! I learned last night what a foolish mistake it was to come here. I know now that I just can't handle young kids. I could hardly stand to come here today. I talked to them this morning and they just laughed and talked behind by back. Now that I know all of this, I don't know what to do. I guess I started out wrong. I think I need to get some new people and start all over again. This time in the beginning I'm going to be tough. Everyone will know from the start who is boss. We won't have the same problems. This time they are going to respect me. I learned last night that you sure can't run a restaurant unless you are respected.

Researcher:–How was it that you learned all this last night?

Subject:–I don't know. I guess I was watching more than usual and I knew we had sold lots of hamburgers. I watched and listened to these kids. If I had stayed blind to this whole thing much longer, they would have walked off with the store. I was just too trusting and I wanted to be their friend. That doesn't work—you can't be the friend and the boss. You can't run a restaurant without respect. No sir, old Harry isn't going to be fooled any longer.

Example III: Qualitative Analysis

Discriminated meaning units expressed as much as possible in S's language and based upon perspective that description was an example of learning	*Discriminated meaning units expressed more directly in psychological language and with respect to relevancy for the phenomenon of learning.*
1. S left restaurant downtown to come here (a new place). S just wanted a small deli. Just what he needed for his retirement and he thought he was rid of all the problems. Now, after what happened the previous evening, S wonders if he can keep it up	1. S reveals personal project involved with experience which makes him doubt if he can sustain the project
2. *(Things were going well for S), he thought, until the night before. S	2. S had assumed that the personal project was being smoothly ful-

* Indicates that response is prompted by a question rather than being entirely spontaneous.

learned so much the night before and now S doesn't know what he should do. *(S found out), S learned, about the girls (waitresses)	filled, but on account of some new knowledge concerning others who are necessary for the continuance of the project, he does not know what to do
3. The night before, with the snow and all, the young crowd came to his place. It was packed and business was great. Then S realized the girls were cheating. S and his helpers must have cooked hundreds of hamburgers. The girls gave their friends all this food and only wrote them a slip for a Coke or a cup of coffee. This had been going on for months, the night before S caught them	3. Due to situational circumstances, S could entertain high expectations concerning his personal project (good financial return for an evening's work), but these expectations were not fulfilled. This lack enabled S to become aware that certain assumptions (that waitresses were honest) concerning the role of others, were not true. S was able to ascertain that the assumptions apparently were not true for some time
4. S really didn't know what to do. S felt like he wanted to hit them, then S felt like crying because of all his hard work trying to make a go of it in his new place	4. As the implications of his new awareness for his personal project became clearer to S, he experiences strong emotional reactions and is at a loss as to the next step
5. S learned that after all these months the girls didn't have any respect for him. S also found out that they didn't give a damn about their jobs. So S fires them—what do they care. All they are concerned about is getting a date for Friday night and giving away S's food	5. S also realizes that other assumptions concerning the others important for his project are not true (waitresses do not respect him; they don't care about their jobs)
6. In S's restaurant downtown it was different. The girls wanted to work. They needed the jobs to keep their families. The kids today don't have a damn about anything. S doesn't know how much money he has lost. S expresses that he has been a fool. S describes himself as stupid	6. Present evaluation of other's role in his project evokes context of former, similar situation for S wherein others' behavior fulfilled his expectations. S describes himself as foolish
7. S learned last night that it was a foolish mistake to come to the new place. S now knows that he just can't handle young kids. S could hardly stand to come to the deli	7. S seriously suspects that launching new project was an error. He makes a negative discovery about himself (can't handle young kids) that is confirmed when he con-

today. S talked to the girls when he came but they just laughed and talked behind his back. Now that S knows of all of this, he doesn't know what to do	fronted others (girls laughed, talked behind his back) that puzzles him and leaves him in doubt with respect to his next step
8. S guesses he started out wrong. S thinks he needs to get some new people and start over again. This time, in the beginning, S is going to be tough. Everyone will know from the start who is boss. S will not have the same problems. This time the girls will respect him. S learned the night before that one cannot run a restaurant unless one is respected	8. S begins to see possibility for a new start and imagines how to begin again. S's role in project as imagined is precisely suited to overcome current problems (S will be tough from beginning; everyone will know who is boss, girls will respect him). S is able to imagine project in this light precisely because of clear awareness of what he believes to be the difficulty. Previously to this moment he lived a more ambiguous role (friend and boss)
9. *(S does not know how he came to learn all this the night before.) S guesses he was watching more than usual and he knew he had sold lots of hamburgers. S watches and listened to the kids. If he had stayed blind to the whole thing much longer, they would have walked off with the store	9. S suspects that he became aware of the threat to his personal project because, due to circumstances (lots of business), he was more aware of the total situation than previously
10. S was just too trusting and he wanted to be their friend. That doesn't work. One cannot be the friend and the boss. One cannot run a restaurant without respect. No, S isn't going to be fooled any longer	10. S summarizes his interpretation of the problem: with respect to the others who are necessary for the continuance of his project he lived an ambiguous role (friend and boss), which resulted in loss of respect. S now sees the establishment of respect as necessary and resolved not to repeat error

Example III: Specific Description of Situated Structure of Learning

A learning situation begins for S when he discovers that a personal project to which he is committed is not being adequately fulfilled due to the behavior of others necessary for the continuance of the project. The actions of the others were apparently not in the interest of S's project for some time, but S became aware of the different intentions of the others only in this situation because, due to certain circumstances, he was more aware of the total situation than he normally was, and when certain expectations of S were not met, the clarification of the lack of fulfillment of those expectations forced S to revise his assumptions concerning the others and their relationship to him and his project. When S realizes that other assumptions concerning his relation to the others presumably helping him in a situation vital for his project are equally false, he becomes emotional and recalls a former situation where the others behaved in line with his expectations. This leads him to the consideration that he may have erred in launching the newer personal project and to another important self-discovery, namely, that he cannot relate well with the type of persons hired in new project if he maintains the same attitude as previously. S then imagines beginning the project again and imagines himself behaving, based upon his new awareness of his difficulty, precisely in the way necessary to execute the new project successfully. This new role reflects a shift in attitude whereby S maintains a single role with respect to the others rather than ambiguously and prereflectively living out two roles. Thus, learning for S consisted in the apprehension of a new meaning in a situation which in turn resulted in the uncovering of false assumptions concerning significant others, in the admission of an incompetent way of relating to the others due to the prereflective living out of two different roles in an ambiguous way, and in the projection through imagination of the possibility of living out the desired one of the two roles unambiguously.

Example III: General Description of Situated Structure of Learning

Learning is the awareness of the necessity to reorganize a personal project based upon the discrepancy between the implicit assumptions brought to a situation vital for the continuance of the project and the perception and understanding of the actions of others in terms of the project in the same situation. It is also manifested in S's discovery of the fact that he is prereflectively and ambiguously living out two conflicting roles with respect to the others involved in the project and in the ability of S to circumvent the difficulty by imagining he can choose to live out the project in terms of the preferred role in an unambiguous way.

Example IV: Naive Description

Learning to drive was important to me at 16 because it meant I no longer needed to depend on others for transportation. So I was excited when my learner's permit came. My first time behind the wheel of the car was on a Sunday in empty shopping center parking lot. I first learned how to start the car, what the PRNDL stood for, and where the emergency brake was. I practiced starting the car about five times and started to feel a little more confident even though the car still seemed huge.

Now I was ready to start to drive. I was nervous again and started to think maybe I wasn't ready to drive, maybe I should practice starting the car some more, as I was confident in doing that. But my teacher assured me I was ready. So I started the car, took the emergency brake off and the car moved a few feet. I remember thinking, "It's moving, it's moving" and then feeling really afraid because I was in control of the car and didn't really know what I was doing. The car moved a few feet and then I put the brakes on. They seemed really tight and jerked both of us forward. I felt I would never be able to put them on smoothly. But after driving a few feet and stopping, I felt a little more confident.

The next step was to take the car on the road. This was the most frightening time for me. The car seemed like a giant boat. I had visions of it going out of control or of my crashing into another car. As I went on to the road and in with traffic I felt that my car was all over the road—that I took up all four lanes. Everyone seemed to be passing me—I seemed to be going slower than everyone else—but if I went faster, I was afraid the car would go out of control. The car also didn't seem to keep straight. I had to keep moving the wheel to keep it straight. When it was time for me to change lanes to pass other cars, I was always afraid that they would come into my lane and hit me or that I wouldn't be able to get back into the other lane. The car just seemed so big I didn't feel in control of it.

After learning to drive—and more important just driving—the car did not seem so big, and I could see it was no different from the other cars on the road. I also began to realize that the car stayed pretty straight without my turning the wheel all the time and that when I passed other drivers, they would stay in their lanes.

I viewed my car in the right perspective as compared to road size and other cars.

Specific Description of Situated Structure of Learning

A learning situation begins for S when an opportunity arises for him to master the control of a vehicle that he is highly motivated to operate. This mastery was apparently accomplished in three phases. With the help of an expert other, S first discriminated the functional parts of the interior of the vehicle and performed the starting operations. The initial achievements give S some confidence, but he also experiences the vehicle in a distorted way (it seems huge). Secondly, S was actually able to move the vehicle, but in limited conditions. As the movement of this second phase arrived, S experienced a desire to remain at the first phase longer because he had confidence there, but the expert other reassured him that he was ready for the next level. In executing the second phase S felt awkward along with thrills and fears simultaneously, the former because of achievement, the latter because he realized he was in control without fully knowing what he was doing. Thirdly, S advanced to operating the vehicle in normal conditions and this aspect was initially most frightening to him. S's perspective of the total situation was distorted (car seemed huge vis-à-vis road and other cars, seemed to move more slowly and nonlinearly, and S did not seem in control). When learning was accomplished after practice, S experienced a balanced perspective with respect to all significant features of the situation (with respect to his car, the road and other cars) and he felt confident.

General Description of a Situated Structure of Learning

Learning is the gradual achievement of mastery over the control of a vehicle, with the help of an expert other, which was experientially organized around three phases: the use of relevant parts of the vehicle, its operation in safe conditions, and its operation in normal conditions. At the beginning of each phase S was simultaneously thrilled and fearful, and learning was experienced as the movement from distorted perspectives on the situation to balanced perspectives as S moved from fear to confidence.

Example V: Naive Description

During August I spent ten days in San Francisco, staying with a couple I had not met before. They were friends of the person I was traveling with. Both of these people are professionals, busy in their respective occupations. They were also caring for the two-and-a-half-year-old son of the man. During our stay, Michael and Marika gave us the use of one of their cars and urged us to enjoy ourselves in the city. They shopped, cooked, cleaned, and also worked. My friend and I took care of our own possessions, trying to interfere as little as possible with the rhythm of the home. I offered throughout the first three days of our stay to help with the maintenance chores, and each offer was politely refused. The five of us were also sharing lots of play time together.

I began to feel uncomfortable with not contributing more to the process of meeting the needs of all of us in the house. I talked with my traveling companion about my discomfort, and he reassured me, saying that Michael and Marika would ask if/when they wanted help. I still felt that Michael and Marika really did want assistance, and that they were not asking for it. I was experiencing some awkwardness with just going ahead and doing things in the kitchen, etc., as I was afraid of messing up plans for meals or being too forward in any way. I was also afraid to check out my suspicions with Michael and Marika directly, because they appeared to be at ease with what was happening. I continued to offer assistance, and the refusals continued also.

The evening of the fifth day of our stay, my friend and I came back from a day in the city. Michael and Marika were painting their kitchen. As I walked in the house and saw them, I felt the fear and awkwardness around actually assisting in some way come over me again. I went into the living room, frustrated that the good feelings of the day were dissipating, my friend came in and sat down with me, asking me what was wrong. I explained that I wanted to help but that I felt sure my offer would be refused. My friend asked me if I really did want to help. I started thinking, "Yes, I do, I would enjoy helping." I realized that my offers had been made timidly, that I had been feeling like a guest and offering to help as if I didn't really have much to offer. I reviewed mentally my approaches to Michael and Marika in the last few days, and realized that I had been expecting refusals from the beginning. I thought that in my own home, I'm more likely to refuse help from a guest or not ask for it even when I wanted it. Still, inside, I felt very positive about working with them to create an easier time with more sharing for us all, and I decided that I had been inhibiting myself out of fear instead of stating what I wanted. I went into the kitchen and said I wanted to help cook dinner. Michael heard me, and I felt that this was because I had made a positive statement. I learned that in this situation I had definite personal wants that I could state, and that I had been inhibiting myself by judging what their response would be in advance.

Brief Elaborative Interview:

E.: When did you first feel you were not getting what you wanted?

S.: Right after being turned down when I asked to help. I felt shut out, at a loss, I didn't know what to do at that point.

E.: When did you first connect the refusals of your help to the way you were asking to help?

S.: I became aware on the second day that I felt like a little girl, like a child. But I did not connect that to how I was asking until my friend asked, in an adult way, if I really wanted to help. His asking was a catalyst to my thinking of how I was expressing myself. I wasn't aware of the depth of my offering, I was offering in a really superficial way as a matter of politeness.

E.: Were you asking only out of politeness?

S.: Well, at first I felt that they were doing all this stuff, and I felt that I should help. I was asking in a really superficial way. I didn't realize that I would enjoy helping.

E.: Did you first ask simply to be polite, and later because you did not want to be left out?

S.: No, for me it wasn't like that. It was like I became more aware of what I wanted. I wanted to be part of that flow in the house and also to share with them that way. I became aware that it's important to me to share with someone like that. To feel like I'm contributing. And that was a lot of what I wasn't aware of in myself. Because there have been other times when I've offered to help people out of politeness and they have said "No, that's O.K." and it's been O.K. with me. But this time it was different, it wasn't O.K.

So, I sort of went through a process of becoming aware of why it wasn't O.K. and then asking to help in a more direct way.

Specific Description of Situated Structure of Learning

S is in a situation where she experiences herself as an outsider, but yet obligated because she received the benefits of the labors and the generosity of others but not the responsibilities. Her initial offers to be of help were politely proffered and politely refused. S was feeling uncomfortable in the situation because she felt that the others would accept help but she was afraid to be directly helpful for fear of seeming forward, but she also was reluctant to verify her expectations in a direct way. S shared her feelings of discomfort with her closest friend in the situation, and he interrogated her about her desire to help in such a way that S was provoked to reflect upon what her real feelings were. S realized then that she did want to help and that her modes of requesting help earlier were really invitations for refusal because they were merely polite and not presented as full genuine offers. At the next opportunity S announced in a more convincing and concrete way that she wanted to help and her help was accepted.

General Description of Situated Structure of Learning

Learning is the awareness that communications are received according to their total expression and not just their manifest intent. With the help of a significant other, S was able to interrogate her real feelings, choose a course of action, and genuinely communicate her decision to others in an adequate way.

Discussion of Phenomenological Psychological Findings in Learning

If we include the first description that was presented in the methodological chapter (the chess example), we have presented a total of five descriptions of learning by naive subjects unfamiliar with phenomenology or the psychology of learning. Before discussing a more detailed analysis of the findings some general points should be mentioned. First of all, all of these descriptions referred to situations that were spontaneously lived through by the subjects without their ever realizing that they might later become data for psychological analysis. Upon being confronted with the question of describing a situation in which they learned, they obviously had to scan their past experience and see what situation stood out for them as a learning one. Thus, they all had to have some precomprehension of what learning was as understood in everyday life, but it is equally clear that this sense is more a lived meaning, as described in our method chapter, than an articulate and precise definition of learning. Thus, in principle, it is conceivable that a subject's description of learning does not meet the more severe criteria of the psychological perspective, but in fact we affirm that all of the examples do fall within the meaning of learning in a psychological sense. The fact that the subjects have the freedom to choose their own example of learning probably accounts for the fact that most examples are highly significant for the subjects in a personal sense.

We shall limit ourselves here to a discussion of four dimensions of these findings. The first fact to point out is that, at a very general level, four of the five descriptions can be subsumed under one type of learning which we might label "Discovery of Discrepancy Between Assumptions and Situation." The chess example, the yogurt one, the restaurant one and the outsider description all fall within this type. The basic structure is as follows: The subject either posits or is existing within a posited project and then comes across a hard fact that is discordant with the assumptions and aims of the project. This makes the subject pause and reflect on what could be the matter, and he or she becomes aware that another perspective in the situation is not only possible, but sometimes actually operating. The awareness of the other perspective brings more precise clarity to a situation which, from hindsight, is now recognized as having been more ambiguous than it seemed prior to the discovery of the discrepancy. Within this type, then, learning is the transformation of the sense of a situation from a lived ambiguity to a degree of clarity as a consequence of changed assumptions with the implications that future situations of the same type would also be met with greater clarity.

Thus, in the chess example, the father seems to assume that his son shared equally in the solemn and sentimental exchange and only saw in the son's behavior examples of what he wanted to believe was there. It took an accidental and dramatic event to break through the father's own dramatic perspective, and the son's limited interest in the chess set was so at odds with the father's perspective that he had to recognize the son as a genuine other, with a perspective of his own, to make sense of the whole experience. The effect was great enough to make the father permanently aware of the possibility of other perspectives.

In the yogurt example, the posited project was the making of yogurt and the belief that hid the ambiguous assumption was the idea that the subject knew the recipe. The discrepant fact once again appeared (the yogurt wouldn't get firm) and while the subject "lucked out" by chance in making the yogurt, she later had to recognize that her making of the yogurt was a chance event and after her genuine discovery, she knew with precision why the "chance yogurt" worked and how to make it again. A change in perspective made her realize both the error in her procedures and why, by chance, the erroneous procedures produced yogurt. In the restaurant example, the posited project was making a success of a small business for retirement purposes when the owner became aware that the day's financial intake did not meet his perceptual expectations, and this discrepancy allowed him to observe more carefully and detect the cheating that his employees were engaged in. While we do not know what the owner ultimately did, we do know that he paused in this project to consider alternatives to the status quo. Thus, what was an ongoing situation for him was transformed into a problematic one, but this was progress because the situation-as-problematic was the reality. The situation's gestalt was totally transformed. Lastly, the outsider also had a posited project: to have fun with her friend during a visit to San Francisco. The discrepancy that arose here was that the hosts were so generous, while extremely busy themselves with their own projects, that the subject unexpectedly began to experience the demand to help meet the everyday exigencies the hosts were encountering. This meant that she had to participate in more than a stereotypically "guest-role" manner. She was unsure herself that she wanted to make this commitment and this broke her out of her "guest role." In each case, therefore, the discrepant fact made the subjects pause, reflect, and discover a hidden aspect of their assumptive world, which when brought to light, helped them respond to their situations more adequately.

The car description is different, and we might simply label it, as the tradition does, skill acquisition. There is a project, the goal is clear, and the process is one of trying to bring one's body to a level of smooth functioning. Precisely because the activity is new to the subject, he expresses awkwardness behaviorally and experiences exaggerated sizes and distances as he lives through the learning process. But there is nothing discrepant in the strict sense in the unfolding of the project; no major assumptions have to be modified and no radically new perspective has to be adopted. The difficulties encountered and the changes required all seem to be within a single expectational set, and that fact makes it a different type of learning. What is consistent with all of the types, though, is that in order for a situation to be experienced as a learning one, the subject has to make a discovery about himself or his way of relating to the world in such a way that all future situations of that type will be handled in a more adequate way.

This leads us to the second dimension that we will discuss briefly, namely, the role of the assumptive world in learning. Situations we encounter in the world are always broader and more intricate than our conscious presence to them, and it seems that we meet this vastness of the world in part with a set of assumptions built up from past experience. This means that often we use sedimented responses to help meet unfolding aspects of new situations, and thus these responses might not be adequate in every way to the unfolding specifics of the new situation. Thus, we often discover that our assumptions are not entirely adequate for the new situation, and hence learning occurs.

However, a more detailed examination shows that how assumptions play their role or are broken through can vary quite a bit and the exploration of this theme could prove to be of value to psychology. In the chess example, the father's own emotional investment in the chess set probably prevented him from thinking about his son's views on chess, or perhaps he was simply reenacting an experience he had had with his own father and assumed his son was sharing in it in the same way. (Whichever of these possibilities is true, if either, does not matter so far as the learning is concerned. We are here suggesting further research on the ways in which the assumptive world prevents us from being fully present to concrete situations, which in turn can develop into learning situations of this type.) In the yogurt example the subject's perception of the instructions was that they were "simple," and thus she quickly committed them to memory. Probably because of this impression of "simplicity" she never questioned that she may have remembered the instructions wrong and thus assumed that something must be wrong elsewhere. The restaurant owner also assumed that his business was going well and assumed that since he had contractual agreements with this waitresses, they would perform adequately and honestly. But this scheme does not fully allow for multiple motivations. The waitresses did want to work and earn money, but they also wanted to be good to their friends. There may also be some ambiguity in the owner himself. He might have also enjoyed having young waitresses about and expected them to behave like more mature married women. Thus, in the first case the emotions were possibly responsible for the assumptions, in the second case possibly "simplicity," and in the third case possibly conflicting motivations. The network of assumptions is never simple, and when current situations reveal some of the ambiguities, it is an occasion for learning to take place.

The third dimension of these findings is the prevalence of the social. While other aspects of traditional psychology have spoken to the role of the social in learning, the verbal learning tradition with which we are dialoguing barely mentions it in large part because of the experimental setting. However, it is omnipresent in our research because its open-ended character allows the social to reveal itself. Thus in the chess example, the father learned the truth about his first son's attitude toward chess through his second son; in the yogurt example the subject discovered her error in her own procedure because of her friend; in the restaurant example the owner realized his project was not going smoothly because of the behavior of the waitresses; in the car example, at a critical moment, the subject wanted to remain at a lower level of performance because of lack of confidence, but the teacher was there to urge him that he could perform at the next level and thus encouraged him to proceed and he succeeded; lastly, the "outsider" was not sure of what she really wanted but with the help of her friend, she was able to pause, decide, and then behave adequately. Thus, in each case, the very constitution of learning as an experienced phenomenon depended upon the presence of others. The social is an instrinsic determinant of psychological reality, and it should be given its due.

The fourth and last dimension to be noted is that the results of phenomenological psychological research provide us with the sense of learning as it is experienced. It is precisely because the phenomenological approach thematizes the meaning of learning that it can provide complementary data and information, but it also means that these contributions should not be judged by traditional criteria. The manner in which meanings are constituted is one thing; whether or not the meanings so constituted are adequate for the objective state of affairs as determined by a fuller perspective is another thing.

These differences are highlighted in the yogurt example. On the one hand, this description shows that learning cannot be identified with successful performance because the subject achieved her goal without having genuinely learned. Learning has to be a certain kind of performance or performance that is accompanied by a certain sense or intelligibility (but it does not necessarily mean that this sense has to be thematically conscious to the subject). It is the discovery of this sense or intelligibility that the phenomenological approach emphasizes. Based on this research it seems that learning is ascribed to situations in which factors that were hiddenly operating are discovered or where a struggle is necessary for proper achievement. These experiential characteristics, of course, do not exhaust the description of learning, but are merely what seem to stand out from the perspective of experience.

The yogurt example also shows that one can experience learning without it being objectively true that learning took place. This happened when the subject, by chance, introduced a modification that corrected an earlier error. Yet, she experienced learning because all of the conditions for the sense of learning to be present were fulfilled. She was attempting a procedure she had never achieved, she met some unexpected discrepancies during the process, she introduced modifications based upon her reflective analysis of the situation, and of course, the procedure was successful. Thus, she experienced learning. The face that she could not have reproduced the procedure successfully later would have retroactively informed her that she did not really learn. However, the implication here should not be that the sense of learning is wholly unreliable—only that it is a limited perspective that does not speak to the total situation. The experiential sense of learning can be achieved but it is not identical to the full objective sense of learning just as the sheer objective performance of a successful procedure does not guarantee learning either. What it does indicate is the complexity of psychological reality and how both experiental and behavorial aspects will have to be included in a full definition of psychological reality. However, a complete understanding of the sense of learning would have to include both correct performance and precise meaning. While a meaning was present in the first part of the yogurt example, it was not the precise one. The precise sense was not uncovered until later, and then the subject could proclaim with confidence that she had learned.

Having briefly discussed the findings concerning learning obtained from a phenomenological viewpoint, we shall now proceed to the remaining essential issues. Is the method really phenomenological? Is it really scientific? And lastly, how do the findings compare to findings emerging from the verbal learning tradition?

The Qualitative Method Is Phenomenological

Earlier, based upon Merleau-Ponty, we accepted the premise that phenomenology was defined in terms of method, which consisted of description, the reduction, the search for essences, and the recognition of operative intentionality. We also modified these criteria as we adapted the phenomenological method to psychological phenomena, and our demonstration of the phenomenological character of the qualitative method will reflect these modifications.

(1) *Description:* Clearly, the qualitative method is descriptive, and at two levels. The original data consist of naive descriptions, prompted by open-ended questions, of experiences of situations by subjects unfamiliar with the researcher's theories or biases. Then the researcher himself describes the structures of the experiences that the subjects lived through and presents his findings descriptively. It should be noted that this emphasis on description does not necessarily rule out quantification (a form of description) but simply that there is no pressure to quantify unless the demand arises intrinsically from the situation.

(2) *Reduction:* That some sense of reduction is in operation in the analyses can also be indicated in two ways. First of all, the very fact that a concrete situation that was lived through prior to any thought about being studied or analyzed can later be taken *as an example* of learning already indicates a reduction. One could say that for a fully rich, lived-through situation in the everyday world to be taken, retrospectively, as an example of learning is to say that it is taken to be meant and intended as learning. Thus, in order to be taken as a psychological reality, it has to be meant and intended as such by the researcher (and implicitly, perhaps naively, by the subject in the reporting of it if not in the

living of it). But that is precisely the definition of the reduction.

The second sense in which the reduction is employed is with respect to the noematic aspects of the subjects' descriptions. It is granted that the subject really lived through the experiences and meanings he describes insofar as they were acts that took place for him or her at a specific place and time. However, what is being referred to is not taken as objective, real truth but only as the correlate of what the subjects believed happened—that is, what the situation meant to them, not what it really was. For example, there could have been no learning for the subject in the yogurt example if she did not believe that she executed the recipe correctly the first time. What made it a learning experience, in part, was the fact that she was confronted by facts that she knew to be contrary to what she believed, and the resolution of the discrepancy was necessary for the learning experience to occur. One could perhaps say that learning consisted in the adequation between what she believed and what was in fact objectively true. Similarly, for the restaurant subject, there is sufficient evidence (for the reader) to question whether or not the degree of learning that took place for the subject was indeed sufficient to meet the objective requirements of the total situation. That is, one wonders whether his resolve is sufficient for him really to change his project, or whether he can really carry out in the world his role as boss as he imagines it, and whether there are not more dimensions of his personality and his relations with the waitresses that have to come to awareness before he can competently change his role. But, still, one cannot deny that the insight into his ambiguous role with respect to the others is a real start, that his awareness of the discrepancy between his implicit assumptions concerning the waitresses and his experience of low financial return from a busy evening is not significant. What all this means is that these meanings for the subject are taken precisely for what they are: meanings of the situation for the subject (but really taking place in the stream of consciousness of the subject). But, again, that is the definition of the reduction. What *is*, has to be ascertained in other ways and then compared to the (reduced) perspective of the subject. While the implications cannot be pursued here at this time, it seems that one could say that unless there is a reduction of some type, one cannot genuinely apprehend the psychological.

(3) *Essences or Structures:* It is also clear that this criterion is met, since the very units of analysis are "meaning units" discriminated within the subject's description and also the meanings perceived by the researcher at the psychological level organize the data, and the ultimate findings are presented as structures, or the most comprehensive invariant meaning, which is what an essence is. However, in line with the modifications introduced in the theoretical discussion of phenomenology, these essences or structures, are not universal, or eternal, because they are not pursued

at that level. On the other hand, they go beyond mere empirical generalities because the method of free variation is used to help discover the invariant for the particular level of analysis being pursued. For example, when it was time to transform the second meaning unit of the yogurt example presented above, the question arose of how to transform the meaning of a recipe into psychologically relevant terms. A number of possibilities can be imagined. Could it be the contents? Is it the problem of remembering all the steps? Is it merely a matter of the timing between steps? No, based upon the sense of the whole description, which sets the parameters within which the most invariant meaning must be ascertained, it has to do with the correctness of earlier phases. The point here, of course, is that one discovers the fittingness of the latter meaning through the process of free variation and after discarding several alternatives. Or if we look at the fifth meaning unit of the restaurant example, the facts are that the subject learned that the waitresses did not respect him, didn't care about their jobs, and wouldn't care if he fired them. What are the essential implications of those facts with respect to the determination of the structure of learning as revealed in this particular description? Again there are numerous possibilities, but the constraints placed upon the play of free imaginative variation by the sense of the whole description with respect to its being an example of learning narrows down the range of optimum choices without necessarily reducing them to a single one. Still, imaginative variation is required. Does the subject's discovery of the lack of respect for him mean that he hired the wrong specific individuals, but not the wrong types? Does their not caring for their jobs mean that he is really helpless with respect to having them behave the way he desires? No, what essentially ties them together is the fact that there are two specific assumptions that he uncritically brought to his new restaurant based upon his experiences in his former place, and what makes the articulation of these assumptions important in this context is the fact that the subject discovers that the assumptions do not hold. However, that insight does not necessarily leap out at one, and even if it did, one would still have to check it out in terms of free imaginative variation. Thus, the method meets the criterion of seeking out essences or structures and the method of free imaginative variation plays a necessary role in the search for meaning.

(4) *Intentionally* Actually, intentionality is not so much directly studied as presupposed. It refers to the fundamental fact that a human being is always directed toward or oriented toward something that is not himself. Usually that means the world, and he cannot be understood except in terms of his being related to the world. Neither of the two above analyses could have taken place in the way they did if the intentional relation was not presupposed. While the discovery of intentionality took place and developed phenomenologically speaking within the context of con-

sciousness, we have already argued (Giorgi, 1970, p. 158), based upon Merleau-Ponty's work, that it can extend beyond the realm of consciousness and other phenomenologists have also made this claim. Mohanty (1972, p. 174), for example, suggests that intentionality should be a characteristic of a range of phenomena understood as subjective. If we accept this description, then it is clear that the above analyses not only presupposed intentionality but actually performed certain "intentional analyses" in the sense that the meanings of situations as related to the understandings and performance of human subjects were precisely what the analyses sought. Indeed, the method employed may even enhance our present knowledge of how to go about performing intentional analyses within a psychological context.

If all of the above points are true, the qualitative method described in this article can be considered to be genuinely phenomenological.

The Qualitative Method is Scientific

In affirming that the qualitative method is scientific, we have to state at the outset that we are not appealing to the natural scientific criteria of science but to a meaning of science which would be grounded in a phenomenological theory of science which, unfortunately, is also only in the process of being articulated (e.g., Kockelmans & Kisiel, 1970). Science, however, even in its most rigorous sense, always allows varied means. In order to have both a broader and more precise sense of science in general, it would be necessary to conduct a series of concrete analyses of both natural scientific and human scientific praxes in order to ascertain the goals and values that the human and natural sciences share. From that perspective, we could then determine under what conditions different manners of scientific implementation may be optimally fruitful (for example, when to employ quantitative description and when to employ verbal description).[5] Lacking such a precise and direct manner of establishing our point, however, we have to turn to indirect means, such as a pragmatic argument and an indirect theoretical argument.

First the pragmatic argument. In order for an activity to be considered scientific, it must be able to be performed by many researchers, the finding should be intersubjectively valid, and there must be a definable method. Clearly, the qualitative method described above is distinguishable and intelligible, and it is also capable of being performed by many people. While the evidence cannot be presented here (although readers can attempt to apply it themselves), the ground for the assertion is based upon my experience in teaching the use of the method in graduate

5. Unfortunately, a work we are contemplating dealing with descriptive sciences and their relation to natural sciences is only in the planning stage.

courses in the Department of Psychology at Duquesne University since 1970. Over and over again I have seen students and colleagues apply the method to both similar and highly disparate phenomena. The same experience provides the grounds for asserting that the application of the method yields results that are in principle (and often factually) intersubjective. I teach the method by submitting the identical description to the class and instruct each student to apply the method individually, and then we come back and compare the findings. Over and over again the degree of spontaneous intersubjective agreement is surprisingly high, and the structure that is presented brings a great degree of consensus. No claim is made that there is 100% agreement, but then neither does traditional science use that high a criterion.

The indirect theoretical argument is based upon the fact that the qualitative method outlined here and the traditional psychological method share the same values but treat them differently because of the differences, ultimately, in the philosophy of science adopted. In order to appreciate this argument, we have to recall why we even found it necessary to seek another way of being scientific with respect to human phenomena in the field of psychology. Our claim was that the natural scientific approach could not do justice to human phenomena because the peculiarly human characteristics were not given sufficient scope to enter into the research situation as they were actually lived. Specifically, we referred to the historical, social, and meaning-giving aspects of human subjectivity. We saw that these aspects did enter indirectly into the verbal learning tradition, but it was despite the method. And yet, at another level, researchers recognize that these dimensions of human reality are important because they are always seriously considered as variables to be controlled. Since we have elaborated this before (Giorgi, 1976), we can perhaps demonstrate this in a briefer way here.

First of all, the fact that humans are influenced by meanings is the reason for the invention of nonsense syllables in the first place (allegedly neutral material). The fact that meanings can be attributed to such presumably neutral materials is the reason that attempts were made to control for the syllables' association value (Glaze, 1928) or their meaningfulness (noble, 1952). Thus, the meaning responding and meaning attributing characteristics of human subjects are acknowledged by the tradition and are valued to be so important as to try to control for these characteristics. The only difference with our method is how to conceive of and work through this problem. The traditional procedure wants to control for meaning by measuring certain characteristic attributes of the items as though they existed "in themselves," even though it is acknowledged that such characteristics (for example, 100% association value) have only probabilistic value, and the establishment of the alleged independent characteristics of the stimulus items require the presence of human subjects other than the ones to be used in the experiment proper, but presumably with like characteristics, and in tasks that are essentially different from the task imposed upon experimental subjects (see pp. 00-00). In our method, the actual meaning that aspects of the situation had for the subjects is first noted (for example, a subject who is used to memorizing numbers memorizes letters by grouping; trying to make yogurt for the first time is attempting to execute a progressive step-by-step procedure never done before), and then one attempts to ascertain its general significance. Our procedure stays closer to the actual experience and hesitates to generalize in terms of abstraction or formalization.

Secondly, we mentioned earlier that Ebbinghaus began the verbal learning tradition solely on his own. He was experimenter, subject, and author of his own manuscripts. While all of this is admirable in one sense, the way the results were presented theoretically implied that man is a solitary learner. The implication of such a procedure is that social influences are so complex (and they are) that the only way to handle them is to remove the subject from them as much as possible and try to understand his behavior in a solitary setting. The tradition has accepted this initial constraint, and all studies of this type are basically that of a solitary learner confronting his material (when group settings are used, the motivation is efficiency, not theory). Moreover, there is almost no way for the social dimension to enter, since usually only individual performance data are recorded and all other aspects are controlled. In our method, while it is true that descriptions have been obtained from a single subject at a time, the very open-endedness of the description with its emphasis on everyday world situations almost guarantees that the role of relevant others, if there is one (and there almost always is), will be made manifest (the role of the friend in the yogurt example and the waitresses in the restaurant example). What makes the social aspect manageable is the fact that the other is considered precisely within the context of the meaning that he or she had for the subject insofar as that is manifested and implied in the description. Thus, the social is recognized as relevant by both methods, except that the traditional psychologist tries to control for it by isolation, and the phenomenological psychologist in terms of the meaning of the other for the subject in that situation insofar as this meaning is made manifest and is implied in the description. Once again, our method is closer to the actual state of affairs.

How about the subject as a historical being? Again, one of the reasons that nonsense syllables were invented was to neutralize the historical factor. Since one could never uncover the whole history of relations that a subject had with language, the problem of control was not solvable. Hence, Ebbinghaus invented a way of presuming no history, since no subject had ever seen the materials before. Thus, in the tradition, one attempts to control for history by assuming no relevant history (just as learning alone was the solution to the social, and no meaningfulness was the solution for the role of meaning). In our approach, because of the open-endedness of the question, the role of relevant aspects of the past are allowed to present themselves insofar as they are relevant to the learner as manifested in his description (thus, in the yogurt example, we shared the first—mistaken—attempt at making yogurt with the subject, and in the restaurant example, we understood the disappointment with the current waitresses better when the subject described the kinds of waitresses he had in his former place). Again, the personal past is made manageable because the role that it plays is controlled by the subject himself, because he reveals as much of it as is necessary to comprehend its relevance for the present insofar as this is manifested and implied in the description. Both traditions value history and want some control of it, but how this is achieved is what differs.

Thus, we conclude that if the method of traditional science and our method share the same values, there must be some overlapping of projects. Of course, the retort would be that what differentiates science is method and not aims, and to the retort we would say—precisely so! Insofar as traditional science adopts a strategy that begins by attempting to eliminate sociality, historicity, and meaning, only to deal with them indirectly as they keep reemerging, one has to raise the question of the adequacy of the initial method. Our theoretical argument at this point would be that traditional science violates a fundamental principle, that is, fidelity to the phenomenon as it presents itself, and it is our contention that there can be no description of human phenomena that lasts at least a relatively brief span of time that does not reveal social, historical, or meaningful characteristics. Our method wants first to be faithful to those characteristics that description reveals and then to proceed systematically and methodically by always allowing the mode of givenness of those characteristics to play a role in the development of the method. In this sense, we would say that our method is more precise, and in the long run, when fully developed, will prove to be more fruitful.

One last remark on this point. To allow the descriptive, human characteristics of human subjects to enter more fully into the design of psychological research is only to make the relationship of the subject and experimenter more parallel, since there is no doubt that the experimenter would argue for his own meaning-giving abilities, as well as for the fact that even as a scientist, let alone personally, social and historical factors played a role in the very design of the experiment. In the older format, an ahistorical, asocial, and ameaningful subject almost literally had no role to play, no ground for interaction, except as an "anonymous one" who contributed the measurable aspects of his performance. For the subject to enter in as a person is not a threat to psychological science, but the very basis upon which an authentic psychological science can be built.

Brief Analysis of the Relationship Between Experimenter and Subject in Research

Now that the qualitative method can be understood to be scientific as well as phenomenological, we feel we are ready to give brief consideration to the third point raised earlier (P. 00) namely, why, despite the convergence between traditional psychology and phenomenological psychology, we still claim the need for a phenomenological psychology. We said previously that a phenomenological analysis of the subject-experimenter relationship would be enlightening for psychological science, and we more or less concluded the last section with the same point. We would now like to present a brief initial analysis so that our reasons for insisting on this point can be made clearer. We cannot do full justice to this topic here, but we will merely point out three interrelated dimensions of the subject-experimenter relationship, which, if explored in depth and pursued to obvious conclusions, can change psychology's self-understanding of the research situation.

(1) *Total versus Partial Consciousness*: This dimension refers to the fact that the experimenter has complete (not absolutely, of course) knowledge of the experimental situation and the subject only partial knowledge, depending upon what the experimenter lets him know. In other words, where it really counts, the experimenter is all-knowing and the subject is mostly ignorant. The experimenter knows the purpose of the experiment, the independent and dependent variables, the hypothesis to be tested and even the most relevant contextual factors. He knows beforehand what aspects of the subject's performance he is interested in and focuses on those to the exclusion of everything else. The subject, on the other hand, knows only the instructions initially and then whatever he experiences in the actual experiment.

Once this structure is clearly understood, it soon becomes apparent that doubts concerning its long-term fruitfulness can easily arise. The experimenter has so constructed the experimental situation that he knows everything humanly possible about it except how the subject will perform and that bit of information is simply integrated into the structure of the situation as conceived by the experimenter. But the experimenter can only do this by fragmenting the unity of the subject's behavior in an arbitrary way because to seize upon an aspect of behavior (for example, an error in reciting a list of syllables) without relating that aspect to its totality is precisely to reify a part because its relations to the whole are not considered. Gestalt psychology has repeatedly shown that contextual relations are equally constitutive of the meaning of the part. However, if the experimenter opens up to more of the phenomenon than merely the narrow performance aspect he has been concentrating on, then he must allow for the fullness of the subject's perspective and that means that *his* (the experimenter's) structuring of the situation has to be merely tentative rather than decisive. As a consequence of following this line of reasoning, a shift in priority takes place: Initially, the experimenter's totality dominates, but then as he allows for more of the subject's perspective to enter, he must surrender momentarily his own priorities, or else remain content with an arbitrary delimitation of the subject's perspective. Thus, instead of experimenter dominance we get something like the following phases of a temporal process as a guideline for research: (*a*) Experimenter perspective total and active versus subject perspective partial and passive; (*b*) Experimenter perspective partial and receptive versus subject perspective total and active; (*c*) Experimenter and subject perspective equal and interactive; (*d*) Experimenter perspective, informed by total subject perspective, is dominant and integrative. The fact that traditional research limits itself to the first phase of the above process indicates that it is being guide by a different set of assumptions and that it is incomplete in its praxis rather than wholly wrong.

(2) *The Known versus the Lived*: Another way of characterizing the experimenter-subject relation is by describing it as the relation between the known and the lived. The experimenter knows about the situation, and the subject lives it. But as in the first case, such a shorthand description is merely a point of departure and not at all adequate, for once seen in this light, a host of implications have to be pursued. The experimenter not only knows, but also lives the situation and sometimes even observes it. Similarly, the subject not only lives through the research situation but also knows something about it (even if it is incorrect) and makes observations in the course of living through it. However, how the experimenter lives through, observes, and has knowledge about the experimental situation is very different from how the subject lives through, observes, and has knowledge about the same situation. A good design must interrogate all of these factors in order to be able to speak with some precision, and it's doubtful whether traditional research deals with these problems in sufficient depth. For example, the experimenter knows the situation in detail, so much so that he can concentrate on what is predefined as the critical behavior in relation to selected aspects of the environment. What he lives during the process of researching is presumably bracketed and rendered noninfluential, but recent literature demonstrates convincingly that this ideal is never reached (Rosenthal, 1976; Friedman, 1967). Consequently, somehow even the lived dimension of research with respect to the research situation must be dealt with for, even if the researcher is physically removed from the situation, as in some cases, that fact does not remove him from the lived imagination of the subject, and moreover, the lived dimension cannot be removed from a researcher's interpretation and communication of his results.

The subject, on the other hand, initially usually only knows *about* the research situation, and in general, what he observes and lives through is very specific, but whether or not these latter two enter into the results of traditional experiments *as* subject's observed data and *as* lived is doubtful. The issue, in other words, is whether the referents of the experimenter's observations are adequate to the subject's lived responses or merely caricatures of them. Because of the emphasis on quantification in traditional psychology, one is often dealing with *measured behavior* as data rather than the *lived behavior* of the subject, and the question of the adequation of the former to the latter is often not raised. In brief, with traditional psychology, one is often dealing with the relation between the known and the observed, rather than the known and the lived. The latter, however, is the more fruitful relation for psychological research.

(3) *Researcher as Variable versus Researcher as Meaningful Presence*: For about a decade now explicit recognition of the fact that a researcher's presence may influence the nature of experimental findings has been general knowledge within scientific psychology, and one consequence of this knowledge is that the experimenter has been viewed as another variable to be controlled. That is, the experimenter is simply another category to be worked into the general prevailing schema of research. From a phenomenological perspective, however, a human presence would have to be conceived as more than a mere variable. Throughout this paper we have been emphasizing that humans attribute meanings to situations and this is equally true of researchers and their human subjects. Thus, instead of the experimenter being a variable for the subject, as indeed the subject is also for the experimenter, phenomenologically, a research situation is conceived of as one in which two humans engage but relate differently to the same situation, and because they relate differently, the meanings experienced by each in the same situation differ, and one of the best ways to find out the respective meanings is by having the participants enter into a dialog and systematically and rigorously pursue all the implications of the different perspectives on the same situation. In other words, a truly comprehensive approach understands the research situation with human subjects to be one in which the same situation evokes different perspectives, purposes, experiences, and behaviors from the participants and a full comprehension should tap into both perspectives (experimenter and subject) as well as their interaction. In short, as has been recently noted (Orne, 1962), the experimental situation is a social situation (indeed, a human one!), and this dimension should not be overlooked. Thus, the experimenter and the subject, in our terminology, are both meaningfully present in the research situation, but in divergent ways that have to be properly explicated each time. This goes far beyond seeing the researcher merely as a variable that is added to traditional research schemas.

Two comments should be made about the above analysis. First, it should be noted, as implied above, that traditional psychology is aware of these problems in its own way. The problem of total versus partial consciousness is approached in the tradition in terms of the question of deception in research (e.g., Kelman, 1967; Hofstee, 1976); the problem of the relationship of the known and the lived in terms of the role of verbal reports in psychology (e.g., Nisbett & Wilson, 1977); and the question of experimenter and subject divergent presences and their implications in terms of the research on research literature (Rosenthal, 1976; Friedman, 1967). But what is true of the traditional psychological literature concerning these issues is that in each case the fundamental approach or philosophy of research is not challenged. The traditionalists try to cope with the problem within the framework of the existing views concerning research. Within the phenomenological perspective, these problems converge with many others to motivate a different way of looking at research in psychology.

The second general comment relates to the fact that a truly comprehensive approach that centers on the essentials of the problem can reveal the genuine interrelatedness of the three problems and thus solve them more adequately. For example, if one understands that the experimenter and the subject bring different perspectives to the same situation, then one can raise the question of the relative priority of perspectives and thus speak to the question of total and partial presence at different moments of the research. Furthermore, when one is speaking of total and partial presence, the question of "to what one is present" immediately arises, and the question of the relation of the known to the observed and the observed to the lived can be addressed. Lastly the very issue of perspectives implies the divergent presence of researcher and subject. Thus, a genuine, comprehensive approach to the problems of research with human subjects can reorient both the understanding and practice of research. Incidentally, even the sketchy outlines of the approach as provided here can show the possibilities of unifying psychology in a more adequate way because if the research situation can be understood as first and foremost a human situation of interaction and dialog, then the possibility of a theoretical link with the therapeutic situation is conceivable because it, too, is a human situation consisting of interaction and dialog, that consists of divergent presences between therapist and client, of total and partial consciousness, and of the problems of the lived and the known, and the lived and the observed. Of course the two situations are not and could never be identical—that is not my point. My point is simply that the theoretical possibility of understanding how two apparently very different situations can belong to the same discipline may be more apparent.

Comparison Between Verbal Learning Tradition and Qualitative Studies of Learning

This topic is too large to cover exhaustively, and in many ways, it is premature even to suggest a comparison because there is not as yet anything like a body of literature in the qualitative area to have recourse to. But still it is interesting to note if there is any way at all in which these two areas of research touch each other despite the different philosophies that motivate their practice.

Of course there are great differences. Most of the early verbal learning studies, with the exception of G. E. Müller, and the Gestalt theoretical approach (e.g., Koffka, 1963/1935) were concerned with the relationship between subject performance and many formal and abstract variables such as item characteristics, number of items to be learned, serial position curves, frequency of presentation, and so on. In short, traditional research dealt with characteristics dictated by either the experimental situation or association theory. Moreover, most of the variables are abstract, and in one sense, can be related to any situation because of their abstractness, and yet, in another sense, are difficult to relate to for the very same reason. For example, many traditional studies deal with either the amount of time it took to learn, the number of errors committed in learning, and the place of errors (serial position curves). Of course, one could say that these factors are all present in our descriptive data. One could conceivably determine how long it took the restaurant owner to perceive that the waitresses were cheating, or one could ascertain how many errors the yogurt maker made in following her recipe, and even the places in the procedure at which the errors were committed. Thus, it would be possible to answer these and related questions, but one also gets the impression that these are not the most relevant facts to seek in our descriptive material. Rather, we would want to know why it took the restaurant owner so long even to discover the fact of cheating, or we would want to know the nature of the error and its implications for making yogurt with respect to the yogurt learning example. While the emphasis on time and errors seems so natural for nonsense syllables, they are not the first things one wants to know when a fully contextual everyday situation is the focus. Thus, a convergence between the tradition and our approach is in principle conceivable, but its significance is dubious because of the abstract and nonpersonal quality of the primary variables in the traditional literature.

When the verbal learning literature departs from the domination of association theory (e.g. Tulving, 1962; Mandler, 1967), then a possible convergence between the two styles is greater because the departure from association theory is a movement toward an active role on the part of a subject, toward a greater role for cognitive interpretation of learning

(Jung, 1968) and to the study of variables such as response integration, stimulus selection, response encoding, mediational factors, strategies of learning, and so on. But all these terms—integration, selection, encoding, mediation, strategies—imply subjective or personal characteristics, and we see them in our own descriptions: The way in which the subject in the yogurt example integrates the new insight learned from her friend into what happened to her, the way in which the subject in the restaurant example was selectively aware of certain aspects of his situation, the way in which the subject distinguished (encoded) between "in the oven for 5 hours" as opposed to "at 110° for 5 hours" or the way in which the restaurant owner allowed his memory of his former place (proximate or remote association?) to mediate between his current difficulty and his imagined solution, and so on. In other words, it is easier to relate to the variables of the literature not under the influence of association theory precisely because human factors are tending to emerge as significant even if they are not met head-on in the most adequate manner because of the residual effects of traditional language and situations. In our view, our type of research would simply hasten this process toward direct human relevance because it operates directly up on the significant human phenomenological variables.

Once again an interesting question presents itself: If the two streams show convergence, what difference does it make where one situates oneself, since they may ultimately merge anyway? Well, it matters, because there is still the question of the adequacy of the merger—if it is merely an ideological or political solution, it may not advance the status of psychology one bit. In addition, since a new framework is what is really needed, how can that come about without the articulations of a new vision with new concepts and new perceptions? Only a theoretically satisfying solution can make genuine headway, and since it is only when the verbal learning tradition left the framework of association theory and traditional experimental design and turned to subject-related variables that it began to investigate variables more in line with the subject's manner of dealing with the materials, it would seem to indicate that more effort in that direction would be desirable.

Another pressure nudging verbal studies and learning theory in general in the direction of everyday world situations is the pressure coming from applied interests which in general find learning theories far too narrow in approach and theoretically far too removed from everyday situations to be of much help (Hilgard & Bower, 1966, p. 581). Other psychologists have also recognized this need and have begun attempts, different from ours but sympathetic in outlook, at qualitative approaches to learning (e.g., Radley, 1976; Marton & Saljo 1976a; 1976b; Torbert, 1972).

Our approach, of course, begins with the everyday situations and therefore has no problem with respect to relevancy for the life-world. Our difficulties relate to ways of languaging our findings, ways of presenting our method and its analyses more efficiently, and in learning how to develop a consistent psychological perspective within which to conduct our analyses. More experience with the method should lead to more adequate solutions to these problems, but it is hoped that the value of the general direction adopted in this paper has been demonstrated.

Postman (1968), in writing about the contributions of Ebbinghaus, listed some of the principles by which he believed Ebbinghaus was guided. One of the principles was, "The second guiding principle is emancipation from orthodox constraints on the scope of experimental inquiry. According to the prevailing doctrine only those mental phenomena which were directly subject to physical influences were to be studied experimentally." (Postman, 1968, p. 150) We believe that we are doing nothing other than this in applying a phenomenological perspective to research in learning with the exception that the human scientific perspective that guides us is not yet as well established as the natural scientific perspective that guided Ebbinghaus. He, at least, could appeal to the legitimacy of the perspective in its own realm and merely had to demonstrate its applicability to mental phenomena. We, unfortunately, not only have to demonstrate the applicability of the human scientific perspective, but also must argue for its very legitimacy.

References

Boring, E. G. (1950). *A history of experimental psychology*. New York: Appleton-Century-Crofts.

Cofer, C. N. (Ed.). (1961). *Verbal learning and verbal behavior*. New York: McGraw-Hill.

Cofer, C. M. & Musgrave, B. S. (Eds.). (1963). *Verbal behavior and learning*. New York: McGraw-Hill.

Colaizzi, P. (1971) Analysis of the learner's preception of learning material at various stages of the learning process. In A. Giorgi, W. Fischer, & R. von Eckartsberg (Eds.). *Duquesne Studies in Phenomenological Psychology I*. Pittsburgh, PA: Duquesne University Press.

Ebbinghaus, H. (1964/1913/1885). *Memory* (H. A. Ruger and C. E. Bussenius, Trans.) New York: Dover Publications (original 1913; German original, 1885).

Ericsson, K. A., & Simon H. A. (1980). Verbal reports as data. *Psychological Review, 87*, 215–251.

Friedman, N. (1967). *The social nature of psychological research*. New York: Basic Books.

Giorgi, A. (1970). *Psychology as a human science*. New York: Harper & Row.

———. (1971). A phenomenological approach to the problem of meaning and serial learning. In A. Giorgi, W. Fischer, & R. von Eckartsberg (Eds.), *Duquesne*

Studies in Phenomenological Psychology I. Pittsburgh, PA: Duquesne University Press.

———. (1976). Phenomenology and the foundations of psychology. In J. F. Cole & W. J. Arnold (Eds.), *Nebraska symposium on motivation, 1975: Conceptual foundations of psychology*. Lincoln, NE: University of Nebraska Press.

———. (1981). Sartre's systematic psychology. In P. A. Schilpp (Ed.), *The philosophy of Jean-Paul* (pp.179–196). Lasalle, IL: Open Court Publishers.

Glaze, J. A. (1928). The association value of nonsense syllables. *Journal of Genetic Psychology, 35*, 255–269.

Gurwitsch, A. (1974). Edmund Husserl's conception of phenomenological psychology. In L. Embree (Ed.), *Aron Gurwitsch: Phenomenology and the theory of science*. Evanston, IL: Northwestern University Press.

Harcum, E. R. (1975). *Serial learning and paralearning*. New York: Wiley.

Hilgard E. (1964). Introduction to Dover Edition of *Memory* by H. Ebbinghaus (H.A. Ruger & C. E. Bussenius, Trans.). New York: Dover Publications.

Hilgard, E. & Bower, G. H. (1966). *Theories of learning* (3rd ed.) New York: Meredith.

Hofstee, W.K.B. (1976). *Deception and disclosure in psychological research: Implications for scientific inference*. Unpublished manuscript, University of Groningen.

Husserl, E. (1977). *Phenomenological psychology* (John Scanlon, Trans.). The Hague: Nijhoff.

Jung, J. (1968). *Verbal learning*. New York: Holt, Rinehart and Winston.

Kelman, H. C. (1967). Human use of human subjects: The problem of deception in social psychological experiments. *Psychological Bulletin, 67*, 1–11.

Koch, S. (1959). Epilogue: Some trends of study I. In S. Koch (Ed.), *Psychology: A study of a science*, vol. 3. New York: McGraw-Hill.

Kockelmans, J. (1971). Phenomenological psychology in the United States: A critical analysis of the actual situation. *Journal of Phenomenological Psychology, 1*, 139–172.

Kockelmans, J., & Kisiel, T. (Eds.). (1970). *Phenomenology and the natural sciences*. Evanston, IL: Northwestern University Press.

Koffka, K. (1963/1935). *Principles of Gestalt psychology. New York: Harcourt, Brace and World (original, 1935).*

Lyon, D. O. (1914). The relation of length of material to time taken for learning. Journal of Educational Psychology, 5, 1–9.

Mandler, G. (1967). Verbal learning. In *New directions in psychology III*. New York: Holt, Rinehart and Winston.

Marton, F. & Saljo, R. (1976a). On qualitative differences in learning I: Outcome and process. *British Journal of Educational Psychology, 46*, 4–11.

———. (1976b). On qualitative differences in learning II: Outcome as a function of the learner's conception of the task. *British Journal of Educational Psychology, 46*, 115–127.

McGeogh, J. A. (1930). The influence of associative value upon the difficulty of nonsense syllable lists. *Journal of Genetic Psychology, 37*, 420–430.

———. (1942). *The psychology of human learning*. New York: Logman Green.

Merleau-Ponty, M. (1962). *The phenomenology of perception* (Colin Smith, Trans.). New York: Humanities Press.

———. (1963). *The structure of behavior* (Alden Fisher, Trans.). Boston: Beacon Press.

Mohanty, J. N. (1972). *The concept of intentionality*. St. Louis, Mo: Warren H. Green.

Müller, G. E. (1911). Zur Analyse der Gedächtnistätigkeit und des Vorstellungsverlaufes I. *Zsch. Psychol.*, Ergbd 5, 403.

———. (1913). Zur Analyse der Gedächtnistätigkeit und des Vorstellungsverlaufes III. *Zsch. Psychol.*, Ergbd 8, 567.

———. (1917). Zur Analye der Gedächtnistätigkeit und des Vorstellungsverlaufes II. *Zsch Psychol.*, Ergbd 9, 682.

Müller G. E., & Pilzecker, A. (1900). Experimentelle Beiträge zur Lehre vom Gedächtniss. *Zsch Psychol.*, Ergbd 1, 300.

Müller, G. E., & Schumann, F. (1893). Experimentelle Beiträge zur Untersuchungen des Gedächtnisses. *Zsch Psychol, 6,* 81–190; 257–39.

Murphy, G. (1949). *Historical introduction to modern psychology*. New York: Harcourt, Brace.

Nisbett, R. E. & Wilson, T. (1977). Telling more than we can know: verbal reports on mental processes. *Psychological Review, 84,* 231-259.

Noble, C. E. (1952). An analysis of meaning. *Psychological Review, 59,* 421–430.

———. (1963). Meaningfulness and familiarity. In C. N. Cofer & B. S. Musgrave (Eds.), *Verbal behavior and learning*. New York: McGraw-Hill.

Orne, M. (1962). On the social psychology of the psychology experiment: With particular reference to demand characteristics and their implications. *American Psychologist, 17,* 776–783.

Politzer, G. (1968/1928). *Critiques des fondemonts de la psychologie*. Paris, Presses Universitaires de France (1st edition, 1928).

Postman, L. (1968). Herman Ebbinghaus. *American Psychologist, 23,* 149–157.

Radley, A. (1976). Teaching psychology: A practical approach to personal learning. *Psychology Teaching*, 1976, *4* (1), 57-62.

Rosenthal, R. (1976). *Experimenter effects in behavioral research.* New York: Irvington Publishers.

Sartre, J. P. (1962a). *Sketch for a theory of the emotions* (Philip Mairet, Trans.). London: Methuen.

———. (1962b). *Imagination* (Forrest Williams, Trans.). Ann Arbor, MI: University of Michigan Press.

Schmitt, R. (1961-1962). In search of phenomenology. *The review of metaphics, 15,* 450–479.

———. (1967) Husserl's transcendental phenomenological reduction. In J. Kockelmans (Ed.). *Phenomenology: The philosophy of Edmund Husserl and its interpretation*. Garden City, NY: Doubleday.

Schütz, A. (1962). *Collected papers I.* (Ed., Maurice Natansen). The Hague: Nijhoff.

Spiegelberg, H. (1960). *The phenomenological movement* (Vols. 1 & 2). The Hauge: Nijhoff.

———. (1964). Phenomenology through vicarious experience. In E. Straus (Ed.), *Phenomenology: Pure and applied.* Pittsburgh, Pa: Duquesne University Press.

———. (1970). Panel discussion. In E. Straus & R. M. Griffith (Eds.), *Phenome-*

nology of memory (pp. 155–158). Pittsburgh, PA: Duquesne University Press.

———. (1972). *Phenomenology in psychology and psychiatry*. Evanston, IL: Northwestern University Press.

Strasser, S. (1957). *The soul in metaphysical and empirical psychology*. Pittsburgh, PA: Duquesne University Press.

Thorndike, E. L., & Lorge, I. (1944). *The teacher's wordbook of 30,000 words*. New York: Bureau of Publication, Teacher's College, Columbia University.

Torbert, W. R. (1972). *Learning from experience toward consciousness*. New York: Columbia University Press.

Tulving, E. (1962). Subjective organization in free recall of "unrelated" words. *Psychological Review, 69*, 344–354.

Underwood, B. J. (1963). Stimulus selection in verbal learning. In C. Cofer & B. Musgrave (Eds.), *Verbal behavior and learning*. New York: McGraw-Hill.

Witmer, L. R. (1935). The association value of three-place consonant syllables. *Journal of Genetic Psychology, 47*, 337–360.

3/The Structure of Thinking in Chess*

Christopher M. Aanstoos

THINKING is almost universally acknowledged to be an important psychological phenomenon. For example, psychology's introductory textbooks identify thinking as "the most significant activity that humans engage in" (Haber & Runyon, 1978, p. 135), "the most uniquely psychological subject" (Marx, 1976, p. 179), "absolutely central to our notions of who we are...one of the principle hallmarks of being human" (Le Francois, 1980, p. 234). Texts on the psychology of thinking in particular, which may be expected to take a more partisan interest, have also long affirmed the key role of the topic of thinking. For example, Humphrey (1948, pp. 1–3) asserted that "thinking is incomparably the most important thing in the world...thinking is vital...we must learn to understand thinking." And Guilford (1960, p. 6) stated that no psychological problem is more important than that of thinking, and that "it is imperative that we understand more about the processes of human thinking."

Despite this recognized importance, psychology has consistantly failed to explicate the phenomenon of thinking. By 1949 this failure was decried as the "essential weakness of modern psychological theory" (Hebb, 1949, p. xvi). By 1959 a text on the psychology of thinking was forced to conclude that "we still have a long road to travel before our knowledge is anything better than speculative" (Thomson, 1959, p. 209). By 1969, a conference on thinking whose stated goal was "to reach agreement on the general nature of thought" still could not even do that (Voss, 1969, p. vi). This lack of foundation clarity continues to be widely noted (Bourne, Ekstrand, & Dominowski, 1971, p. 8; Bruner, 1978, p. vii; Hunt & Poltrock, 1974, p. 227), and has led to the conclusion that thinking is the

*This research was supported by West Georgia College Faculty Research Grant #8426

most "difficult" (Haber & Runyon, 1978, p. 135), "frustrating" (Guilford, 1960, p. 6) or "intractable" (Weimer, 1974, p. 6) of all psychological phenomena.

It was on the ground of this continuing disillusionment with its ability to understand thinking that psychology recently embraced the now dominant information-processing approach with its alluring promise of a method suited to the complexities of the subject matter. The pioneering efforts of Allen Newell and Herbert Simon have deservedly earned for them the recognition as the founders of the information-processing approach to psychology (Newell, Shaw, & Simon, 1958b; Newell & Simon, 1961, 1972; Simon, 1978, 1979; Simon & Newell, 1964, 1971). Their basic premise is that the person, like the computer, is an information-processing system, whose thinking can therefore be demonstrated with computer simulation models. This information-processing approach conceptualizes thinking as essentially symbol manipulation in the same sense that computer processing is. In other words, thinking is viewed as a series of elementary or primitive processes, combined serially according to explicit, predetermined rules, each process of which is a formally definite operation for the manipulation of information in the form of elemental and discrete symbols. Since the computer simulation program is taken as a precise model of how thinking proceeds, Newell and Simon's (1972, p. 5) fundamental methodology has been to design computer programs capable of replicating human performance in order to provide concrete demonstrations of the requisite processes.

How can the validity of such a model be determined? Newell and Simon first sought to validate it by recourse to the argument of sufficiency; that is, if a program contained all of the statements required for the computer to perform a task that requires a person to think, the program can be taken as a simulation of thinking (Newell, Shaw, & Simon, 1958b, pp. 151-153; Newell & Simon, 1961, pp. 2012-2013; Simon & Newell, 1964, p. 282). And, from the beginning, Newell and Simon chose chess playing as the "type case" (Newell, 1955) or "natural arena" (Newell, Shaw, & Simon, 1958a) of such a task. Indeed, chess playing has become so important a task for computer simulation efforts that it is now referred to as the "fruit fly" of that field (Hearst, 1978, p. 197). Although chess programs have never attained the playing strength that overly optimistic early estimates claimed they would (Simon & Newell, 1958), the best recent ones have exhibited considerably improved capabilities. However, the criterion that similarity of results alone could establish the validity of the computer model was eventually acknowledged to be inadequate, after it was pointed out that similar results were no guarantee that they had been attained in a similar manner (de Groot, 1978, pp. 387-388; Gunderson, 1964; Hearst, 1967, p.32). For example, airplanes can fly, but that result is not simulation of birds flying because they do not fly in the same way (Simon, 1980, p. 76-77). Most information-processing theorists now admit that it is the processes themselves that must be simulated, and not merely the results (Simon & Newell, 1971, p. 147; Simon, 1980, pp. 76-77). But this requirement led to an additional problem: the lack of data on how human thinking actually proceeds. This question is so problematic because the information-processing approach sought to simulate thinking before it understood thinking, presuming to know the very phenomenon that needed to be disclosed.

Some information processing researchers have attempted to fill this gap by searching for similarities between the steps taken by computer simulation programs and protocols spoken by human subjects engaged in solving the same problem (Newell, 1977; Newell & Simon, 1961, 1972). Such comparisons can be quite ambiguous because of the differences between the computer language of the simulation program and the ordinary language used by the human subject (Boden, 1972, p. 111; Simon & Newell, 1971, p. 148; Kendler, 1981, pp. 362-363). To insure fidelity under these circumstances, a rigorous analysis of the human protocols in their own right should be the necessary prerequisite. But this has not been done. Instead information/processing preconceptions have biased these comparisons in ways that can be severely criticized (Aanstoos, 1983c; Frijda, 1967; Wilding, 1978, p. 171). Even Newell's (1977) more thoughtful effort to specify a means of protocol analysis that would be helpful "for developing theory rather than for validating theory" remains faithful to inferred information-processing preconceptions, as its aim is to identify the presumed elemental "operators" applied to a presumed "problem space" to change incrementally a presumed "state of knowledge."

Advocates as well as critics are increasingly recognizing that efforts to improve simulation programs are reaching an impasse, limited by a lack of understanding of how people actually think, and that this impasse can be remedied only by a direct investigation of human thinking (Charness, 1978, p. 35; Hearst, 1978, p. 200; Neisser, 1976, pp. 7-8; Newell, 1973, pp. 303-304; Raphael, 1976, pp. 284-285; Wilding, 1978. p. 176). This gap is precisely the sort of deficiency phenomenologically based research. For that reason, this author conducted an empirical phenomenological study of thinking exemplified during chess playing (Aanstoos, 1983b). The method used in that research will be outlined in the next section, after which the results will be summarized.

METHOD

Subjects

Five highly skilled chess players were used as subjects in this study. It was decided to obtain subjects across the range of competitive ability claimed by today's best computer chess programs, to facilitate a more clear-cut comparison of results. Fortunately, a standard evaluation of chess-playing ability was available: the rating system devised an used by the U.S. Chess Federation to rate its members on the basis of their tournament results. These ratings are strictly performance based and are stratified by levels, each of which is identified by a particular term. The subjects in this research represented the following levels: Master, Candidate Master, Category I, Category II, and Category III (in the remainder of this article, these subjects are identified as S.1, S.2, S.3, S.4, and S.5, respectively). Subjects were recruited by means of an advertisement placed in the Pittsburgh Chess Club's newsletter and by posters displayed at two U.S. Chess Federation tournaments. None of the subjects knew the researcher, and none were involved in psychology, either as students or as professionals. All subjects were male, and they ranged in age from late teens to mid-thirties. Subjects were paid for their participation in this study. The amount of money, specified, and agreed upon in advance, was $20.00 each for the Master and Candidate Master, and $15.00 each for the others.

Procedure

Each subject played one game of chess, having the white pieces (and so making the first move), against an assistant of the researcher. Each subject played against a different assistant, matched as closely as possible with the subject's own level of skill. Each game was played on a separate occasion, always at the same location, a quiet room in the researcher's house. The researcher did not remain in the room while the game was in progress.

Before the game began, the subject was given a page of written instructions to read and an Informed Consent form to read and sign. These specified that the subject was to "think out loud as completely as possible all of the thoughts you are having throughout the game. . .exactly as they occur to you." This basic instruction was repeated redundantly in the various ways that pilot studies had demonstrated to be most clearly understandable.

The subject then played a game of chess against the researcher's assistant and thought aloud throughout the game. The subject's entire thinking aloud was tape recorded. The opponent was prevented from hearing the subject by wearing headphones through which music was continuously played. The researcher's assistant (the subject's opponent) wrote down the moves of the game for the researcher.

After each game, the subject was interviewed by the researcher. In addition to noting whatever commentary the subjects had to give about the game itself, three specific questions were asked of every subject. The first question was "Do you feel that you were able to say your thoughts aloud without any problem?" All subjects said they had been able to do so. The second question was "Do you feel that having to think aloud interfered with your game in any significant way?" All subjects answered that it had not. One subject (S.4) noted that it helped him to see that he didn't use his opponent's time to think very effectively. The third question was "Do you feel that the ability you showed in this game was fairly representative of the games you've played recently?" All subjects responded affirmatively. Indeed, one who lost (S.2) even said that he had been making the same sorts of blunders in his recent tournament games.

Next, an assistant of the researcher transcribed the tape recordings. Then another assistant compared these typed protocols to the tapes in order to correct any discrepancies. Then a portion of each protocol was set aside for in-depth analysis. The portions to be analyzed in-depth were selected from points at which the games were still relatively evenly balanced, and leading toward an important turning point. For S.'s 1, 2, and 3, this segment went from the beginning of the game to the early middle game. For S.'s 4 and 5 this segment was taken from the late middle game. The remainder of the transcripts served as background for the researcher's understanding of the segments. (The interested reader may find these transcripts in their entirety in Aanstoos, 1983b.)

Data Analysis

Phenomenological methods recognize and seek to describe the instrinsically intentive relation of the person to some subject matter. Indeed, that is the meaning of its most important discovery: intentionality—that consciousness is consciousness of something. Hence, rather than preconceiving the protocols as "bits of behavioral responses" for the sake of methodological orthodoxy, they are understood as a description of the relation of the subject to the intentional world (see Aanstoos, 1983c, for a more extended discussion of this use of think-aloud protocols). In such an analysis "the task of the researcher is to let the world of the describer. . .reveal itself through the description" (Giorgi, 1975b, p. 74), in order to disclose the structure of the phenomenal field as it was lived. A phenomenological method achieves this aim through a rigorously specified means of engaging the naive descriptions and discerning their psychological sense. First formulated by phenomenological philosophers, this method has recently been adapted to psychological research by Giorgi. It consists of the following steps: bracketing, intuiting, describing.

Bracketing. In order to attend to thinking, or any phenomenon, as it is lived, it is first necessary to "take what is experienced just as it gives itself in any instance, and thus begin where we must begin" (Husserl, 1977/1925, p. 42). In other words, to understand the subject's world, one must first arrive at it by a suspension, or bracketing, of all presumptive constructs about it. Such bracketing "slackens the intentional threads which attach us to the world and thus brings them to our notice" (Merleau-Ponty, 1962/1945, p. xiii). In that way, the naturalistic bias which conceives the world as extrinsic and simply there as a thing in itself is overcome, and the world as intended, or meant, is allowed to come into view.

By this bracketing operation, a phenomenological method aims to achieve a direct contact with the world as lived (Merleau-Ponty, 1962/1945, p. vii). This reduction does not result in the disinterest of the researcher but rather in the suspension of all narrowly confining interests preceding attention to the phenomenon, in order to become fully interested in the phenomenon itself. By so deliberately avoiding concentrating attention on any particular predetermined aspect, the researcher is able to escape the danger of finding only what one expects to see. Instead, one adopts an attitude of "open-ended presence to the phenomenon that is unfolding" (Giorgi, 1976, p. 313). Giorgi (1975b) identified this first step as "initial familiarizing" and demonstrates concretely how its achievement is brought about by reading the transcript as a whole, attuned not merely to the linguistic content, but to the intentional, or lived experience. For example, in this case, the conception that thoughts are discrete symbols that happen to be passing through short-term memory is set aside, in order to discern their significance for the subject. Allowing the subject's thinking to come into view meant that the researcher had to give it priority over questions regarding the objective accuracy of the subject's judgment, for thinking was not to be prejudged by the standards of logic. For example, when a subject thought that a particular move was "forced," then it is as a forced move that it is an object of thought for him, regardless of whether or not another analysis of it could demonstrate otherwise.

Intuiting. The next step was to grasp to essential psychological meanings through a direct intuiting. In this way, the phenomenological method aims to bring the phenomenon itself to self-showing, to "return to the things themselves" in order to bring their meaning to self-evidence (Husserl, 1962/1913 pp. 48-50). Phenomenological methods are noninferential in the sense that there are no hypotheses to be tested. Evidence resides not in the probabilistic support for a hypothesis, but the description of the essential significance of the phenomenon.

These essential meanings are not at all self-evident in advance however. They must be brought to a self-showing and can only be made self-evident through rigorous effort. It is this work that the eidetic intuiting strives to accomplish. A concrete exemplification of the manner in which such essential meanings are brought to a self-showing has been provided by Giorgi (1975a, 1975b) who proceeds by way of identifying meaning units, specifying their central themes, and then articulating their psychological sense or meaning. For the present study, these procedures were carried out as follows:

1. The researcher read the protocol, attuned to the question of the meaning of thinking. Each time a transition in meaning was perceived (always in regard to the sense of the whole within which it participates) it was delineated. The result was that each protocol was delineated into its constituent meaning units.

2. Next, the phenomenal themes of each meaning unit that had allowed it to emerge as a constituent in the first place were clarified and made explicit. This description of the lived experience of the subject retained its embeddedness in the naive perspective of the subject. The aim of this step was simply to provide a phenomenal description of the meaningful themes of each constituent. Such a phenomenal description is not yet a psychological understanding, rather it is that which has to be comprehended psychologically.

3. Next each of these phenomenal descriptions of the meaning units was reflected upon in order to discover what it revealed about the psychological significance of thinking, in that situation for that subject. It is at this step that the researcher aims to transform the phenomenal description into a properly phenomenological understanding by laying bare the immanent significance therein.

Describing. At this step, the structural meanings achieved were organized into a systematic structural description in order to grasp the relation of the essential meanings through their coherence. Merleau-Ponty (1963/1942, p. 130) identified this primordial coalescence of any phenomenon as its "structure," which he elucidated by showing that "situation and reaction are linked by their common participation in a structure in which the mode of activity proper to the organism is expressed." He added that this notion of structure does not imply that the organism knows the structure and attempts to realize it. Rather, it is significant as a structure for the one who grasps it as such (1963/1942, p. 159). Hence, it may be said that structure is the explicit thematization of the implicit dialectic "situation and reaction," of world and person. The comprehension of this "immanent meaning" (Merleau-Ponty, 1962/1942, p. 184) or "immanent significance" (Merleau-Ponty, 1962/1945, p. 258) is the aim of this step of the phenomenological method.

Following the guidelines of Giorgi (1975a, 1975b) and Wertz (1983), this procedure consisted of two phases. The first task was to describe the situated or individual structure for each of the empirical cases. These ideographic descriptions remained anchored in the concrete experience of the particular subject, and thus were the systematic structural statements of the essential psychological significances that were grasped in the preceding step.

Then, the second task of this operation was to interrogate those individual structures in order to proceed from them to a description of the structural significance of thinking in chess in general, by retaining those features that were essentially invariant across the particular cases. In other words, the analysis proceeded from the individual to the general by means of its articulation of the "essential generality" of each particular instance examined. Another way of expressing this movement is that it is a disclosure of the essence of the phenomenon, or the essential theme of all its variations. It must be clear that the theme is expressed in its concrete variations, and only in its concrete variations. It is "not a thing which rests in itself" (Merleau-Ponty, 1963/1942, p. 159). The way to the invariant theme of the variations was by "cross checking" the essence of each variation (Merleau-Ponty, 1975/1964, p. 26). In this step, not only were the empirical variations checked against each other, but against other possible variations imagined by the researcher as well. Empirically obtained variations can never exhaust the realm of all possible variations. Instead, they provided the starting point, a set of exemplar cases, which had to be completed through the use of imagined variations (a procedure first employed by Husserl, e.g., 1977/1925, p. 53). Each constituent of the individual structure was varied, and the question asked, "if this were changed, would this phenomenon still be this phenomenon?" In that way, the researcher was able to proceed to the essential generality that was then described as the general structure of thinking as it is exemplified during chess playing.

RESULTS

Levels of Specification

This presentation will provide the final result of the analysis: the general structural description of thinking, as it is manifested in chess playing. The high level of essential generality of this structure will then next be elaborated concretely in the Discussion section. A structural description may be developed with varying degrees of specificity or completeness, depending on the audience for whom it is to be presented. These results, for example, have been presented in various brief formats (e.g., Aanstoos, 1983a). The most concise description of the general structure of thinking that was formulated as a result of this research is the following:

> Thinking as it is exemplified during chess playing is a process of discovering and making explicit certain implicit possibilities that are taken by the thinker to be present in the position. These possibilities are experienced as dynamic currents of force, avenues of virtual action that hold the ambiguous promise of transforming the position. This effort of making such possible transformations explicit is therefore essentially telic in the sense that the aim is to achieve a favorable transformation of the position within the overall aim of winning the game. Thinking concerns itself with these possibilities in three ways: by taking them as questions, by characterizing them as possibilities in their own specificity, and by determining their pragmatic appropriateness to the context of the game. In doing so, thinking thematizes the relation of these possibilities to the position as a whole. In other words, thinking grasps this relational unity through the way that it is implied by the possibilities. This relational unity is itself a network of implications, with both temporal and spatial references to further possibilities. Temporally, it implies relations between past, present and future moves. Spatially, it implies relations between pieces on the board. Thinking grasps this relational unity from the particular perspective of the player, illuminating only those aspects of it that appear as relevant from that point of view. The specific means by which thinking determines the implicitory significance of its possibles is by grasping their if—then relations within the larger referential unity of the position.

The language in such a statement is necessarily precise in order to condense so much material so concisely. But after a certain point, such condensation begins to exact a price in comprehension among those readers who are not familiar with the complete individual analyses from which it was derived. Unfortunately, such a concise statement cannot adequately disclose the rich and varied texture of thinking provided by the descriptive data. The phenomenon of thinking defies cursory explication. That is the reason for the repeated failure of the psychology of thinking. To do justice to such a complex phenomenon, the complete and detailed structural description that was developed as the culmination of the data analysis must be presented. That description is the following.

The General Structural Description

Thinking is necessarily thinking about something. Hence, its structure includes two constituents: a specific (noetic) act by which it intends an object of thought, and the (noematic) object of thought itself. These two constituents are strictly correlated as a bipolar structure, in that there could be no object of thought without an act of thinking, nor could there be an act of thinking without an object of thought. Though writing, by its sequential nature, requires that they be described alternately, it is important to realize their essential correlation. In this general structural description, first the noetic pole, the act of thinking, will be described, and then the noematic pole, the objects of thought. In each case, however, sufficient mention of the other will be made so that their correlative status will be clear. After that, thinking's structural involvement with other moments of psychological life in chess playing will be described.

The noetic structure of thinking. In chess playing, thinking's own proper intending of its objects is the explicitation of the possible. In other words, thinking is the act of making explicit the implicit possibilities which are the symbolic objects of thought. Thinking explicitates previously prethematic possibilities by thematizing how they are implied, or symbolized, by the configuration of the position in the chess game. Through this thematization of possibility, thinking predelineates a possible future. That is, it discloses the future implications of the present position. In that sense, thinking is essentially future directed, or telic. The apprehension of this telic dimension is itself founded on thinking's aim, which is to determine the most efficacious possible transformation of the present position in order to facilitate the thinker's effort to win the game. Thus thinking is pragmatic. To summarize: Thinking is pragmatically and telically explicitative of a symbolic dimension.

Thinking explicitates its objects through three different modes of apprehension: interrogation, characterization, and fulfillment. Though typically unfolded within a phasic temporality, these various modalities cannot be said to be strictly sequential. Rather, any one mode may be initially focal. While it is, the others are cooperative as ground, lending significance to the focal mode. For example, it is often the case after the opponent has just made his move that thinking begins by characterizing a particular theme of that move and then shifting to interrogating it more deeply. S.3, for instance, first characterized his opponent's third move as "threatening my king pawn," and then interrogates the significance of that threat. In this case, the focal mode is characterizing, but this apprehension rests on both interrogating (what the opponent's move threatens) and fulfilling (countering the threat) even though these modes are initially present only as ground. Another example of the relations of thinking's modalities is revealed by those occasions when thinking shifts from interrogating to fulfilling. For instance, as soon as S.5 questions the possibility of a particular rook sacrifice, he immediately shifts to a fulfilling mode, simply noting that "I need those rooks," without any intervening specific characterizing of that need. Instead, the sole characterization—their indispensability—is simply ground for the conclusion not to sacrifice one. Nor do the latent modes of apprehension necessarily emerge focally prior to every shift from thinking to some other psychological act. For example, thinking can shift to memory following its interrogatory mode. Such a shift is especially typical during the opening moves. At the beginning of the game, for instance, subjects' questioning of what opening to play evokes their memorial attunements to previous games. Another variation of this point is thinking's shift to another psychological act directly from its characterizing mode. S.3's shift directly to a decision of what move to make after having characterized the dynamics of his opponent's previous move provides an example of that variation.

Thus, thinking's different modes of intending objects of thought are structurally rather than linearly related. Specifically the structure of their relation is that each is latently co-present with and may be evoked by each of the others, even when not all three are focal in every act of thinking. Such instances are not inherently less efficacious. Their utility is preserved by the demand character of the game, which at points renders unnecessary thinking's bringing focally to bear all three modes of explicitation. Each of these three modes must next be described in some more detail.

As *interrogation*, thinking thematizes a questionableness about the position. The concrete way by which thinking as interrogation raises this questionableness involves possibilizing, projecting, and seeking justification. That questionableness irrupts within previously taken-for-granted facticities, and reveals a gap as that which is to be completed. Subject S.1 provides an apt illustration when, after noting several possible moves his opponent could make, says, "I'm not sure how this opening works, if he, if he can develop his king bishop."

Thus, in the mode of interrogation, thinking addresses itself to and thematizes a prethematic questionableness as an indeterminant significance horizonally present within a more complacent certainty. This horizonal questionableness is itself evoked by more implicit moments of interrogation. Thus, interrogation unfolds as an ensemble of questioning, pulsating between the horizonal and the thematic. The next several meaning units following the one quoted above provide ample exemplification of this unfolding ensemble of implicit questioning, culminating with: "Um. I'm not sure where all my pieces ought to be going. Maybe I play bishop to rook three. I've got to think about that. Maybe I should just play, ah, maybe if bishop to knight five I should play bishop to rook three right away, to trade, to keep him from castling. That's an interesting idea."

Such questionableness is never devoid of contextual inherence. Rather, it is evoked by the referential network characterized by thinking (see below), toward whose possibilities for transformation it is directed. Specifically, interrogation takes up the beginnings, or subbeginnings, or new beginnings, for transformative possibilities. The example just cited illustrates this point well. Another is S.2's "Wonder what he'll play against me." Of course it must be kept in mind that the use of the term "beginning" here refers to its meaning as such for the subject, not to any objective or logical standard.

Two different kinds of questions are raised by interrogation: those which seek a single answer that is taken to be determinable and definite, and those for which such answers are not sought (although these are still assumed to be answerable). This distinction is related to that between forcing and virtual types of possibilities (see below). It is revealed especially by whether the subject questions some move he thinks he should make versus some move he merely considers wanting to make. An example of the former type of question is S.1's "Maybe I should play pawn takes pawn right away." An example of the latter type of question is S.2's "Where do I want my queen bishop developed? Knight two maybe? King three? Knight five?"

As *characterization,* thinking thematizes possibilities by apprehending how they are implied by both general principles and especially by the position as a network of spatial-temporal references (see below). Thinking does not attend to the entire network of referential relations, but precisely only to those that appear to offer relevant transformative possibilities. These are predelineated by thinking's characterizing an "if-then" structure, in which thinking thematizes what is implied by explicitating the relatedness between two features or possible moves (see below). In this mode, thinking is concerned with the answerability of thematized possibilities which may be either specific move continuations or more general positional characteristics. In either case the possibilities (as gaps within the facticities) have the character of being fill-able, completable, determinable. To fill in the gap, thinking as characterization strives to discover a necessary positional advantage or a forcing continuation by which the particular transformation may be achieved. The compelling quality of such characteristics, however, are highly relative (see below, under Objects of Thought).

Some examples of both combinational and positional characterizations are in order. An example of the former type is S.4's characterization of the continuation: "Knight takes pawn, pawn takes pawn, queen takes pawn, I don't get anything back. Ffh." This instance is particularly exemplary of a number of aspects of such characterizing. It demonstrates thinking's grasping of the relatedness of the moves and thinking's sense of the determinability of what is being characterized, but it also demonstrates something more. It shows thinking's characterizing being guided by, and elucidating, an implicit contact with a balance of a dynamic tension of force. That concern will be described more fully below, as an object of thought.

Besides combinational characterizing, thinking also characterizes positional features as such. Some examples of such moments include thinking's characterizing: balanced development; a lack of attacking possibilities; a troublesome knight; control of the center. Two important aspects of such characterizing stand out: positional characterizing is typically the result of a prior questioning; and it is through such characterizing that thinking contacts the medium and long-range future of the game. The sense in which the game's future is an object of thought will be described more fully in the section on the noematic structure of thinking (see below).

As *fulfillment*, thinking establishes the embeddedness of the possibility within the referential network. That enables thinking to bring a sense of closure to its explicitation of the role of that possibility in the transformation of the position. It distinguishes those possibilities that affect the dynamics in a fundamental way from those that do not. For example, S.1 noted, "Knight to rook seven is, is flashy but, but bogus." That move was grasped as not fundamentally able to affect the transformation of the equilibrium because S. grasped that the opponent could still maintain it by making a particular move. Thus, its apparent capacity to affect the equilibrium depended on the opponent not making his own best move. In this mode, thinking thematizes such criteria. In other words, as fulfillment, thinking involves demonstrations of the applicability and the necessity of the thematized possibility. It does so by means of "if—then" structures (see following section on Objects of Thought). In this mode, thinking seeks to achieve a reorganization of the field of possibles such that the ambiguity about the future is dissolved. Such a thoroughgoing clarification is sometimes achieved, but most typically it is not. Rather, the transformative capacity of the possibilities remains beyond the circle of necessity, retaining a peripheral instability, which then evokes subsequent interrogation.

The noematic structure of thinking. The objects of thought are intentional objects, and as such must be distinguished from the transcendent objects which are thought about (for examples the chess pieces on the board). However, part of the essential meaning of the object of thought is its relation to that which is thought about, and this relation will be articulated as part of its noematic structure.

The object of thought presents itself as a possibility capable of factical completion. Its manifestation as a possibility is through that which "could," "might," or "may" be. It has four essential attributes: it is symbolic, pragmatic, telic, and ambiguous. Regarding the first, the object of thought is essentially *symbolic* in that it has no existence apart from its participation in a referential totality of meanings to which it refers and through which it is expressed (see below for a more complete specification of this referential totality). Regarding the second, the object of thought is *pragmatic* in that it has the character of an action possibility:

the possibility of effecting a transformation in the dynamic relations in the position. An example is S.3's "bishop to knight five, which can go from there to rook four to knight three, attacking his king pawn." Regarding the third attribute, the object of thought is *telic* in the sense that it refers to the future. Usually, this attribute is obvious, but it is even descriptive of thinking's thematizing a past possibility, that is, something that was previously possible but now no longer is. Even then it illuminates the ongoing relations among the pieces. An example is "Bishop takes knight didn't work because of queen takes, knight takes pawn, and ah, knight takes pawn himself. Or he could even just play knight takes pawn." The telic dimension of such an object delineates what the future does and does not now portend. Regarding the fourth attribute, the object of thought essentially presents itself as an *uncertainty*. But uncertainty here must be seen as a quality of the intentional object (that is, as lived), not a mathematical array of objectively determinable alternatives, for it is the lack of foreclosure rather than the availability of legal moves that founds uncertainty. That was especially exemplified by the subjects' manner of playing opening moves by rote.

In the course of a chess game, thinking intends many different objects of thought. These include: a move, the initiative, a positional feature, the opponent, and the network of referential relations in the position. While a possible move, and particularly the next move, is the most thematically central object of thought, all these objects are structurally related to the network of spatial-temporal relations, whose implicatory or referential character provides the basis for thinking's determination of the sense or meaning of these other objects. This network of spatial and temporal relations is repeatedly delineated, revised, and maintained by thinking.

Thinking's thematization of spatial relations in the position includes both global spatial-dynamic tensions as well as specific spatial relations. An example of the former is S.2's sense that there is "a lot of space advantage" to be won on the queenside. Another, even more general spatial determination is S.4's sense that a particular move will leave his opponent "cramped." An example of a specific spatial relation is S.2's sense that his opponent's knight, if moved to its typical place, "blocks in his queen bishop."

The position is also grasped as being temporally related to past and future possibilities. S.3 notes that it is a "crucial time" in the game. S.1 wonders if it might be "too late" to play a previously thematized move. S.4 considers that his opponent might want to play a "waiting move" to change the temporal flow of the game.

Both the spatial and temporal relations mutually imply each other, and so form a *spatio-temporal network* of relations. These relations, however, are not closed in upon themselves, but imply, or refer to, the possibility of transformation. Their relational structure is an implicatory, or referential, one, such that the meaning of each constituent is not that of an isolated unit, but rather that of a participant in a totality, referring to other possibilities. For example, after a possible move, the spatiality may be so rearranged that a well-posted knight now becomes easily dislodged. The transformation of the spatial relations can even refer to the emergence of new possibilities that are not yet thematic. For example, S.4 noted, "Maybe this brings on some new possibilities with my bishop to there." Hence, this referential network is not a collection of elemental pieces on a geometrically uniform board, but a field of differential forces and tensions carved out by and defined according to their dynamic-actional relations.

Thinking does not thematize this referential network in its totality, but neither are its relations grasped randomly. Rather, it is precisely those whose pragmatic character is most evident (see above). These are grasped by means of an *"if—then" structure,* in which thinking delineates what is implied by explicitating their referential significance. This "if—then" structure takes a variety of forms, their essential structural commonality being an effort to penetrate the opacity of the future possible unfolding of the implications of the present position by extending its referential arcs in order to explicitate what they imply. Actual types of this "if—then" structure include: (1) a specific move in both the "if" and the "then" clauses, (2) no move in the "if" clause and a specific move in the "then" clause, (3) a specific move in the "if" clause and a specific or global evaluation of the position in the "then" clause, (4) a goal in the "if" clause and a goal in the "then" clause.

The first type is the most common, and in fact may form compound "if—then" structures by taking its "then" clause as an "if" clause for a new "if—then" structure, or by combining with the second type. Even in its pure form, there are many varieties of this type of "if—then" structure. The three most important will be presented here. The first is "If move X is made by one player, then the other can make move Y." Two examples are "If I go there, he can move his queen back"; "if he does play knight to king bishop three right—knight to knight five—right now, I'll play pawn to king rook three." The second variation of this type is "If move X is made by one player, then the other must make move Y." Examples include "He can play bishop to king two, and I have to retire to king four in frustration"; "if he'd play knight to the king bishop three, I'd have to kick it out with my king rook pawn." the third variation of this type is: "if move X is made by one player, then he can no longer make move Y." For example, S.2 noted that if his opponent moved his knight, it would prevent him from then moving his bishop.

In the second type of an "if—then" structure, a move by one player is deliberately omitted. That serves to make explicit what possibilities would be implied if they are not blocked by the player whose move is omitted. Thus, the structure is "If no move is made by one player, then the other can make move Y." For example, S.3 noted during his own turn a particular move his opponent could make were it his turn instead ("If it was his move, bishop takes queen would win"). This type may be compounded with the first one and so makes explicit the implications of a series of moves by one player. In this case the structure is "If one player makes move X, and the other makes no move, then the first player can next move Z." Examples include S.1's considering what his opponent will do the turn after making his next move, without interposing S.'s own intervening move; S.3's noting "I can play pawn to queen three here, and then queen knight to queen two."

With regard to the third type, a specific move may imply a global significance rather than another specific move. In that case, the structure is "If one player makes move X, then positional consequence A will follow." An example is S.3's noting that his kingside would be weaker after a particular move. Sometimes the resulting global significance remains prethematic. For example, S.2's sense that a "great game" would follow a particular center pawn advance after castling.

In the fourth type, a particular goal is grasped as implying the possibility of the achievement of another subsequent goal. In this case, the structure is "if goal 1 is achieved, then goal 2 can be." For example, S.2 determines that if he can "control" a particular square, he can subsequently occupy it with his own piece. Another example is S.5's sense that if he can gain control of the seventh rank, he will then have checkmating possibilities.

One final point about this "if—then" structure is that there is a variant of it that is also a thematic object of thought. This variant may be identified as the "since—then" structure, as it is a preceding move (rather than a future one) that is taken as referring to the possibility or necessity or foreclosure of a subsequent move by the same or the other player. For example, S.3 determined that since his opponent's last move resulted in an attack on his bishop, he must now back it up on his next move. While such "since—then" structures occur quite frequently after the opponent's moves, they are typically anticipated prior to that move as an "if—then" structure. Hence, their referential significance has already been largely delineated by the subject. When that significance has not been so delinated, the move presents itself to thinking as "a very strange-looking move" precisely because it lacks referential relatedness. At those times, it is up to the "since—then" structuring to weave it into the referential network.

A summary of the referential network as an object of thought is in order at this point. Thinking grasps the position not as a collection of isolated units, but as a symbolic network of spatial and temporal references, of implicatory referential arcs. These referential arcs are contacted as being there in the position, but they must be uncovered. Thinking grasps them by making thematic, by making a theme of, that which is implicit. That is, thinking is an explicitation of the implications. But how does thinking contact the implications to be explicitated? Implicity—that is the tacit dimension of thinking. In that way, possibilities that seem to come to mind capriciously or "out of the blue"—those referred to as "intuition"—are precisely the implications that were implicitly referred to by these referential arcs. An example is a point in S.1's game when thinking thematizes, seemingly "out of the blue," a move the opponent could make next. Even the subject is unclear about the basis for the move, suggesting that the opponent might want to play it "out of curiosity" to "see what happens." Evidently, the subject's curiosity has also been piqued by the move. It becomes clear through the rest of the meaning unit that the move carries with it a set of referential implications. Thematizing that move called thinking to make these implications explicit, which it promptly begins to do: "I suppose if he plays bishop to knight five I play bishop to king two and then follow up with knight to knight five later or something." Thus, the referential arcs disclose the meaning of the spatial-temporal matrix. Indeed, that disclosure is their essential role for thinking, and is taken as such by thinking. For example, after following out such a referential arc, S.5 explicitly noted "which means I have to move the queen." While the spatial-temporal matrix may be focal, its referential implication or meaning may be horizonal. Furthermore, these referential arcs are transformed with every move. Thus, thinking takes as its task the explicitation of the consequences of these transformations. And, lastly, in doing so, thinking distinguishes between necessary (or forced) and contingent (or virtual) possibilities, necessary ones being those that are directly and immediately implied, whereas contingent ones are those that are only potentially implied by the referential network.

These referential arcs imply possibilities which themselves can effect the transformation of that referential totality; hence there is a dialectical relationship between the referential network and the possibilities implied. Most thematically central is the next move or continuation of moves that can be made. It is here that the intentional object of thought participates in the transcendence that is thought about: the chess game itself. As an intersubjective reality which thinking contacts only perspectivally, the chess game provides the foundation for the answerability which is a profile of the objects of thought. That is, it is by virtue of their relation to this transcendent reality that the objects of thought possess their character of possibility-that-is-to-be-filled-in. This completability eludes final realization in thinking, yet exerts a demand on thinking. That is, answerability includes a normative significance: each possibility presents the meaning that "maybe this is what should be done" (in the sense that it may be the most efficacious way to effect a change in the game in favor of the thinker). This "should" dimension is particularly evident when the object of thought is what move to make next, as that is precisely when the transcendent object must be effected. It is through its proximal relatedness with the game itself that the next move in particular acquires its demand, or telic, character. An apt example is S.1's wrestling with the idea of making a particular pawn trade. He sees it as something he had "better" do, even though it is something he "hates" to do, and feels it is a "pity" to have to do.

The next move as an object of thought, however, is itself subservient to another object of thought wherein its own telic character is ultimately found. This other object of thought, which remains highly implicit itself, is the final result of the game as a future possibility. As objects of thought, the next move is related to the final result by another object of thought, which is sometimes implicit and sometimes explicit: the initiative, or capacity to force the action to a certain extent by the use of offensive threats that force the other player to parry them in limited, defensive ways. This sense of dynamic force or momentum unites the next move (as an explicit and primarily spatial object of thought) with the final result (as an implicit and primarily temporal object of thought). This unity is possible because both have spatial and temporal characteristics (for instance, the next move is never thought about in isolation from the temporal flow, but always as embedded within a plan or combination), and because "initiative" is structurally essential to both.

As an object of thought, *initiative* or momentum is a profile of the game as a whole. For example, S.2 sensed that his position was such that "I got to have a great game." It is specifically revealed through the dynamic balance of offensive opportunities or threats and defensive necessities. This balance is not summatively determined, however, but on the basis of the thinker's capacity to control the transformative flow of the next few moves by being able to force the other player to make defensive moves. When a certain move has the character that it "has to" or must be made as a consequence of the forcing nature of the other player's initiative, that character differs from the "should" character that other moves have at other times. S.1 provides an example of this distinction. He thinks that "pawn takes pawn" is a move he "should" have made, but now thinks "I have to retire to king four." In the former case, it was a move he should have made in order to keep the momentum, whereas the latter move is one that he must make for having lost the momentum. Generally, this balance of opportunities is grasped only implicitly until there is a change or impending change in the balance, in favor of either player. At that point it becomes an explicit object of thought. For example, as S.1's own attacking possibilities are blocked, he became aware of the need to keep his queen defensively posted, sensing that his opponent "may be counterattacking there pretty soon." This change may be an increase or a decrease in the offensive capacity of the player who is already considered to have the momentum, or a disturbance of, or reestablishment of, a state of relative equilibrium. The exact shift in the equilibrium may not be clear, only that it needs to be reevaluated. For example, S.3 finds his hoped-for breakthrough of his opponent's defenses stalled and reexamines the momentum: "Yup, this isn't too bad a game now. Though for a while I was smashing him. Nah, he's not smashing me, I still have all the trumps but, he's not doing too bad."

Another category of objects of thought has to do with the *opponent's intentions.* While the opponent himself remains a highly implicit object of thought, what the opponent may be thinking about is repeatedly thematized as an object of thought. As an object of thought, the opponent's intentions emerge through an imaginal shift of perspective, based on the implicit presumption that the opponent's thinking is no different than the subject's own. For example, S.1 "doubts" that his opponent will fail to block a possibility that he would block. This implied identity is most clear in those cases where a subject thinks a particular move fulfills a particular question. An example is S.4: "I think he wants to move his rook back there." However, it also extends to those instances wherein the subject, still uncertain about the implications of a particular move that the opponent could make, thinks that the opponent is also interested in, but uncertain about, that move as well. A previously cited meaning unit of S.1 also applies well here; he was curious about a move, and so he assumed his opponent was too. But the opponent's thinking, as an object of thought for the subject, is not simply projection, for it always retains a certain impenetrability about it. Indeed, sometimes it is the very opacity of the opponent's intentions that is the object of thought. S.2, for example, wonders what opening his opponent will play, then later wonders what he is thinking, and then where he will move a particular piece. More frequently, it is grasped as ambiguously likely, partially illuminated by some specific characteristic of the position. An example is S.1: "He just plays, probably just plays bishop to ah, bishop takes knight." Sometimes the opponent's intention is not illuminated by the position but by his bodily comportment. For example, at one point S.4 thinks that his opponent has given up hoping to be able to retain a piece by how hard he depressed the bell after the move: "He punched that clock, punched that bell pretty hard, that means he must have dropped it." The implicit basis for thinking's concern with the opponent's intentions is the pattern of rhythmic alternation whereby each player takes a turn at transforming the referential network. While this dialectic remains highly implicit, it provides the structural coherence for thinking's taking the opponent's intentions as an object of thought.

Thinking's involvement with other modes of psychological life manifested in chess playing. Thinking is not the only psychological modality brought to bear in playing chess. Playing chess is properly an action of the whole person, in which many psychological modes are elicited as a unity. Indeed, while thinking "casts about" in a sea of possibility, it is flanked by shores of facticities given by other psychological modes. Thinking initially relates to these facticities by taking them as a springboard, from which thinking itself emerges. That is, thinking emerges within the gaps in these factically givens. It de-structures them by relating them to the possibilities which are the proper objects of thought, in the service of returning psychological life to the field of the factical, but now a facticity transformed by its possibilization. Thus, thinking, whose intentional objects have the character of possibility, occupies an intermediate position, linking modalities whose intentional objects have the character of facticity. Often it bridges two moments of the same mode, for in the actual flux of a chess game, thinking is both evoked by and also evokes the emergence of these other modes. In that sense, thinking is involved with these other modes as a two-sided dependency. The relations of thinking with these other psychological modes must be addressed next, each in turn. While this description will detail these other modes only in terms of their relation with thinking, it should be recognized that each of them could also be made the focus of an analysis of how each is exemplified during chess playing. But that would be another investigation, and is beyond the scope of this one.

Thinking's relation to *memory* is one of the most pervasive and crucial in chess playing. Memory of the rules of chess (how the pieces are moved, and so on) is of course essential for being able to play chess at all. But that memorial infrastructure does not become an object of thought. Rather, in those instances in which thinking relates to memorial objects, those with which it is involved are memories of one's general stock of chess expertise and memories of previous games. These memorially givens are evoked on the basis of their relevance or similarity to the present game. Yet similarity is not an exact duplication. That is because the memorial object is ultimately not a particular configuration of pieces, but a theme, or idea. In thematizing it, either its essential similarity may be focal or its essential difference may be focal, depending on how the memorial object is related to the present position. An example of the former case is S.1's determination that the position reached so far in the game is essentially similar to that of a previous game: "as in the Bisguier game." The relation with that game also provides an example of the latter case, when later the present game diverges essentially from the previous one. S.1 now memorially thematizes how it differs: "It would be like the game with Bisguier except I'd be a, tempo down." This example reveals the distinction between essential versus inessential similarity. The configuration of the pieces is still basically like that in the previous game, but the tempo is different (whose side has the next move). And the subject recognizes that that essential difference means that the similar features no longer indicate an essential similarity.

Thinking's relation to *perception* is also crucial. Perception of course is involved in chess playing especially visually as the player looks at the pieces on the board for virtually the entire game. Indeed, subjects often used visually based terms: a position "looked" good for example, or "let's see" about a particular move possibility. The sole occasion when another sense modality was used was by S.2. While considering his 22nd move, he said "that sounds pretty good." That followed a quick, superficial synthesis of a possible combination. Perhaps he couldn't yet "see" it, but it sounded right to him (at that same time he was also not "seeing" the material balance accurately, which is quite a blunder for a player of his caliber). But what is thinking's relation to perception such that at some point it almost merges into it, or fails to? Perception thematizes the immediate physiognomies of the position, especially right after it has been transformed by the opponent's making a move. For example S.4 notes: "Ah, he plays rook to D eight." In that sense, perception provides a starting point for thinking. But the relationship is more complex than that, for thinking also evokes perceptual reorganizations. These are achieved by thinking's clarification of the referential arcs of the spatial-temporal network. For example, thinking founded a perceptual reorganization upon taking up the opponent's perspective for subject S.1. It was specifically when thinking thematized the position as if it were the opponent's turn that the perceptual field is reorganized such that he now sees the relation between the opponent's bishop and his own queen. A second example of thinking's capacity to evoke perceptual reorganizations is provided by subject S.4. Only after thinking has thematized a possible future move that S. could make does S. perceive a particular dynamic relation that his opponent's knight has with his own pieces. He now grasps perceptually a certain configuration of these pieces ("the knight hook") that he had not previously perceived as a configuration. Thus, even though the pieces were not moved at that point, the perceptual field itself is re-gestalted or reorganized as a consequence of thinking's thematization. While such a reorganization comes as a surprise, it would be inaccurate to understand it as a merely fortuitous coincidence. Indeed, thinking does not simply evoke them, it provokes them, so frequent and important are such perceptual reorganizations to the course of the game.

Thinking's relation to *affect* also provides an example of a two-sided dependency, in that each can evoke the other. A player's first reaction upon seeing his opponent's move (already within its implied significance) may be an affective one; he may be shocked, surprised, even frightened. Such reactions then evoke thinking to thematize the implicit significance. On the other hand, thinking may in its turn evoke affect, such as relief or frustration. An example is S.1. His frustration at being unable to achieve the aim of his speculative opening gambit mounts and mounts, until it nears the point of "hair-tearing frustration." Perhaps the notion of a two-sided dependency here is not even sufficient to grasp the intertwining of affect and thought in chess, for it is an intensely emotional experience for the serious player. S.1 "curses" himself for having "missed a shot here." S.2 becomes quite depressed over his blunder late in the game. S.4 castigates himself as a "dummy" for thinking he had a possible combination when he didn't, and writhes in agony when he feels his opponent's capacity to defeat a particular possible continuation: "Ooh, he's got me crunched now." Even when not verbalized, the affective experience of the chess game is expressed bodily, through gestures and comportment. Thought and affect are brought to bear as a unity during chess playing, a relation well grasped by chess masters themselves. Vitale Sevastianov, president of the Soviet Chess Federation, summed this relation concisely by noting that "through chess a human being is able to unite his mind and feelings" (quoted by Bert, 1981, p. 30).

Thinking's relation to *imagination* is a complicated variant of a two-sided dependency. Certainly it is the case that either can evoke the other. Just as imagination as the evocation of the possible founds thinking's "if—then" structuring, so too does thinking's questioning call forth imagining. But in imagination, the mode of givenness is changed; specifically, they are not posited as questions, as uncertainty. Rather, the imagination serves thinking by projecting its object, such as a move, into a future, but then it is thinking which takes up that future possibility as a question. For example, S.4 considers the imagined possibility of a bishop sacrifice. The imagination simply presents that possibility as a possibility. It then becomes an object for thinking's questioning.

Thinking's relation to *empathy* is also important. One of the ways that the subject intends his opponent's possibilities and intentions is by empathically taking up the opponent's perspective. For example, S.4 feels that his move has surprised his opponent. And S.3 empathically feels at one point that his opponent "is really thinking hard now." Often this empathic sense occurs by virtue of the subject's having been in that position in previous games himself. S.1, for example, thematizes such a time. Thus, empathy provides facticities for thinking to take up.

Thinking's relation to *anticipation* and *judgment* is also important. These are listed together here, as they are both typically founded on thinking as its outcomes or its means of returning to facticity. But there is an essential difference between them. When thinking passes into judgment, the subject remains mindful of the uncertainty character of the intentional objects. For example S.3's judgment that his next move "should protect everything" reveals this mindfulness. In anticipation however, there is a falling toward the future within a forgetfulness of uncertainty, in which possibility is foreclosed and questionableness submerged. For example, S.2's anticipation that "I got to have a great game" just before making a particular move reveals this blinding enthusiasm—he lost that game.

Finally, a word should be added about thinking's relation to *motivation.* There seems to be an intrinsic motivation which founds thinking without being evoked by it, thus in the manner of a one-sided dependency. Specifically, thinking in chess as pragmatic is founded upon the motivation of wanting to win the game. While the motive of wanting to win the game is the way by which motivation interfaces with thinking, it is possible to analyze more deeply concerning the motivational significance of chess playing. While that analysis is largely beyond the scope of this research, some interesting leads did emerge from the data. For example, all of the subjects spoke not merely of attempting to defeat their opponents, but of wanting to thrash them in some more primordial way: to "tear him apart" (S.1), or to "smash him" (S.4), for example. And often, in their distracted moments, subjects' thoughts drifted onto physical sports competitions, for example, S.2 onto baseball, S.3 onto hockey. Lastly, there was also an obscure sexual connection. After thinking of taking control of "the long diagonal" (the diagonal formed by the squares extending from one corner of the board to the opposite corner), S.2 then became distracted by thoughts of his girlfriend. Fine (1967) has conjectured a latent sexual significance to chess playing, which he considered oedipal in nature.

DISCUSSION

The results of this research bear critically on the view of thinking promulgated by the information-processing approach. This critical significance will be discussed in terms of both quantitative and qualitative issues. First, the quantitative differences will be described. Then, ten specific qualitative differences will each be elaborated in turn.

Quantitative differences. Subjects searched far less than information-processing models proposed by Newell and Simon. In fact, the continuations they thematized in the time between making one move and the next (thereby including the time during which the opponent made his intervening move) never involved more than 62 positions. This maximum is lower than de Groot's (1978/1946, p. 319) finding of a maximum of 76 for his experimentally provided position but within the range he found of 20 to 76. Also, the average number of positions included was far lower than de Groot's. Partly that difference can be accounted for by de Groot's having preselected difficult positions, whereas in an actual game some positions are much less complicated. Also, however, the subject's embeddedness in the game contributes to his being able to focus more narrowly than could de Groot's subjects, who were presented with a position in the middle of a game they had not even seen develop. This difference reconfirms that structural description already presented concerning the role of the previously constituted horizons in the thematization of future possibilities, and is also compatible with Luchins (1960) finding that creative thinking is facilitated to the extent that the subject participates in the formulation or creation of the problem on which he subsequently works. The significance of this embeddedness was not only missed by de Groot (see Aanstoos, 1981) but is essentially overlooked by information-processing models.

Another quantitative difference was in the number of beginning moves thematized. Clarke (1971, p. 190) had suggested that one reason that chess programs search many more variations than people was because programs include two or three times the average number of possible first moves in their search as people do (four to seven as opposed to two). That difference is also confirmed and accounted for by these findings. And the anomaly of the information-processing model's much larger searching must be seen to be inherent precisely because its search method is structurally different from human thinking. The only exception to such exhaustive searching by a computer program is that proposed by Atkin (1972; Atkin & Witten, 1973). His program analyzes positions in terms of maximizing the values of a position according to a grid of 53 dimensions. However, that program cannot play chess, and its sterile description of a position so neglects taking dynamic and tactical possibilities into account (such as imminent piece captures or checks) that its method has been judged to have "quite obviously no relationship with human chess thinking" (Bell, 1978, p. 92).

Uncertainty. Many theorists have tended to describe thinking as a process whereby one choice is selected from among various alternatives. Obviously, such a "decision making" or "problem solving" view of thinking is the one employed by information processing, as well as by those they take as precursers (especially de Groot and Selz). Such a perspective is wider than that, however. Writers as far removed from the information-processing model as Dewey (1910) and Bolton (1972) have also characterized thinking as beginning with a "forked-road situation" in which an obstacle blocks the way of goal-directed activity. Bolton (1972, p. 9) adds that the chosen alternative is selected by applying a set of rules and that "thinking is therefore essentially a matter of judging and evaluating objects and events." Berlyne (1965, p. 276) also argues that "conflict is a major influence in the initiation of directed thinking." he then links this notion of conflict with that of the formal, mathematical concept of "uncertainty" provided by information theory:

> The mathematical truth that information implies prior uncertainty corresponds to the biological and psychological truth that the role of information

> in animal life is contingent on conflict, the behavioral equivalent of uncertainty. Information will be valuable to an animal only when it prevents or relieves conflict. (Berlyne, 1965, pp. 278-279)

It is partly the wide acceptance of this linkage of uncertainty, as the presence of alternatives, with information, in its formal sense, that is responsible for the current high status enjoyed by the information-processing approach. It mathematized and mechanized the taken-for-granted view of thinking as decision making. But such a view is incomplete, for it considers thinking only within an already explicit field of choices. The results of this study showed that thinking also involves the delineation of that field of possibles, through an interrogatory or questioning mode. Furthermore, these findings show that this thematization of the possibles is not merely propaedeutic to thinking, but is an essential constituent throughout the thinking process. In that sense, these findings are closer to Green's (1966, pp. 11-12) position. He asserted that the "sterile stages model. . . has led nowhere" and proposed simultaneous rather than serial activities, specifically including an "assimilating" activity. Berlyne himself had noted that the term "question" seemed relevant to the thinking process. However, he prejudged its role on the basis of information theory and took it in the following sense: "the questioner will be faced with a set of alternative events to which an uncertainty value can be assigned" (Berlyne, 1965, p. 285). As already noted, the results of this study do not support such a mathematical conception of uncertainty. Instead, the research showed that uncertainty is more accurately described by the Gestalt psychologists (especially Wertheimer, 1945) as a stress, strain, or tension. In other words, while uncertainty is an essential constituent, it is best understood as a lived experience rather than as a mathematical array. The subjects experienced uncertainty not necessarily when there was a large number of objectively available moves, but precisely when there was no prior foreclosure of them, as there typically was when a combination was being followed through. Indeed, that is the meaning of a combination.

Look ahead. The information-processing model had posited a look-ahead function that proceeded in a linear, move-by-move, counting-out fashion, to a predetermined depth. The results of this study also include data in which such move-by-move sequences are taken as objects of thought. However, in contradiction to the information-processing model, such move-by-move sequences were always embedded within thinking's overarching contact with an implicit sense of the flow of the game as a whole. This relation of the particular move to the flow of the game was achieved by thinking as a unity through a sense of "initiative" as a telic characteristic. And it was that unity that guided thinking's looking ahead, even in the absence of any counting-out sequence. For example, S.1 refrained from moving his queen at one point based on thinking that he would need it where it was to counteract his opponent's future attack on that side of the board. That looking ahead involved no specific sequence of counting out at all, but was based on the sense that the initiating was changing toward his opponent. As another example, thinking about the consequences that a move in the middle game had for the end game was typical for the subjects, yet that is something no model based on a sequential look ahead can simulate. In other words, the results show that the information-processing model's problem cannot be resolved simply by lengthening its look ahead to a farther depth. Rather, they indicate that thinking looks ahead in an essentially different way.

Purposiveness. The information-processing model had posited predetermined heuristic rules as guiding thinking to certain moves and not others. The results of this study do show that general principles are involved in thinking in chess. However, rather than simply adhering to predetermined guidelines as sheer facticities, thinking took them up as guidelines, as objects of thought. As such they were questioned as possibilities. For example, S.4 followed the principle of posting a knight on the sixth rank when he had the opportunity to do so, as an explicit following of a maxim that it is advantageous to do so. But the maxim itself was thematic as a question, and following it meant extending that questioning to the position on the board. In other words, the maxim did not serve to conclude thinking, but to evoke it. So, even when followed, maxims serve as signifiers rather than as rigid rules. Perhaps an even more clear example of this difference between thinking's flexibility and the model's rigidity occurred in those instances when thinking took up again as questionable the very possible moves it had already rejected. For example, S.1 repeatedly reconsidered playing "pawn takes pawn" after having decided against it "on general principles." Such data provides ample support for the distinction that thinking determines the applicability of guidelines within the context of the game or situation, in contrast to the predetermination that is made for the program's heuristics.

Goal seeking. The information-processing model asserts that thinking is essentially serial processing, able to pursue only one goal at a time. The descriptive results are also revelatory on this point, for they show thinking pursuing a multiplicity of goals simultaneously. More specifically, they show this simultaneity is possible because the goals are related to each other as theme and horizon. For example, S.2's pursuit of the goal of controlling the center was thematic and his goal of maintaining the initiative was horizonal. Both could be pursued simultaneously because of their intrinsic relatedness at a structural level. This finding undercuts Newell and Simon's (1972, pp. 796-797; Simon & Newell, 1971, p. 149) argument against such multiplicity, for they had based their argument on the demonstration that a person cannot do two unrelated tasks simultaneously. This understanding of the structural relatedness of thinking's goals needs also to be distinguished from the information-processing model's use of goals and subgoals (Newell & Simon, 1972, for example). Such a model achieves a goal by breaking it down into steps, called subgoals, and then establishes subroutines to solve these subgoals one at a time in order to narrow the difference between the present state and the goal state. It would appear that thinking also includes this use of goals and subgoals. For example, S.1 wondered whether to open the long diagonal in order to attain greater offensive threats. To read that as compatible with the information-processing model, however, is to miss a crucial distinction made evident in the structural analysis. The difference is that, for thinking, the former (in this case, the open diagonal) is not one small step on the way to the latter (in this case, greater offensive threats). Rather, the latter, as initiative, is the horizonal meaning of the former. The open diagonal, as theme, is not isolated from its horizon as if it were one step on the way toward something other than itself. Rather it is embedded in that horizon specifically by means of a referential unity of implications.

Memory. In information-processing models, memory serves thinking by storing an enormous amount of information in the form of isolated bits. This research showed that objects do indeed serve thinking, but in a much more concise and organized form. It is concise because memorial objects are taken up as objects of thought only as they are appropriate to the present game. Thinking's capacity to grasp this essential similarity is what enables it to make more limited yet more effective use of memory. The effectiveness of thinking's use of memorial objects is also dependent on another structural difference with the computer model: the memorial objects are recalled as dynamic wholes—for example, S.1's remembering of his previous game against Bisguier. Indeed, it is only because it is recalled as a whole that he can discriminate its essential similarity.

Overall sense of the task. Two important differences may be noted here between the results of the descriptive study and the information-processing model. For the model, the game is incrementally put together, since a game that is constructed incrementally can only be evaluated statically. In contrast, thinking is guided by an overall sense of the game, which it evaluates dynamically. One obvious way by which that is repeatedly manifested is through thinking's tendency to provoke reorganizations in the subject's perceptual grasp of the position. Chase and Simon's (1973a, 1973b) PERCEIVER program had no such capacity. This overall sense that unites any individual move within the flow of the game is possible because each move refers to a larger whole (the referential unity) and because the shifting balance of offensive opportunities and defensive necessities is itself an object of thought (as "initiative"). This overall sense is not an artifact of incremental objects but is itself their telic structure. Similarly, it is "the initiative" as an object of thought that founds the dynamic evaluations typical for the subjects. S.1 and S.4, for example, continued to regard their position as superior to their opponents' even while they were down a pawn in material.

Level of knowing. Information processing models function completely on the basis of formal and explicit criteria. The descriptive data, however, reveals that thinking is guided by a tacit awareness of objects of thought that remain implicit. For example, all of the subjects recognized certain moves as significant even without being able to specify wherein their significance lay. This difference may be most crucial to the information processing model, for its whole approach is based on the belief that thinking can be represented as a formal, explicit system. In contrast, the subjects' thinking was guided by the implicit referential significances of the position. An example from the descriptive results is the role that a sense of closure, as an implicit and nonformal characteristic, had for thinking. The importance of closure to the directedness of thinking was in fact suggested by Harrower (1932) as possibly playing a similar role in thinking as it does in perception.

Role of experience. Information-processing models seek to explain intuition on the basis of stored patterns from previous experience. But, as in the use of memorial objects in general (see above section on Memory), the elemental and predetermined nature of the program's stored patterns differ from the wholistic and contextually relevant patterns the subjects used from their previous experience. And, with regard to the issue of intuition in particular, analysis of those instances wherein a subject thematized a particular move "out of the blue" as it were, reveals that it is the explicit thematization of a possibility that had already been referred to implicitly before that. This explicitation of a previously implicit object of thought therefore does depend on previous experience in that the object of thought had been previously experienced implicitly. However, it does not require, nor arise from, an array of thousands of elemental and predetermined patterns. This finding is also significant for its methodological implications. That significance is discussed more fully elsewhere (e.g., Aanstoos, 1983c).

Expectations. Though absent from information-processing models, expectations were frequent objects of thought for all subjects. They concerned not only the position (for example: "there's got to be something here though. I just know there's got to be something here" by S.4), but also the opponent's intentions (for example: "after pawn to queen three as I expect him to play" by S.3). These expectations are not inferences or calculations, but the temporal adumbrations (given through the referential arcs) of "initiative" as an object of thought.

Opponent's style. A sense of the opponent's "chess personality," likewise absent from computer-processing models, was a common object of thought for the subjects. Wiener, a pioneer in cybernetics, had anticipated the importance of this aspect, when he criticized Von Neumann and Morgenstern's (1947) theory of game playing for omitting it. He noted that "naturally, as always is the case with chess, you will come to a judgment of your opponent's chess personality" (Wiener, 1961/1948, pp. 171-172). The descriptive results reveal that this sense of the opponent emerges in the course of the game. At first, the opponent is grasped almost anonymously, simply as "the opponent." Early thematizations of the opponent are based on the subjects' empathically putting themselves in their opponents' perspective. There is a phase of questioning the opponent's ability by some subjects (notably S.4). Then eventually, the opponent's style coalesces as a specific object of thought. For example, S.1 concluded "now I have some kind of idea of what kind of player I'm dealing with . . . take everything in sight, especially when you're down in material."

Conclusion

Taken in their totality, these differences constitute a significant critique of the information-processing model of thinking. The basic conclusion supported by this critique is that it is time psychology set aside its presuppositions about thinking. Rather than rely on a computational model of thinking in which discrete elements are processed according to predetermined rules, the psychology of thinking needs to begin with the recognition of thinking as a genuinely explicitative process of bringing to clarity an ambiguous, referential network of possibilities.

References

Aanstoos, C. M. (1981). [Review of de Groot's *Thought and choice in chess*]. *Journal of Phenomenological Psychology, 12,* 131-139.

——— (1983a). A phenomenological study of thinking. In A. Giorgi, A. Barton & C. Maes (Eds.), *Duquesne studies in phenomenological psychology* (vol. 4). Pittsburgh, PA: Duquesne University Press.

——— (1983b). *A phenomenological study of thinking as it is exemplified during chess playing.* (Doctoral dissertation, Duquesne University, 1982). *Dissertation Abstracts International. 43,* 2726-B.

——— (1983c). The think-aloud method in descriptive research. *Journal of Phenomenological Psychology, 14,* 150-190.

Atkin, R. H. (1972). Multidimensional structure in the game of chess. *International Journal of Man-Machine Studies, 4,* 341-362.

Atkin, R.H., & Witten, I. H. (1973). Mathematical relations in chess. In A. G.

Bell (Ed.), *Computer chess: Proceedings of a one day meeting on chess playing by computer.* Chilton, England: Atlas Computer Laboratory.

Bell, A. G. (1978). *The machine plays chess?* Oxford: Pergamon.

Berlyne, D. (1965). *Structure and direction in thinking.* New York: Wiley.

——— (1975). Behaviorism? Cognitive theory? Humanistic psychology? To Hull with them all! *Canadian Psychological Review, 16,* 69-80.

Bert, A. (1981, November). The FIDE reports. *Chess Life,* pp. 29-32.

Boden, M. A. (1972). *Purposive explanation in psychology.* Cambridge, MA: Harvard University Press.

——— (1977). *Artificial intelligence and natural man.* Hassocks, England: Harvester.

Bolton, N. (1972). *The psychology of thinking.* London: Methuen.

Bourne, L., Ekstrand, B., & Dominowski, R. (1971). *The psychology of thinking.* Englewood Cliffs, NJ: Prentice-Hall.

Bruner, J. S. (1978). Foreword. In A. Burton & J. Radford (Eds.), *Thinking in perspective.* London: Methuen.

Charness, N. (1978). Human chess skill. In P. Frey (Ed.), *Chess skill in man and machine.* New York: Springer-Verlag.

Chase, W. G., & Simon, H.A. (1973a). The mind's eye in chess. In W. G. Chase (Ed.), *Visual information processing.* New York: Academic Press.

——— (1973b). Perception in chess. *Cognitive Psychology, 4,* 55-81

Clarke, M. R. (1971). Some ideas for a chess compiler. In A. Elithorn & D. Jones (Eds.), *Artificial and human thinking: Report of the NATO symposium on human thinking.* San Francisco: Jossey-Bass, 1973.

de Groot, A. D. (1978). *Thought and choice in chess* (2nd ed.). The Hague: Mouton (Originally published, 1946).

Dewey, J. (1910). *How we think.* Boston: Health.

Fine, R. (1967). *The psychology of the chess player.* New York: Dover.

Frijda, N. H. (1967). Problems of computer simulation. *Behavorial Science, 12,* 59-67.

Giorgi, A. (1975a). An application of phenomenological method in psychology. In A. Giorgi, C. Fischer & E. Murray (Eds.), *Duquesne studies in phenomenological psychology (vol. 2).* Pittsburgh, PA: Duquesne University Press.

——— (1975b). Convergence and divergence of qualitative and quantitative methods in psychology. In A. Giorgi, C. Fischer & E. Murray. (Eds.), *Duquesne studies in phenomenological psychology* (vol. 2). Pittsburgh, PA: Duquesne University Press.

——— (1976). Phenomenology and the foundations of psychology. In W. Arnold (Ed.), *Nebraska symposium on motivation* (vol. 23). Lincoln, NE: University of Nebraska Press.

Green, B. F. (1966). Current trends in problem solving. In B. Kleinmuntz (Ed.), *Problem solving.* New York: Wiley.

Guildford, J. P. (1960). Basic conceptual problems in the psychology of thinking. *Annals of the New York Academy of Sciences. 91,* 6-21.

Gunderson, K. (1964). The imitation game. In A. R. Anderson (Ed.), *Minds and machines.* Englewood Cliffs, NJ: Prentice-Hall.

Haber, A., & Runyon, R. P. (1978). Fundamentals of psychology (2nd ed.). Reading, MA: Addison-Wesley.

Harrower, M. R. (1932). Organization in higher mental processes. *Psychologische Forschung, 17,* 56-120.

Hearst, E. (1967, June). Psychology across the chessboard. *Psychology Today,* pp. 28-37.

——— (1978). Man and machine: Chess achievements and chess thinking. In P. Frey (Ed.), *Chess skill in man and machine.* New York: Springer-Verlag.

Hebb, D. O. (1979). *The organization of behavior.* New York: Wiley.

Humphrey, G. (1948). *Directed thinking.* New York: Dodd, Mead.

Hunt, E., & Poltrock, S. (1974). The mechanics of thought. In B. Kantowitz (Ed.), *Human information processing: tutorials in performance and cognition.* Hillsdale, NJ: Erlbaum.

Husserl, E. (1962). *Ideas* (W. Gibson, Trans.). London: Collier (Originally published 1913).

——— (1977). *Phenomenological psychology* (J. Scanlon, Trans.). The Hague: Nijhoff. (Originally published 1925).

Kendler, H. H. (1981). *Psychology: A science in conflict.* New York: Oxford University Press.

Le Francois, G. R. (1980). *Psychology.* Belmont, CA: Wadsworth.

Luchins, A. S. (1960). On some aspects of the creativity problem in thinking. *Annals of the New York Academy of Sciences, 91,* 128-140.

Marx, M. (1976). *Introduction to psychology.* New York: Macmillan.

Merleau-Ponty, M. (1962). Phenomenology of perception (C. Smith, Trans.). London: Routledge & Kegan Paul (Originally published 1945).

——— (1963). *The structure of behavior* (A. Fisher, Trans.). Boston: Beacon Press (Originally published 1942).

——— (1964/1975). *Maurice Merleau-Ponty at the Sorbonne.* Bulletin de psychologie, 236, *18* (Trans. under A. Giorgi by the Duquesne University Psychology Department, 1975, unpublished manuscript).

Neisser, U. (1976). *Cognition and reality.* San Francisco: Freeman.

Newell, A. (1955). The chess machine. *Proceedings of the 1955 Western Joint Computer Conference,* 101-108.

——— (1973). You can't play twenty questions with nature and win. In W. G. Chase (Ed.), *Visual information processing.* New York: Academic Press.

——— (1977). On the analysis of human problem solving protocols. In P. N. Johnson-Laird & P.C. Wason (Eds.), *Thinking: Readings in cognitive science.* Cambridge: Cambridge University Press.

Newell, A., Shaw, J. C., & Simon, H. A. (1958a). Chess playing programs and the problem of complexity. *IBM Journal of Research and Development, 2,* 320-335.

——— (1958b). Elements of a theory of human problem solving. *Psychological Review, 65,* 151-166.

——— (1961). Computer simulation of human thinking. *Science, 134,* 2011-2017.

——— (1972). *Human problem solving.* Englewood-Cliffs, NJ: Prentice-Hall.

Raphael, B. (1976). *The thinking computer: Mind inside matter.* San Francisco: Freeman.

Simon, H. A. (1978). Information processing theory of human problem solving.

In W. K. Estes (Ed.), *Handbook of learning and cognitive processes* (vol. 5). Hillsdale, NJ: Erlbaum.

——— (1979). Information processing models of cognition. *Annual Review of Psychology, 30,* 363-396.

——— (1980). The behavioral and social sciences. *Science, 209,* 72-78.

Simon, H. A., & Newell, A. (1958). Heuristic problem solving: The next advance in operations research. *Operations Research, 6,* 1-10.

——— (1964). Information processing in computers and man. *American Scientist, 52,* 281-300.

——— (1971). Human problem solving: The state of the theory in 1970. *American Psychologist, 26,* 145-159.

Thomson, R. (1959). *The psychology of thinking.* Baltimore, MD: Penguin Books.

Von Neumann, J., & Morgenstern, O. (1947). *Theory of games and economic behavior.* Princeton, NJ: Princeton University Press.

Voss, J F. (1969). *Approaches to thought.* Columbus, OH: Merrill.

Weimer, W. (1974). Overview of a cognitive psychology: Reflections on the volume. In W. Weimer & D. Palermo (Eds.), *Cognition and the symbolic process.* Hillsdale, NJ: Erlbaum.

Wertheimer, M. (1945). *Productive thinking.* New York: Harper & Row.

Wertz, F. J. (1983). From everyday to psychological description: Analyzing the moments of a qualitative data analysis. *Journal of Phenomenological Psychology, 14,* 197–241.

Wiener, N. (1961). *Cybernetics* (2nd ed.). Cambridge, MA: MIT Press, (Originally published 1948).

Wilding, J. (1978). Bits and spaces: Computer simulation. In A. Burton & J. Radford (Eds.), *Thinking in perspective.* London: Methuen.

4/Self-Deception: An Empirical-Phenomenological Inquiry Into Its Essential Meanings

William F. Fischer

Is self-deception the invariant characteristic of all psychologically defensive activity (Frenkel-Brunswick, 1939; Hilgard, 1949; Schafer, 1976)? Is it intrinsic to all instances of neurotic behavior (Mischel, 1974)? Can psychoanalysis be described as "a systematic study of self-deception and its motivations" (Hartmann, 1964, p. 335)? Does self-deception explain the lack of validity of subjects' responses to self-report personality inventories (Meehl & Hathaway, 1946)? Is self-deception to be grasped as a moral problem, that is, as an expression of man's fundamental project to flee from a recognition of his intrinsic freedom (Sartre, 1953, 1956), or should it be understood as an inevitable consequence of certain patterns of child rearing (Freud, 1953-1966)? These are only some of the questions that have generated the considerable literature that this phenomenon has accrued in recent years.

In my own efforts to come to grips with the psychological as well as the philosophical contributions to this literature, I have discovered that, as a whole, they may be organized around three distinguishable yet interrelated issues. Hence I offer the following schema as a heuristic means of differentiating among them.

1. *What are the essential meanings of self-deception?* While every researcher of this phenomenon has recognized the priority of this question, only some have appropriated it as their dominant concern. Others, such as those who have been concerned with related topics, have addressed it in only a preliminary manner. Among the first group, that is, among those who have been primarily concerned with this question, Demos (1960), Siegler (1962), Canfield and Gustafson (1962), Penelhum (1966),

Schafer (1976) and Sackeim and Gur (1978) have all approached it by performing logico-linguistic analyses of self-deception when it is grasped as a concept. That is to say, they have attempted to specify the necessary and sufficient behavioral criteria that are *logically implied* when people use this concept to explain someone's actions. Others, such as Sartre (1953, 1956), Fingarette (1969), Solomon (1977), have approached self-deception as a phenomenon, that is, as a human activity to which one may be present in an understanding way. Hence, in their efforts to characterize its essential meanings, they have reflected upon imagined and/or actual first as well as secondhand descriptions of others being self-deceptive. Among those who have addressed this question in only a preliminary manner, that is, among those who have been preoccupied with related topics, are Frenkel-Brunswick (1939), Meehl and Hathaway (1946), Hilgard (1949), Murphy (1970, 1975), and Mischel (1974). These researchers have been interested in the relations of self-deception to such phenomena as the meanings of psychological defensiveness, the meanings of being neurotic, lying on psychological tests, and so on. As working hypotheses, they have characterized self-deception as maintaining illusions about oneself, as distorting one's perceptions so as to bolster one's self-esteem, and the like.

2. *What are the different types of self-deception? In terms of what strategies is self-deception enacted?* For the most part, the authors who have focused upon this question have tried to reinterpret the psychoanalytic mechanisms of defense as descriptions of self-deception. Among these I would include Frenkel-Brunswick (1939), Hilgard (1949), Murphy (1970, 1975), Mischel (1974), Schafer (1976), and Solomon (1977). Sartre (1953, 1956), on the other hand, has tried to describe the ways in which consciousness, as he conceptualizes it, deceives itself in terms of the basic structures or dimensions of human reality, for example, facticity-transcendence, being-for-itself/being-for-others, past/present/future, and so on.

3. *What is the significance of self-deception in human life?* For most of the researchers who have addressed this question, the significance of self-deception lies in its relations with particular other phenomena, for example, with one's sense of identity and/or self-esteem, with the meanings of being neurotic and/or psychologically defensive, with the meanings of being emotional, with brain physiology, and so on. Among them I would include Frenkel-Brunswick (1939), Meehl and Hathaway (1946), Hilgard (1949), Fingarette (1969), Murphy (1970, 1975), Mischel (1974), Schafer (1976), and Gur and Sackeim (1979). For others, such as Sartre (1953, 1956) and to some extent Solomon (1977), Sackeim and Gur (1978), and Fingarette (1969), the significance of self-deception lies in its implications for a general theory of human consciousness. That is to say,

if self-deception is a possibility, if not an actuality in all human relationships, then any ontological characterization of human consciousness must reflect this.

I realize that a comprehensive theory of self-deception can be achieved only when the answers to all three of these questions are known and integrated. As an initial effort toward this end, I will direct my attention to the first question, that is, to a characterization of the essential meanings of self-deception. In choosing to proceed in this fashion, I am in no sense diminishing the importance of the other two questions. In fact, it is my implicit comprehension of the significances of self-deception, as well as my still-to-be articulated sense of the variety of its types, that motivates me to first address and clarify the question of its essential meanings.

REVIEW OF THE LITERATURE

As I have described in the schema presented above, only some of the researchers of self-deception have devoted themselves primarily to the question of its essential meanings. Among these, some have used the methods of linguistic analysis while others have availed themselves of what could loosely be described as the methods of phenomenology. These two groups are most relevant to my purposes. Those who have been preoccupied with related topics have offered operationalized, common-sensical conceptions of self-deception. For the most part, their specific contributions have been assimilated by the researchers of the first two groups. Still, limitations of space as well as a concern for redundancy mitigate against an exhaustive review of the contributions of the language analysts and the phenomenologists. Hence, I will focus upon those whose works I found to be most stimulating as well as most representative of the approach of their group.

Fingarette

In *Self-Deception*, Herbert Fingarette (1969) tries to come to grips with this phenomenon as a way in which human beings frequently live out their engagements in the world, that is, self-deceivingly. Central to his effort is a concern with characterizing self-deception in a nonparadoxical manner. That is to say, he wants to avoid the dilemma which seemed to confront those who had asserted that consciousness was necessarily transparent to itself. They had to explain how a person could be said not to know what he was believing and/or doing when he was, by prior conceptualization, necessarily present to all of his beliefs and/or actions. At the same time, Fingarette wants to avoid the necessity of postulating two subjects, such as, an ego and an id, or a conscious system and an unconscious system, in one person. In other words, he wants to describe how it is possible for self-deception to occur while still maintaining the unity of the person and the ambiguity of his presence to himself. Further, he feels that previous efforts to achieve such a description have failed and he suspects that an appropriate clarification of this phenomenon will illuminate the meanings of both consciousness and psychopathology. Hence, Fingarette attempts to present "a coherent, intelligible, and large-scale map of self-deception" (1969, p. 10).

When he reviews the linguistic analyses of Demos (1960), Siegler (1962), Canfield and Gustafson (1962), and Penelhum (1966), Fingarette finds that their inability to represent self-deception in a nonparadoxical manner was due to their failure to recognize its "deep paradox." To be more specific, the linguistic analysts had preconceived self-deception to mean that a person held two logically incompatible beliefs simultaneously but did not notice that this was the case. Hence, the person was said to be self-deceived with regard to the conflicted character of his beliefs. Fingarette, on the other hand, argues that insofar as "this at most mildly odd condition" was posited as the essential meaning of self-deception, these theorists had failed to "appreciate that the deep paradox of self-deception lies in the element of knowing, intentional ignorance" (1969, p. 29). That is to say, for Fingarette, the real paradox of self-deception lies in the fact that when one deceives oneself, *one systematically avoids* confronting and recognizing oneself as actually living, as well as believing in, certain valuations of the states of affairs of one's world. Hence, an adequate characterization of this phenomenon must take into account not only the logical relations among a person's beliefs, but also and even more importantly, the person's efforts to know as well as not know himself in terms of those beliefs and the engagements that express them.

In his attempt to achieve such an adequate characterization, Fingarette proposes a fundamentally different approach to the phenomenon. Instead of preconceiving self-deception to be a matter of logically incompatible beliefs held unwittingly by an essentially passive consciousness which was presumed to be totally transparent to itself, he first argues that consciousness, that is, human subjectivity, should be grasped in terms of a purposive, "volitional/actional" model. That is to say, he argues that human subjectivity is not confined to perceptual and cognitive activities, themselves understood as merely reflecting the world. Human subjectivity, or consciousness, is also concerned with and determines, through its prototypically linguistic skill of "spelling-out," that which the person will explicitly know about himself. In other words, Fingarette rejects the conception of the person as immediately and necessarily knowing, in the sense of explicitly realizing, that he was engaged in the world in this or that particular way. Rather, coming to know oneself explicitly in terms of one's engagements is to be conceptualized as a process that depends upon whether and how one articulates, that is, spells out to oneself, those engagements. Further, Fingarette rejects the assumption that people are necessarily inclined to spell out their engagements to themselves. Rather, he argues that if the person is to know himself in terms of them, then there must be a special reason for doing so. By the same token, there may be a special reason for not spelling out one's engagements, for not explicitly realizing that one is engaged in the world in a particular way. In either case, whether one spells out one's engagements to oneself, or whether one systematically avoids doing so, there is always a special reason and this is provided by the person's "general policy commitments" as well as by his "tacit assessment" of his engagement.

Although Fingarette does not fully clarify what he means when he speaks of a person's general policy commitments, the implication that I have derived from his discussion is that it refers to a person's implicit decision to know himself in only certain ways. Hence, the possibility of knowing himself in conflicting ways is precluded. In other words, the person has already decided, presumably on the basis of past events, such as childhood experiences, and relationships, that he must be such and such a kind of person and that contrary self-significations of his engagements are unacceptable. Therefore, insofar as any present engagement is suggestive of such unacceptable self-significations, the engagement is not spelled out. Thus, Fingarette claims that the avoidance of spelling out some engagement is not an ad hoc decision but, rather, represents the living out of an already enacted general policy commitment.

As a means of clarifying his idea of a person tacitly assessing his engagements and thereby discovering reasons to either spell them out or not, Fingarette discusses (1) how a person relates to himself when he engages in the activity of spelling out, (2) what are the consequences of tacitly assessing an engagement as not-to-be-spelled-out, and (3) how a person's general policy commitments guide him when he tacitly assesses his engagements. With regard to the question of how the person relates to himself when he engages in the activity of spelling out, Fingarette states that, "spelling out is an activity which is not itself spelled out except when there is a special reason to do so" (1969, p. 43). In other words, even when one makes it explicit to oneself that one is engaged in the world in a particular way, presumably on the basis of some tacit assessment of that engagement, one does not necessarily spell out that tacit assessment, that is, how it provided reasons for making one's engagement in the world explicit. The clarification of that assessment and its reasons would occur only if there were another reason, presumably based upon another tacit assessment, for doing so.

As the reader may have already surmised, the upshot of all this is that, for Fingarette, people become thematically aware of themselves as engaged in the world in certain ways only to the extent that they have tacitly chosen to do so. Whether or not they choose to become explicitly aware of that choice and its reasons depends upon another tacit assessment and the reasons that it discovers. By the same token, people systematically avoid becoming aware of themselves as engaged in the world in certain ways only to the extent that they have tacitly chosen that avoidance. Whether or not they choose to become explicitly aware of that choice and its reasons, that is, their general policy commitments, depends upon another tacit assessment and the reasons that it discovers. Hence, self-deception entails the systematic avoidance of spelling out certain of one's engagements *and* the systematic avoidance of spelling out the tacit assessments of those engagements on the basis of which one chose to avoid spelling them out. Stated alternatively, self-deception is the effort *not* to know oneself in terms of certain of one's engagements *as well as* the correlative effort *not* to know the basis upon which, that is, one's general policy commitments, as well as the fact that, one has chosen not to know oneself in those terms.

As a consequence of tacitly assessing certain engagements as not to be spelled out, the person must elaborate a "cover story" in order to account for noticeable discrepancies and inconsistencies which others may point out in his behavior. This cover story is a "protective attempt on the part of the person to use elements of the skill he has developed in spelling out as inventively as possible in order to fill in plausibly the gaps created by his self-covering policy. . . . Out of this protective tactic emerge the masks, disguises, rationalizations and superficialities of self-deception in all its forms" (1969, p. 50). Moreover, it is essential that the self-deceiver not spell out what he is doing in constructing his cover story and that he tells himself exactly what he tells others.

It is precisely because he tells himself exactly what he tells others that the self-deceiver is sometimes perceived as sincere. The discrepancy between what he says and what he does, however, undermines the initial perception of him as sincere. For this reason, the observer who is present to the self-deceiver often experiences the latter as paradoxical, that is, as someone who really seems to believe that he is really doing one thing, which is what he tells us, while he is obviously doing something else. Furthermore, the observer experiences the self-deceiver as capable of experiencing the truth of what he is doing if he wants to. Fingarette argues that the observer experiences the self-deceiver as paradoxical because he falsely assumes that the self-deceiver is automatically explicitly present to what he is doing. If, however, it is realized that a person explicitly grasps the meanings of his engagements only when he spells them out to himself, then, according to Fingarette, the paradox disappears. That is to say, the observer realizes that it is not a matter of simultaneous sincerity and insincerity, but rather, a matter of selective and purposeful self-understanding.

To say that self-deception is a matter of selective and purposeful self-understanding is to assert that there are particular concerns that guide the individual when he tacitly assesses certain engagements with regard to the possibility of spelling them out. As Fingarette himself asks, "why should it matter whether or not we spell out something we are doing or experiencing in any case, or why should our refusal constitute so peculiarly human, so peculiarly demoralizing an illness as self-deception?" (1969, p. 65). In other words, what is at stake when one tacitly assesses one's engagements? What is being defended or preserved when one refuses to spell out some engagement, when one explicitly refuses to understand oneself in terms of it?

Fingarette attempts to come to grips with these questions when he states, "self-deception turns upon the personal identity one accepts, rather than the beliefs one has" (1969, p. 67). Implied in this assertion is the idea that self-deception has little to do with what one believes and everything to do with how one defines oneself in terms of one's engagements. Still, I would ask, isn't believing such and such in a given situation a way of being engaged therein? If that is so, then what one believes is important, since it is also in terms of said belief that one defines oneself in that situation. I think that Fingarette means to imply, although he does not say so, that it is not one's beliefs per se that are important, but rather, how one grasps oneself in terms of those beliefs.

In any event, Fingarette goes on to suggest that to understand self-deception we must first realize that who one is for oneself is a function of how one avows, or fails to avow, certain of one's engagements. Hence, the origin or ground of self-deception is this process of avowing personal identity, that is, the more or less systematic effort at creating an explicit understanding of oneself and at maintaining that understanding in the face of contradictory meanings. Therefore, Fingarette claims that self-deception is purposeful, since it seeks to maintain the integrity of one's avowed personal identity. Further, self-deception is the refusal to spell out those actual engagements which contradict one's avowed self-understanding. Obviously, if one were to avow those engagements as one's own, then one would undermine one's established personal identity; at the very least, one would render that identity ambiguous.

Finally, Fingarette points out that when we disavow certain engagements by refusing to spell them out, when we refuse to understand ourselves in terms of them, we isolate them, we refuse responsibility for them, and we further incapacitate ourselves with regard to our possibilities of spelling them out. All of this occurs as a function of our silent, implicit, but fundamental project of self-synthesis or identity-avowal. It is as a correlate of this ongoing project that self-deception arises as an intrinsic possibility for the maintenance of one's already avowed personal identity. Hence, for Fingarette, self-deception presupposes "the capacity of a person to reject such identification, and the supposition that an individual can continue to be engaged in the world in a certain way even though he does not acknowledge it as his personal engagement and therefore displays none of the evidences of such acknowledgement" (1969, p. 91).

In summary, Fingarette feels that he has overcome the paradox of self-deception as it appears in the theories of those who have preconceived this phenomenon in terms of the co-presence of logically incompatible beliefs. He further feels that he has surpassed that paradox with his understanding of the person as engaged in the project of synthesizing a personal identity, that is, of avowing as well as disavowing certain engagements in the world. Self-deception, therefore, is not a question of the logic of one's beliefs, but rather, is more adequately understood as an unwillingness to make explicit certain of one's engagements in the world; self-deception is in the service of synthesizing and maintaining a consistent personal identity.

While I am both intrigued by and impressed with the depth, as well as the comprehensiveness, of Fingarette's "large-scale map of self-deception," I am still troubled by his conception of the person as tacitly assessing his engagements and thereby finding reasons either to spell them out (avow them) or not to (disavow them). The fact that this process of tacit assessment is said to be guided by a general policy commitment does not help. If the success of one's efforts at self-deception depend upon one's tacit assessments of engagements remaining tacit, that is, unreflectively, and if tacitly assessing some engagement means that one unreflective considers the self-significations of that engagement, thereby discovering reasons to either avow it or not, then I would like to know how do the self-significations of a certain engagement show themselves as unacceptable and still remain unreflective or implicit?

Although I have other questions of Fingarette's theory, they pertain more to the significance of self-deception than to its essential meanings. To some extent, they shall be raised later in the Discussion section of this paper. The question that I have just raised, however, seems especially relevant to Fingarette's claim to have surpassed other paradoxical conceptualizations of self-deception. That is to say, doesn't Fingarette's own theory still imply that one knows what one doesn't want to know, that is, the unacceptability of the self-significations of one's engagement(s) and hence one's reason(s) for not spelling them out? Because of the unspelled-out character of his conceptualization of tacitly assessing, I can only answer that at this point I do not know. Perhaps my own research will shed some light on this issue.

Sartre

As Fingarette has noted in his discussion of Jean-Paul Sartre's (1953, 1956) conceptualization of "mauvais foi," the examples which the French Existentialist analyzes are "clearly cases of self-deception" (1969, pp. 92-93). Hence, while I shall bear in mind Sartre's evident intention to emphasize the belief character, as well as the moral dimension, of this phenomenon, that is, by characterizing it as "bad faith," I will also accept the looser translation of "mauvais foi" as self-deception. In this way, I may include a brief exposition of this philosopher's psychologically intriguing analysis in my review.

If one is to grasp Sartre's understanding of self-deception, one must first comprehend something of his ontological characterization of human reality. Further, by beginning with a description of his preconceptions as to the being of human consciousness, as well as that which is other than human consciousness, the reader will be able to appreciate the fact that at least in part, Sartre used is analysis of self-deception as a means of elaborating upon his preconceptions. That is to say, the reader will be able to appreciate the fact that Satre's approach to self-deception was not unequivocally phenomenological, in other words, he did not interrogate it as a phenomenon in its own right, nor without a priori principles to which his conceptualization was required to conform. Rather, as I have already suggested, his analysis, while often fascinating and provocative, was also in the service of exemplifying his already operative understanding of the being of human consciousness in its relations with itself, others, and its world.

Within the complex network of causally determined, space/time relations that constitute physical reality, that is, within the realm of what Sartre terms being-in-itself, human consciousness emerges as an emptiness, a non-thing, a locus of freedom, which is characterized as being-for-itself. Condemned to be free, never given to itself as complete or finished, as simply what it is once and for all, human consciousness must continually choose its particular mode of being in each situation. Hence, human consciousness is described as a lack, a freedom that also seeks to possess the being of a thing, that is, being-in-itself. This fundamental desire of human consciousness to attain a mode of being that could be characterized as in-itself-for-itself, as being what it is once and for all and, at the same time, as being totally free to change itself, is revealed in the phenomenon of human anguish. It should be understood that this anguish is not simply before the world of things in their being what they are, but rather, it is primarily before its own non-thing-ness, its own never simply being what it is, its own freedom. Stated succinctly, human consciousness is anguished by its ever-present necessity to choose its own mode of being.

Sartre contends that human consciousness, in its efforts to escape from its anguish and the burden of its freedom, attempts "to apprehend. . .(itself). . .from without as an Other or as a thing" (1956, p. 82). Further, it is this refusal to accept, as well as act upon, the truth of its freedom, it is this effort to constitute itself as a thing, that, for Sartre, is the essence of self-deception.

In the section of *Existential Psychoanalysis* (1953) entitled "Bad Faith," Sartre presents his complex and sometimes convoluted analysis of self-deception. He begins by describing this phenomenon as "hiding a displeasing truth or presenting a pleasing untruth" (p. 157). In this regard it is extremely important to realize that for Sartre, human consciousness or being-for-itself is necessarily transparent to itself. This is an a priori assumption, Sartre is not interested in discovering it or demonstrating it; he is concerned with working out its consequences. Further, he insists that this necessary transparency of consciousness to itself both discloses the essentially self-deceptive character of human consciousness and constitutes it—self-deception—as a moral problem.

To continue, Sartre asserts, "it follows first that the one to whom the lie is told and the one who lies are one and the same person, which means that I know in my capacity as deceiver the truth which is hidden from me as the one deceived. Better yet, I must know the truth very exactly *in order* to conceal it more carefully—and this not at two different moments" (1953, pp. 158–159, his emphasis). Hence, insofar as Sartre proposes that human consciousness is totally transparent to itself, he precludes the possibility of it's ever being unaware of, or absent from, its efforts at self-deception. Still, its presence to itself is prereflective or nonthetic, that is, it is an implicit, unreflective consciousness of itself. In essence, then, "that which affects itself with bad faith must be conscious (of) its bad faith since the being of consciousness is consciousness of being (conscious)" (1953), p. 159). In other words, since human consciousness is, by definition, prereflectively present to itself in its relations with that which is not human consciousness, it must also be prereflectively present to itself when it attempts to deceive itself about those relations.

Clearly, the significance of these passages for our understanding of Sartre's conceptualization of self-deception lies in their implication of the moral responsibility of human consciousness. Insofar as it seeks to evade or deny its freedom, it must be prereflectively conscious of itself as so doing. If this is true, if human consciousness can do nothing of which it is genuinely ignorant, then there can be no place in Sartre's existential psychoanalysis for anything like a hidden or autonomous unconscious. There cannot be two discrete agencies within a single, transparent-to-itself consciousness. There can only be the unity of the psyche which, for reasons of assumed principle, is necessarily clear to itself, at least unreflectively. Hence, self-deception is essentially a moral problem, an evasion of one's responsibility. It is human consciousness itself which chooses to deceive itself; it is human consciousness which is aware that it is deceiving itself; and it is human consciousness alone which can overcome its deceptions through purifying reflections.

Still, I would like to ask of Sartre, if consciousness is necessarily transparent to itself, at least unreflectively, then how does self-deception happen? How can a consciousness that is transparent to itself hide from itself, fool itself? By using a few *imagined* examples, Sartre attempts to describe as well as analyze the unfolding of this phenomenon. In so doing, he reveals that for him, a given instance of self-deception always organizes itself around at least one of three dimensions, or structures of human reality. These are: transcendence/facticity, being-for-oneself/being-for-others, and the interrelations of past/present/future. So that we may deepen our understanding of his conceptualization, I will briefly sketch some of the meanings of these dimensions, or structures, by using one of Sartre's own examples to characterize the exposition.

Consider the case of the flirt who has consented to go out with a particular man for the first time. She is aware of his intentions toward her, as well as of her own need to make a decision with regard to them. However, rather than face the possible self-other significations of the situation and the decision that it calls for, she prefers to "concern herself with what is respectful and discreet in the attitude of her companion. . . she does not want to see the possibilities of temporal development which his conduct presents" (1953, pp. 172-173). In other words, she limits herself, (her thoughts) to certain explicit meanings of the present situation. This is accomplished by imagining and/or thematically focusing upon the man as sincere and respectful in the same way that a table is imagined and focused upon as round or square. That is to say, in only allowing certain qualities of the man to be present for her, in fixing him in them, she avoids any cognizance of the "desire cruel and naked (which) would humiliate and horrify her" (1953, p. 173). Yet, in her own desire, which she does not thematize, she still seeks his desire, even if she "recognizes it only to the extent that it transcends itself toward admiration, esteem, respect. . ." (1953, p. 174). She does not know what she wants and she does not want to make the decision that would reveal to her, as well as to her partner, what she wants. In order to satisfy her, he must approach her as if she were totally free, a purely spiritual personality unfettered by desire, and yet, at the same time, as if she were a totally desirable object, a purely lust-inspiring body. In other words, she demands to be treated as an in-itself-for-itself. But she, herself, lives these aspects of herself, that is, her lofty spiritual/intellectual interests as a personality and her desirous body as contradictory and incompatible. She can neither "coordinate them nor surmount them in a synthesis" (1953, p. 175).

To speak of the facticities of this woman's situation is to refer to her concrete reason for being there with the man, that is, she desires him and she desires his desire of her. Yet, she also insists upon understanding herself as transcending these sensual, if not base, interests, as being solely concerned with lofty, aesthetic, and intellectual matters. Further, she cannot reconcile who she is as revealed through their respective desires and who she is as revealed through her transcendence of them. In her self-deception, she "seeks to affirm their identity while preserving their differences" (1953, p. 175). That is to say, she acknowledges her facticity—her desires—only to the extent that she transcends them with lofty, aesthetic, and intellectual interests. She does the same with her partner, seeing in his "moves" nothing but admiration, respect, and esteem. Hence, she totally separates her facticity from her transcendence of it, but she affirms the former as really being the latter; in other words she affirms her reasons for being there with him, and he with her, as exclusively lofty, aesthetic, and intellectual. As Sartre says, "bad faith. . .must affirm facticity as *being* transcendence and transcendence as *being* facticity in such a way that in the instant the person apprehends one, he can find himself abruptly faced with the other" (1953, pp. 175-176), his emphasis). Thus, in the instant that she apprehends her own and/or her partner's desire, she can find herself abruptly faced with admiration, esteem, and respect, on her own lofty ideals and interests.

When the man takes her hand in his, the situation is again transformed. She is faced once more with the urgency of making a decision. "To leave her hand there is to consent in herself to flirt, to engage herself. To withdraw it is to break the troubled and unstable harmony which gives the hour its charm" (1953, p. 174). Rather than make a decision and thus experience her freedom, rather than affirm or repudiate their respective desires, she leaves her hand there but does not notice that she is doing so. "She does not notice because it happens by chance that she is at that moment all intellect. . .her hand rests inert. . .neither consenting nor resisting—a thing" (1953, p. 174). What has happened here? According to Sartre, although she can sense the presence of her own body, as well as the activity of his hand holding hers, "she realizes herself (by engaging in lofty, sentimental speculation) as *not being* her own body and she contemplates it as though from above, as a passive object to which events can *happen*, but which can neither provoke them nor avoid them because all of its possibilities are outside of it" (1953, p. 175, his emphasis). That is to say, she has again escaped the experience of herself as making a decision with respect to her own and/or her partner's desires by constituting herself as an in-itself-for-itself, that is, a thing-body over which she has no control that is somehow attached to a lofty spirit of pure intellect and freedom.

The fact that human reality frequently involves the alternatives of being-for-oneself and being-for-others is another fundamental dimension or structure around which self-deception may organize itself. To speak of being-for-oneself and being-for-others, is to refer to the fact that who one has chosen to be in a particular situation often runs counter to who others would have one be. In its efforts to deceive itself, to escape from a recognition of the contradictory character of these alternatives and hence to escape from a recognition of itself as choosing one of them rather than the other, human consciousness will either negate the differences that exist between these alternatives, or seek to establish itself as nothing but an object for others, as nothing but the role that they (society) demands of it.

Finally, the possibility of deceiving itself is also available to human consciousness in the manner in which it may live out the essentially ambiguous character of its temporality. That is to say, insofar as human consciousness has chosen and continues to choose its modes of being in each situation, and insofar as it understands itself in terms of these chosen modes of being, it is faced with itself as having been, as being, and as committed to become a particular "who." Further, it is faced with the fact that each of these modes of being and hence, each of these images of itself, have been chosen by it. Hence, to understand itself exclusively in terms of any one of them, or to understand its present or future possibilities as having been totally determined by its past choices, is to flee from its essential freedom. Thus, human consciousness both is and is not what is has been, what it is, and what it has chosen and committed itself to become. It is all of them in their unfolding as well as in their ambiguity. Insofar as it attempts to represent itself to itself as merely one of them, for example, as just its past or future, insofar as it tries to treat itself as having the character of a thing, as just this, it is fleeing its freedom and hence, it is deceiving itself.

In summary, then, we can see that for Sartre, the project of self-deception is always in the service of being a particular "who" without experiencing oneself as having freely chosen that mode of being. The ultimate intention of the different strategies of self-deception is to put consciousness out of touch with itself so that it doesn't have to face the anguish of its freedom to choose, nor the responsibility for its choice. Instead, it hopes to enjoy the security of being an in-itself-for-itself, that is, a being which is completely what it is without its consent and, at the same time, a being that is totally free to change.

Still, I want to ask how can consciousness, especially a consciousness that is necessarily transparent to itself, accomplish these feats of self-trickery? It is true that Sartre has offered some intriguing characterizations of how self-deception is maintained, for example, the reversal of facticity and transcendence, as well as what is at stake in this project. Nonetheless, he has not told us how he avoids the paradox to which Fingarette, as well as others, were so sensitive.

In his concluding discussion, Sartre describes belief as the essential problem of self-deception. He asks, how, if consciousness is always present to itself, can it believe in those ideas which it itself has created in order to deceive itself? His answer is that "the project of bad faith must itself be in bad faith" (1953, p. 204). That is to say, consciousness chooses its understanding of the conditions under which it acts and grasps itself. Certainly there is truth to this, but why doesn't it realize that it is deceiving itself, that its choice of ideas is one-sided and self-serving? How can it believe in its efforts to deceive itself when it is present to their self-deceiving purposes? Sartre's answer to these questions is that this choice of ideas is spontaneous and unreflective, like the decision to go to sleep. This too may be true, but why doesn't this choice become reflective, especially since the ideas that have been chosen matter so much? In other words, the problem of the paradox is not eliminated by simply asserting that these decisions and choices are made and lived unreflectively. If one assumes, as Sartre does, that human consciousness is necessarily present to itself, that is, present to that which it is deceiving itself about and present to the fact that it is trying to deceive itself, then it is necessary to describe how it can so successfully avoid a reflective realization of that presence.

Sackeim and Gur

Whereas Fingarette and Sartre used variations of the phenomenological method in their efforts to conceptualize the essential meanings of self-deception, H. A. Sackeim and R. D. Gur (1978) as well as Gur and Sackeim (1979) appropriated the methods of linguistic analysis in theirs. Furthermore, they alone attempted to verify experimentally the results of their work. That is to say, they alone have demonstrated that in an experimentally created situation, subjects behave in ways that conform to the operationalized behavioral criteria that emerge when the concept, self-deception, is linguistically analyzed. Hence, since their efforts are the most recent, as well as the most thorough, and since at least some of their research is typical of the linguistic-analytic approach as it occurs in psychology, I will review their strategies as well as their conceptualization.

Having initially characterized self-deception as a concept that philosophers, literary writers, and psychologists have used in a wide variety of contexts, Sackeim and Gur then assert:

> Considering the role given to self-deception in several areas of study, it is surprising that psychologists have not attempted to define what is meant by this term. Furthermore, there have been no previous experimental investigations that have examined the appropriateness of characterizing individuals as self-deceived. Rather, self-deception has served as an explanatory construct whose conceptual boundaries and construct validity or ontological status are undetermined. (1978, p. 143)

In their efforts to rectify this unsatisfactory state of affairs, Sackeim and Gur undertook a conceptual, that is, a logico-linguistic, analysis of self-deception. Following this, they performed a series of experiments (Sackeim & Gur, 1979; Gur & Sackeim, 1979) designed to test whether the concept, as analyzed and operationally defined, existed as a behavioral reality. They also constructed a self-deception questionnaire (SDQ) with which they attempted to strengthen the validity of their logico-linguistic analysis, as well as to measure the relations of self-deception to lying and to a willingness to acknowledge personal psychopathology.

Since, in the present paper, I am primarily concerned with the essential meanings of self-deception, I will confine my review to their logico-linguistic analysis and to its elaborations as these have been implied by their subsequent research. Prior to characterizing these efforts, however, I would like to describe their overall strategy as I have understood it. Such a description should help to differentiate their approach from that of Fingarette and Sartre, as well as from my own empirical-phenomenological orientation.

In setting out to determine the meanings of self-deception, now understood as a concept that people use widely, albeit divergently, Sackeim and Gur first distinguished between a logical and an epistemological approach to their task. That is to say, they made a radical distinction between what constitutes self-deception as a concept whose constituent meanings or behavioral criteria are logically related, and that which constitutes self-deception as a phenomenon that people experience. Further, they chose to address themselves to the former, that is, to the determination of the behavioral criteria that must be co-present if the concept is to make *logical* sense. Hence, they rejected, presumably as unscientific, the exploration of that which people experience, whether in relation to themselves or to others, when they speak of self-deception. Obviously, in making such a choice the rules of linguistic logic were given priority over the experienceable meanings of the phenomenon, that is, its phenomenal logic. I stress this point because in my own empirical-phenomenological efforts, which I shall describe later, the meanings of the spontaneously occurring phenomenon, as they appeared to everyday people, were given priority.

Sackeim and Gur also chose to appropriate the logic of other-deception, or lying to another, as the paradigm for their analysis. However, they recognized that such a choice would inevitably lead them into the paradox that Fingarette has described if they also assumed that consciousness was necessarily transparent to itself. That is to say, they recognized that it is paradoxical to assert that one both knows and doesn't know what one believes, feels and/or desires if one also assumes that one is necessarily present to the actual existence of these beliefs, feelings and/

or desires as one's own. Hence, Sackeim and Gur assumed that consciousness was not necessarily transparent to itself.

Ultimately, Sackeim and Gur determined that there are four interrelated behavioral criteria which are necessary and sufficient for the logical use of the term, self-deception. In other words, they asserted that the following conditions must always be co-present if one is to make logical sense in asserting that another is self-deceived:

1. the individual holds two contradictory beliefs (*p* and not*p*);
2. these contradictory beliefs are held simultaneously;
3. the individual is not aware of holding one of these beliefs (*p* or not *p*), and
4. the act that determines which belief is and which belief is not subject to awareness is a motivated act.

Aside from the assumption that consciousness is not necessarily present to itself, there is another assumption that qualifies these criteria. Sackeim and Gur propose that the motivated act that determines which belief is not subject to awareness is not itself planned or reflectively considered. In support of this proposal, the authors offer the following analogy: "just as one cannot go to sleep while reflecting upon going to sleep, one cannot determine between beliefs to be denied while reflecting upon that determination" (1978, pp. 149-150). They also suggest that since they have assumed that consciousness is not necessarily transparent to itself, one can be motivated to act in a particular way, that is, to remain unaware of one's belief, without being aware of such a motivation.

In their subsequent experiments and reflections, Sackeim and Gur elaborate upon their conceptualization of self-deception. A detailed analysis of these experiments and reflections, especially their strategy, would be exceedingly revelatory of the difference between positivistic and linguistic, as opposed to empirical-phenomenological approaches and research methods. However, this is not my purpose, at least in this paper. Further, since I have spent considerable time reviewing other conceptualizations and approaches, and since I am concerned with spatial limitations, I will bypass this otherwise intriguing enterprise and move on to a characterization of Sackeim and Gur's understanding of self-deception.

As a result of their logico-linguistic analysis as well as their subsequent experiments and reflections, Sackeim and Gur develop a conceptualization of self-deception along the following six themes:

1. the interrelated behaviors and conditions that constitute the essential meanings of self-deception are that an individual who actually holds two discrepant beliefs simultaneously, unreflectively chooses to be

aware of only one of them, thereby avoiding a thematic cognizance of his inconsistency and thus negating the anxiousness that would attend to such a cognizance.

2. self-deception is a real phenomenon, that is, there are empirically verifiable behaviors and conditions which fulfill the criteria that were determined to be the logically definitive meanings of the concept, self-deception.
3. As an explanatory concept of construct, self-deception is "a superordinate category of instances of motivated selective transparency in consciousness" (1978, p. 171). Hence, behaviors such as repression and other defense mechanisms are special instances of it. That is to say, there are a number of different types of behaviors and conditions all of which fulfill the criteria of the concept as it has been logico-linguistically analyzed.
4. Although it is not the case that every instance of self-confrontation leads to self-deception, it is the case that every instance of self-deception occurs in a situation of self-confrontation. Self-confrontation situations arise when individuals become aware of conflicts between their wants and/or needs and the environment, or conflicts among their wants and/or needs. It is understood that individuals vary considerably in the degree to which they are vulnerable to such conflicts and hence to their discovery.
5. Self-confrontation situations tend to induce a "metacognitive state," self-consciousness, which serves a self-regulatory role. When in states of self-consciousness, individuals are more likely to have a heightened awareness of their discrepant beliefs. Hence, self-consciousness tends to engender anxiety.
6. Individuals may attempt to avoid the anxiety engendered by a self-conscious, heightened awareness of their discrepant beliefs by actually leaving the field, that is, by fleeing the situation, or by unreflectively choosing to be selectively aware of their beliefs, that is, by self-deception.

If I now attempt to integrate these themes and thereby summarize Sackeim and Gur's conceptualization of self-deception, I would say that for them, it is an empirically verified concept that subsumes a variety of behaviors all of which are undertaken in an effort to avoid the anxiousness which an individual has begun to experience as he becomes self-consciously aware of the inconsistency of his beliefs. Moreover, this becoming self-consciously aware of the inconsistency of his beliefs is itself a phenomenon that has emerged because the individual has been self-confronted, that is, he has become aware of a conflict among his own needs and/or desires. In other words, *self-deception is an effort to alleviate one's anxiousness in the face of one's ambiguity or multi-sided-ness by unreflectively and yet selectively avoiding any cognizance of one of the beliefs through which one's ambiguity has made itself manifest.*

My comments and questions concerning Sackeim and Gur's conceptualization of self-deception have two foci: their approach, that is, their methodological strategy, and the content of their formulations. With regard to the former I would ask what is the value of the original linguistic analysis of the concept, self-deception, if it does not include certain of the latter's most essential features, for example, the anxiousness which is said to emerge with the cognizance of one's discrepant beliefs, the necessary presence of the self-confrontation situation in its role of inducing the anxiousness, and the motivating role of that anxiousness in enacting the unreflective choice to be selectively aware of one's beliefs? It is not that I question the relevance or import of these aspects of self-deception. On the contrary, it is that I fail to understand why, if they are so essential to the meaning of the concept, they did not emerge in the linguistic analysis. After all, the subsequent experimentation was undertaken in an effort to verify the existence of the concept as a behavioral phenomenon.

With regard to the content of their formulations, I would ask Sackeim and Gur is self-deception only an effort at avoidance? Isn't there also an affirmation or reaffirmation of oneself as unambiguous, as without conflicting beliefs? Further, if one becomes anxious in one's self-consciousness of "possessing" discrepant beliefs, and if self-deception is an unreflective effort to become selectively unaware of that discrepancy, then hasn't one already cognized that which is to be avoided? How can one not know that which one already knows and on the basis of which one has become anxious? It doesn't help to assert, or assume, that the choice to become unaware of one's discrepant beliefs is unreflective. That which motivated this choice, that is, one's presence to one's discrepancies and the anxiousness that arose therein, has already happened. Aren't we left, then, with a paradoxical characterization of self-deception? Finally, regardless of the problems cited above, isn't there the implication that who one is for oneself, for example, one is a person whose beliefs are either consistent or discrepant, constitutes the fundamental concern which founds the possibility of self-deception?

SUMMARY OF THE LITERATURE REVIEW AND COMMENTS

We have seen that both Fingarette and Sartre approached self-deception as a phenomenon whose essential meanings were to be discovered through analyses of first- and secondhand, as well as imagined experiences of the other being self-deceptive. According to the former (Fingarette), self-deception is the tacit, unreflective effort to realize and/or sustain a particular self-understanding to which one is already committed. This is accomplished by disavowing, that is, by refusing to articulate explicitly those self-significations of one's engagements that would undermine that self-understanding. According to the latter (Sartre), self-deception is the immoral project to know oneself in such a way that one avoids experiencing the anguish and responsibility that attend to one's freedom to choose a particular mode of being. This is accomplished by constituting oneself as already determined with regard to that mode of being. That is to say, although one otherwise grasps oneself as totally free, one simultaneously understands that one had no control over the enactment of some particular mode of being. Further, the project to deceive oneself with respect to one's freedom to choose, as well as one's responsibility for the mode of being that has been chosen, is itself undertaken in such a way that one does not experience oneself as having freely chosen it.

We have also seen that Sackeim and Gur first approached self-deception as a concept whose essential meanings could be determined through a logico-linguistic analysis. When the authors performed this analysis and when the constituent meanings of the concept, that is, its behavioral criteria, were operationally defined and demonstrated to be empirically verifiable, then Sackeim and Gur proceded to offer an elaborated characterization of it. This latter characterization included their reflections upon the results of their logico-linguistic analysis, as well as their assessments of the findings of their empirical demonstration. Hence, they suggested that self-deception is a family, or "superordinate category," of behaviors, all of which involve a selective presence to oneself and all of which are motivated by an interest in assuaging, if not eliminating, the anxiousness which has emerged in a self-confrontation situation as one has begun to experience one's own ambiguity.

As the reader may have already grasped, these three characterizations of self-deception have much in common. First, all emphasize the turning away or refusing movement of this phenomenon. For Fingarette, this is enacted in one's tacitly assessing some engagement as not-to-be-spelled-out, that is, as not to be avowed as mine. Further, this turning away or refusing movement is both compounded and safeguarded by another—the refusal to spell out one's tacit assessment of the engagement as not-to-be-spelled-out. For Sartre, the turning away movement is revealed in the chosen reversal of transcendence and facticity, or in the chosen insistence that one is *only* being-for-oneself *or* being-for-another, or in the chosen total identification of oneself with one's past, present, or future. For Sackeim and Gur, the turning away movement is enacted in one's motivated, chosen selective presence to oneself, that is, in the fact that certain aspects of oneself remain systematically nonfocal and unacknowledged.

Aside from their emphasis upon the turning away or refusing movement of self-deception, all three characterizations also suggest that it is a family of strategies for realizing and/or sustaining a particular self-understanding. Fingarette, with his notion of a "general policy commitment," which is said to guide the process of tacitly assessing one's engagements, emphasizes the unacknowledged but already chosen character of that self-understanding. Sartre, in a similar vein, emphasizes both the in-itself, thing-like character of that self-understanding and its immoral, irresponsible nature. That is to say, he stresses the fact that insofar as the individual insists upon understanding himself as determined with regard to some mode of being, he is attempting to free himself from the anguish and responsibility that would attend to recognizing himself as the one who has chosen or is choosing his ways of being. Sackeim and Gur, on the other hand, point toward the unambiguous character of that sought after self-understanding. In other words, they suggest that through one's selective presence to one's beliefs, desires, attitudes, and so on one constitutes oneself as no longer discrepant. Hence, one need not be anxious.

Finally, each of these theoretical characterizations, especially the one offered by Sackeim and Gur, points toward the relations of self-deception and anxiety. The reader will recall that these theorists posited that self-deception is motivated by one's interests in assuaging, if not eliminating, one's anxiousness insofar as this has emerged in one's self-confronting experience of oneself as holding conflicting beliefs. In a somewhat similar vein, the relation of self-deception to anxiety is alluded to in the thought of Fingarette when he asserts that the decision to not spell out some engagement is based upon the tacitly assessed fact that its self-significations are "unacceptable," that is, they are such as to undermine one's already chosen self-understanding. Finally, Sartre also alludes to this relationship when he claims that it is the wish to avoid one's anguished sense of responsibility before one's freedom that motivates the self-deceptive project.

As I have already indicated in the comments that I made after characterizing each theorist's conceptualization of self-deception, I am impressed with and sympathetic toward many of the understandings that they have achieved. Still, I would like to raise the following questions:

1. Whether one is said to be disavowing one's tacitly achieved and lived knowledge of the unacceptable self-significations of one's engagements (Fingarette), or refusing to acknowledge and appropriate responsibly one's unreflectively lived presence to oneself as having actually chosen one's particular mode of being (Sartre), or unreflectively avoiding an awareness of the potentially anxiety-provoking character of one's contradictory beliefs (Sackeim & Gur), how is it that in the course of one's disavowing/refusing/avoiding one does not explicitly discover that which is being disavowed/refused/avoided? In other words, if one is *actually present*, either tacitly or unreflectively, to that which is to be disavowed/refused/avoided, then how does it show itself as such and still fail to be explicitly discovered?

2. If being self-deceptive is in the service of realizing and/or sustaining an already chosen self-understanding, then how, from the perspective of the self-deceiver, is that self-understanding being threatened? Again, how does that being-threatened show itself?
3. If anxiety is a significant motivational factor or constituent of the self-deception situation, then how does the self-deceiver experience and live this?
4. Finally, how does the self-deceiver's behavior mitigate the threat to his self-understanding and effectively affirm, at least for the moment, who he would understand himself to be?

It was in an effort to answer these questions and hence to further clarify the essential meanings of self-deception that the present study was undertaken.

Method of the Present Study

Although he never tells us so explicitly, it seems fairly clear that Sartre's conceptualization of self-deception (bad faith) is based upon his analyses of imagined and perhaps actually experienced instances of *the other being self-deceptive.* Fingarette, on the other hand, seems to have derived his theory from literary examples as well as from his reflections upon the writings of the philosophical analysts, Sartre, Kierkegaard, and Freud. Finally, Sackeim and Gur chose to avoid what they termed "the epistemological approach," that is, the effort to ascertain the meanings of self-deception by analyzing people's actual experiences of it. As we have already seen, they chose, instead, the path of logical analysis. Hence, none of these theorists, and to the best of my knowledge no one else, has tried to analyze systematically that which people experience when they are present to themselves as having engaged in self-deception.

It is not the purpose of this paper to discuss the reasons for this omission. For most psychologists they revolve around certain widely held preconceptions as to the nature of scientific inquiry. That is to say, they distrust and discount in advance the scientific utility of their subjects' experiences. Since I, myself, do not subscribe to these preconceptions but, instead, espouse an existential-phenomenological attitude toward the scientific search for the truth, I do not feel obliged to avoid or discount the experiences of my subjects. On the contrary, I feel that if I want to understand the meanings of self-deception, it is essential that I ask people what they experience when they are present to it, whether in their own actions or in another's. This is precisely what I did.

To be more specific, each student in a graduate psychology class was asked to find a subject who was not a psychology major and who was willing, on the basis of a recent realization, to describe a situation in which he/she had been engaged in self-deception. It should be understood that the graduate students did not hide the fact that they were seeking to understand this phenomenon; the subjects were told this explicitly. Hence, each subject was given the following instructions:

> I am interested in learning more about what happens when people try to deceive themselves. Would you be willing to write a description of a situation in which you tried to deceive yourself? Further, would you please include in your description a characterization of what you did in your effort to deceive yourself, e.g., how did you think about the situation, what did you tell yourself and others about it, etc.? Finally, would you also describe how you came to realize that you had been trying to deceive yourself?

Each subject was also told that when the graduate student had read his/her description, he/she would be interviewed about it in order to make sure that its contents were fully understood. Typically, these interviews, which were recorded on tape and then transcribed, took place a few days after the graduate students had received the subjects' descriptions. It is important to note that when they conducted these interviews, the graduate students, while open to new information which the subjects might spontaneously offer, did not themselves ask questions which were not already grounded in the explicit descriptive material of the subjects' written characterizations. Hence, the interview questions posed by the graduate students were of the form: Could you please tell me a little more about that?

Results

In all, thirteen descriptions of being self-deceptive were collected and elaborated through subsequent interviews. Each was analyzed according to a method that has been fully described elsewhere (Fischer, 1974). The final result of these analyses was *a general psychological description of being self-deceptive.* It asserts that:

> The possibility of deceiving oneself arises when three interrelated conditions are co-present: (1) when one is already committed to a particular understanding of some phenomenon of one's world, (2) when certain emerging significations of that phenomenon render that understanding ambiguously uncertain, and (3) when one anxiously lives this ambiguous uncertainty as threatening not only one's commitment to that particular understanding, but also, albeit horizonally, one's commitments to related understandings of other phenomena.
>
> To deceive oneself about the now ambiguously uncertain character of one's particular understanding is to deny, refuse or otherwise

negate the signifying nature of one's anxiousness before that ambiguous uncertainty. That is to say, it is to turn away from the possibility of taking up and allowing that anxiousness to inform, if not transform, that understanding. At the same time, it is to rigidly reaffirm the latter, or some variation thereof, as still unambiguously certain.

While the foregoing constitutes a general characterization of the situation and behavior of the self-deceiver, the development of any particular instance of self-deception varies with the interrelations of: (1) the form and source of the emerging significations which have rendered one's already posited understanding ambiguously uncertain, (2) the type of cognizance with which one lives one's anxiousness in the face of this, and (3) the manner in which one denies and/or explains away this ambiguously uncertain understanding, thereby assuaging one's anxiousness as well as rigidly reaffirming one's already posited understanding. Hence, in the development of any particular instance of being self-deceptive, that which has rendered one's already posited understanding ambiguously uncertain may be the emergence of one's own thoughts, recollections, desires, feelings, etc., or the occurrence of another's suggestions, gestures, etc. Further, one may live one's anxiousness in the face of this ambiguous uncertainty without explicitly cognizing it, or one may grasp that anxiousness as a discrete fact but still negate its signifying nature. Finally, one may attempt to intellectually refute or befog the ambiguously uncertain character of one's understanding; one may attack, accuse or otherwise bully the other who has introduced it, or one may flee the situation altogether and immerse oneself elsewhere. Whatever way one may attempt to deny and/or explain away one's uncertainty, one seeks to assuage, if not eliminate, one's anxiousness and, at the same time, rigidly reaffirm one's already posited understanding as still unambiguously certain.

Discussion

Admittedly, this general psychological description of being self-deceptive is both dense and abstract. Hence, before I discuss its import for the questions that were posed earlier (p. 39–40), I first want to clarify and exemplify the meanings of its constituent theses. Then I will elaborate upon its implications and finally, I will consider its significance for the literature that was reviewed above.

1) *Clarifications and Exemplifications*

As the first paragraph of the general psychological description states, three interrelated conditions co-constitute the situation in which the possibility of self-deception arises. The first of these is that one is already committed to a particular understanding of some phenomenon of one's world. In using the expression, some phenomenon of one's world, I am referring to some past, present, and/or anticipated relationship, project, or event, the meaning of which one has already posited. In describing one as already committed to such an understanding, that is, to one's already posited meaning, I am attempting to characterize the fact that one now lives it as a given, that one is disinclined, if not adamantly unwilling, to consider alternative meanings of the phenomenon. How one comes to posit and commit oneself to such an understanding I will discuss later, but for the present, I offer the following examples:

> A young man was seeking to arouse the affectional interest of a young woman. Having already convinced himself that he was "God's gift to women," that because of his "sexy-smooth style" he was "irresistible," he was sure that "she would fall for (him)," that "she would jump at the chance to make it with (him)."
>
> A young woman who originally experienced herself as alone at a new job, as severed from her past relationships, as uninvolved in any serious present relationship and as anxious about her ability to make friends and be accepted by a new group, suddenly found herself invited to participate in a social group composed of fellow employees. She immediately understood this invitation and the possibilities that it generated as "the best thing that could have happened to (her)," as "the answer to all of (her) problems," and as "giving (her) the chance to be somebody."

The second condition of the situation in which the possibility of self-deception arises in that certain emerging significations of the phenomenon that has been already understood render that understanding ambiguously uncertain. That is to say, heretofore unknown, unrecognized, and/or unaccepted profiles of that phenomenon have begun to reveal themselves and in so doing they have contradicted aspects of one's already posited understanding. As the examples will demonstrate, these heretofore unknown, unrecognized, and/or unaccepted profiles may reveal themselves in the form of one's own thoughts, feelings, and so on or in the form of an another's actions, suggestions, and so on. Whatever their form and source, in beginning to reveal themselves they have rendered one's already posited understanding ambiguously uncertain. Consider the following:

> When the young man who was described above made his "pitch" to the young woman whose affectional interest he was seeking to arouse, she responded with a mixture of laughter and wary, even disdainful, looks.

While eagerly anticipating the possibilities that would be hers if she accepted the invitation to join the social group that was composed of fellow employees, the young woman who was described above suddenly recollected the anonymous social wisdom that warned against personal involvements with co-workers. In other words, while she enthusiastically contemplated "an end to (her) loneliness," "a chance to meet new people and get involved," as well as an opportunity to be somebody more than just a clerk-typist, she recalled "you shouldn't get involved in your place of work."

The third condition of the situation in which the possibility of self-deception arises is that one anxiously lives the ambiguously uncertain character of one's already posited understanding as threatening not only one's commitment to that particular understanding, but also, albeit horizonally, one's commitments to related understandings of other phenomena of one's world. Again, consider the following:

When the young woman responded to the young man's "pitch" with a mixture of laughter and wary, even disdainful, looks, he was suddenly disrupted and confused. Further, he became vaguely aware of his suddenly unsettled stomach and pounding heart. In other words, in living out his already posited understanding of the situation as one in which there was no doubt that he would successfully arouse the young woman's affectional interest, he was anxiously affected by the significations of her actions; they contradicted his already posited understanding and thereby rendered it ambiguously uncertain.

When the young woman who had been invited to join the employees' social group and who had eagerly anticipated the possibilities that it would generate recalled the anonymous social wisdom that warned against such involvements, her sense of the invitation as "the best thing that could have happened to (her)" was suddenly undermined. The possible meanings of accepting the invitation that she had already posited and to which she immediately commited herself were now ambiguously uncertain. She felt "confused, uneasy and troubled."

In summary, then, the possibility of deceiving oneself arises when one is faced with a possible transformation of one's world as one already understands it and when one anxiously lives this possible transformation as threatening one's commitments to that already understood world.

The second paragraph of the general psychological description characterizes the two dialectically interrelated meanings of all acts of self-deception. They are: (1) that one turns away from the possibility of taking up and exploring one's anxiousness in its significations, thereby preventing it from informing, if not transforming, one's already posited understanding, and (2) that one denies and/or explains away the sudden ambiguity of one's already posited understanding thereby rigidly reäffirming that understanding, or some variation thereof, as still unambiguously certain. If we now continue with our exemplary subjects, we find:

> Although he noted that he was disrupted, confused and uncomfortable—"but only for a moment"—and although he sensed that the young woman was not responding as he had expected, the young man who sought to arouse the young woman's affectional interest did not suspend his understanding of himself as "irresistible," nor of her as eager to "jump at the chance to make it with (him)." Further, he did not explicitly cognize, much less explore, the significations of his anxiousness before her responses to him and the ambiguous uncertainty which they had introduced. Rather, he ambivalently dismissed the intrusive phenomenal manifestations of his anxiousness as well as her wary, even disdainful looks, as only tangentially relevant, i.e., as merely signifying his own surprise in the face of her "hesitancy." Quickly telling himself that "she's a shy girl and if I push her too hard she gets scared," he focused his attention upon a positive sense of her laughter and further told himself that "if I just go slow, it'll all work out just as I thought it would."
>
> Although she was "uneasy and troubled" at the recollection that "(she) shouldn't get involved in (her) place of work," the young woman who was described above did not suspend her already posited understanding of the meanings of the invitation to join the employees' social group. Correlatively, she did not take up and explore the significations of her sense of being uneasy and troubled. Nor did she try to comprehend the co-present significations of her "urgent desire to throw (herself) into the group" as an active participant. Instead, as she began to experience her eagerly postulated possibilities as no longer certain, as she began to feel "that they were slipping away," she reassuringly told herself that "the warning was only relevant if the people in authority, the administration, frowned upon employee socializing." Since this was obviously "not the case at this place of work" and since "everyone else was doing it," she happily concluded that "by socializing with (her) fellow employees (she) would not only be a more enjoyable person (herself), (she) would also be a better worker."

The remainder of the general psychological description thematizes how the interrelated constituent issues that co-constitute the unfolding of particular instances of self-deception may vary. As the reader may readily surmise, these variations allow for considerable stylistic differences in the way that individuals live out their respective instances of being self-deceptive. For example, some, whether or not they have explicitly cognized their anxiousness, invariably attack, accuse, or otherwise bully another when their already posited understandings have been rendered ambiguously uncertain; others typically leave the situation, that is, put the problem "on the shelf," while still others typically resort to all manner of intellectual arguments and refutations, whether these are directed toward their own thoughts or are aimed elsewhere. With regard to the issue of whether they have cognized the anxiousness that they are now living, some invariably do not. That is to say, they live the intrusive phenomenal manifestations of that anxiousness, for example, their sudden confusion, their pounding hearts and unsettled stomachs, and so on, as ambivalently present signifiers. In so doing, they intend them as the discrete, relatively prethematic foci of a discomforting state of affairs that is itself lived as to be immediately transformed. Others explicitly cognize the fact of their anxiousness, but still refuse to grasp and articulate the ambiguous uncertainty that is occasioning it. That is to say, they refuse to recognize and explore its signifying nature. Hence, it is treated as a thing in itself, some thing that happens to them and is to be explained away, for example, "I guess I'm just the nervous type." Still others become explicitly cognizant of the fact as well as the signifying nature of their anxiousness. However, when this happens they typically live out an unreflective, yet overriding interest in eliminating the ambiguous uncertainty and thereby assuaging their anxiousness as well as preserving their already posited understandings. That is to say, their recognition that they are anxious before the possibility that some phenomenon of their respective worlds may have a radically different meaning does not necessarily imply that they will explore the ambiguous uncertainty to which they are present nor accept as significant the emerging significations which are occasioning it. Still less does it imply that they will discover and accept transformations of their original understandings.

On the contrary, to the extents to which these understandings were themselves integral constituents of their general grasps of their respective worlds, that is, to the extent to which they were intrinsically related to their understandings of other phenomena, they will be intensely devoted to maintaining them as unambiguously certain. Hence, even if these individuals begin to explore the currently questionable status of their understandings as well as the emerging significations which are rendering them ambiguously uncertain, they will do so with the lived intent of preserving as much of them as possible and of minimizing, if not totally negating, the relevances and significances of the significations that are emerging.

As I have suggested earlier, the question of how one comes to posit and commit oneself to one's original understanding of the phenomenon in question is important and deserves discussion. What can we discover about the sources or grounds of that already posited understanding? Further, what functions does it as well as one's self-deceptions about its certitude fulfill?

It is clear from my subjects' descriptions that their original understandings of their respective phenomena were prefigured by their already operative projects vis-à-vis themselves, others, and the world. For example, the young man who sought to arouse the affectional interest of the young woman was already engaged in the "defensive" project of proving to himself that he was "God's gift to women." That is to say, rather than discover, face, and explore his anxiousness and its significations with regard to his sexual attractiveness, he posited himself as "sexy-smooth" and "irresistible." In the instance of this particular woman, he convinced himself that "she would jump at the chance to make it with (him)" even before he actually approached her. In other words, rather than acknowledge that although he was interested in her, she might not be attracted to him, rather than face the ambiguously uncertain, anxious character of his project with her, he immediately understood, that is, posited, her as eagerly desirous of him. Subsequently, when her responses to his actual overtures threatened to undermine that understanding, when, by dialectical implication, her responses also threatened his general project of verifying himself as "God's gift to women" and "irresistible," he self-deceptively sustained these understandings and their self-other-world significations by refusing to take up and explore his anxiousness.

In a similar fashion, the young woman who was invited to join the social group that was composed of fellow employees was already living her present loneliness as well as her uncertain sense of being able to make new friends as an acutely distressing state of affairs. Clearly, its significations, for example, that she might remain lonely, that she might be unacceptable to others, and so on, were lived as to be abolished/surpassed as soon as possible. Hence, her immediate understanding of the invitation as "the best thing that could have happened to (her)" is readily comprehendible. However, when that understanding and the possibilities that it had generated were rendered ambiguous by her thought, "you shouldn't get involved in your place of work," when "the answer to all of (her) problems" began to reveal itself as potentially problematic, then she self-deceptively struggled to sustain it. That is to say, rather than allow her anxiousness to signify certain still implicit but threatening implications of the invitation and her eagerness to assent to it, rather than let her "uneasy and troubled" cognizance of the thought bring her back to the significations that were to be abolished/surpassed, she convinced herself that her thought was irrelevant and that her original, already posited understanding of the invitation was still valid.

If I try to state that which seems to be essential in these examples, as well as in the descriptions of my other subjects, then I would say that a major source or ground of one's original understanding of the phenomenon about which one deceives oneself is that system of self-other-world projects that one is currently living and in terms of which one is attempting to co-create as well as understand one's relations to oneself, others, and the world. In other words, one posits and commits oneself, at least initially, to a particular understanding of some phenomenon of one's world because it renders that phenomenon amenable to one's general projects; it constitutes that phenomenon as lending itself to one's efforts at being who one would have been, be, and/or become. Further, if that understanding is threatened by certain emerging significations, then one may deceive oneself as to its unambiguous certainty so as to avoid facing one's anxiousness before the possibility that one's current self-other-world projects are impossible and that alternative significations of one's relations to others and to the world may, in fact, be true.

2) *Implications*

Although the clarifications and exemplifications that I have just presented contain a number of implications for the questions that were posed on pages 137–38, I will now try to elaborate these in a more systematic fashion. The first question asked: if one is actually present, either tacitly or unreflectively, to that which is to be disowned/refused/avoided, then how does it show itself as such and still fail to be explicitly discovered? In other words, if one is actually present to the emerging significations which are rendering ambiguously uncertain the already posited understanding to which one is committed, then how do they show themselves as threatening that understanding and still fail to be recognized as such, let alone accepted as informative if not transformative?

As the general psychological description states, the possibility of deceiving oneself arises when one is already committed to a particular understanding of some phenomenon of one's world. That is to say, one has posited what it meant, means, and/or could mean and one is disinclined, if not adamantly unwilling, to consider alternatives to this. Stated positively, one is oriented toward verifying/elaborating/actualizing one's understanding rather than discovering new profiles or significations that might call for its reformulation. Now, in rendering one's already posited understanding ambiguously uncertain, the emerging significations, although present, are hidden by that which they threaten. In other words, one is thematically present to the threatened, that is, to the already posited understanding to which one is committed, rather than to that which threatens it. Further, in being present to this threatened understanding, one is anxious, and the intrusive phenomenal manifestations distract one's attention as well as one's ease; they themselves constitute a problem that demands remedial action. Stated somewhat differently, the emerging of one's anxiousness, whether this is explicitly cognized as such or not, intervenes and overrides one's presence to the emerging significations. Hence, the latter, as well as the informed/transformed understanding of the phenomenon which they might occasion, constitute the prethematic, horizonal, virtually present meanings of the situation whose thematic, explicit face is one of an already posited and valued understanding, which is now ambiguously uncertain. In this way, the emerging threatening significations are lived but not recognized, let alone accepted, as such. They and the informed/transformed understanding of the phenomenon in question, are virtually present, that is, they are meanings of the situation that could be discovered *if* the self-deceiver were not engrossed in assuaging, if not eliminating, his anxiousness by restoring as unambiguously certain his already posited understanding.

The second question asked: if being self-deceptive is in the service of realizing and/or sustaining an already chosen self-understanding, then how, from the perspective of the self-deceiver, is that self-understanding being threatened? Recall that the self-deceiving situation is one in which the self-deceiver's already posited understanding of some phenomenon of his world is threatened, that is, rendered ambiguously uncertain. Also recall that when this happens, the self-deceiver anxiously lives this ambiguous uncertainty as threatening not only his commitment to that particular understanding, but also, albeit horizonally, his commitments to related understandings of other phenomena. But what are these phenomena? As I have described in the preceding section, they are the past, present, and/or anticipated relationships, projects, or events of his world. That is to say, they are the phenomena in terms of which he understands himself as a historical being related to and involved with others and the world. Hence, when his understandings of these phenomena have been rendered ambiguously uncertain, his understandings of himself have been threatened.

The third question asked: if anxiety is a significant motivational factor or constituent of the self-deception situation, then how does the self-deceiver experience and live this? The answer to this has been thoroughly presented in the preceding sections, *Clarifications, and, Exemplifications.* At this point it should be sufficient to say whether or not the self-deceiver explicitly cognizes his anxiousness, he lives and/or experiences it as an unpleasantly intrusive distraction that is to be assuaged, if not eliminated, and that is not to be taken up as significative of a potential transformation of his world as he has already understood it.

The fourth and final question asked: how does the self-deceiver's behavior mitigate the threat to his self-understanding and effectively affirm, at least for the moment, who he would understand himself to be? The answer to this question has also been thoroughly presented in the preceding section. Suffice it to say that the self-deceiver, in turning away from the signifying character of his anxiousness and in rigidly reaffirming his already posited understanding of the phenomenon of his world that has been rendered ambiguously uncertain, sustains the understanding of himself that is implied in and confirmed by that world.

3) *Dialog with Fingarette, Sartre, and Sackeim and Gur*

At this point I would like to reconsider the formulations of Fingarette, Sartre, and Sackeim and Gur. More specifically, I would like to characterize the manner in which their respective conceptualizations of being self-deceptive both converge with and diverge from my own. As a means of facilitating this characterization, I have chosen two questions around which to organize my presentation: (1) how does a person's abiding concern with who he has been, is, and/or can become found the possibility of being self-deceptive? and (2) how is the self-deceiver present to those emerging significations which could occasion a transformation of his already posited understanding of (some phenomenon of) his world?

Clearly, the phenomenon of being self-deceptive strikingly reveals that to be a person means that one is concerned with the constituent personal truths or significations of who one has been, is and/or can become. Further, while these truths or significations are not given in advance, they are posited as well as discovered and/or avoided in the unfolding situations of one's life. Still further, it is through one's self-other-world relations and projects that one attempts to co-create and realize the personal truths or significations of one's life. Hence, I could say that being self-deceptive is an effort to avoid/refuse those personal truths which would conflict with or render ambiguously uncertain others to which one was already committed. At the same time, it is an attempt to reaffirm the latter rigidly as unambiguously certain.

Although Fingarette, Sartre, and Sackeim and Gur all allude to, if not explicitly acknowledge, man's abiding concern with who he has been, is, and/or could become, and although they all point toward, if not thematize, its foundational role for the emergence of being self-deceptive, each does so in a different way. Both Fingarette and Sartre explicitly acknowledge man's abiding concern with the constituent personal truths or significations of his life. Further, both thematize this concern as founding the possibility of being self-deceptive. For Fingarette, human development can be described as a process of self-synthesis, that is, a more or less systematic effort at creating an explicit self-understanding. As I have already stated, he claims that the manner in which one creates such a self-understanding is through identity avowal, through spelling out, acknowledging, and assuming responsibility for one's engagements in the world. Fingarette also affirms that being self-deceptive is correlative of this process; it is the refusal to spell out, acknowledge, and assume responsibility for one's engagements—those that one's general policy commitments have predetermined to be precluded from one's self-understanding.

For Sartre, human being or consciousness is fundamentally concerned with who it has been, is, and/or can become. Further, although it has no choice but to choose freely and create these significations, it inevitably seeks to escape the anguish and burden of its freedom. That is to say, it desires to also possess the being of a thing, being-in-itself; it desires to know itself as having been determined to be such and such a kind of person once and for all. Hence, for Sartre, self-deception is the immoral flight of consciousness from its actual, albeit unreflective, presence to itself as having truly chosen its modes of being and as being free to alter or remake these choices.

In a somewhat more restricted manner, Sackeim and Gur also allude to man's abiding concern with his unfolding identity. They do this by thematizing the importance of self-confrontation situations and the self-consciousness which said situations are alleged to induce. They also speak of self-consciousness as having a self-regulatory role. With regard to the foundational function which self-consciousness has for being self-deceptive, Sackeim and Gur assert that becoming self-conscious of the inconsistency of one's beliefs/needs leads to, or generates, anxiety. Being self-deceptive is then conceptualized as an effort to alleviate that anxiety. In other words, being self-deceptive is understood as an effort to affirm that who one has been, is, and/or can become is consistent and unambiguous.

With regard to the question of how the self-deceiver is present to those emerging significations which could occasion a transformation of his already posited understanding of (some phenomenon of) his world, the formulations of Fingarette, Sartre, and Sackeim and Gur all diverge from my own. They assume that the self-deceiver is actually present, albeit tacitly or unreflectively, to the threatening, emerging significations of the phenomenon in question. By implication, they also assume that the self-deceiver is even present to the informed/transformed understanding of that phenomenon which recognition/acknowledgment of these significations would occasion. In other words, Fingarette, Sartre, and Sackeim and Gur all assume that the self-deceiver is unreflectively present to the actual truth of the phenomenon in question and that he lives this truth as to be disavowed/refused/avoided. On the basis of my data and analyses, I cannot agree with this.

My subjects were not actually present to the threatening, emerging significations of the phenomena of their respective worlds. Certainly they were not present to the informed/transformed understandings which these significations, if recognized/acknowledged, would occasion. Rather, while they were immersed in their self-deceptive activities, these significations and the actual truths of the phenomena in question were only *virtually* present; they existed as that which could have been explicitly discovered only if my subjects had suspended their already posited understandings and taken up *as significative* the intrusive phenomenal manifestations of their anxiousness. That to which my subjects were actually present, both unreflectively as well as somewhat reflectively, were the intrusive phenomenal manifestations of their anxiousness as well as the ambiguous uncertainty of their already posited understandings. One could say that they were present to themselves and the understandings to which they were committed as threatened rather than present to that which was threatening. Further, they each devoted themselves to activities that intended the negating/discounting of their understandings-as-threatened, rather than to an authentic exploration of and reflection upon their sense of being threatened.

The reader should realize that if the self-deceiver is not actually present, even tacitly or unreflectively, to the threatening significations and the transformed understandings, then Fingarette's characterization of the paradox is inaccurate. The self-deceiver does not tacitly assess the actual meaning of his engagement; he does not find it unacceptable and then choose not to spell it out. Hence, he does not really know that which he will refuse to know and avow explicitly. Rather, confused and disrupted by the intruding manifestations of his burgeoning anxiousness and faced with the ambiguous uncertainty of his already posited/valued understanding of the phenomenon in question, he chooses to turn away from these potential signifiers which, if he would take them up as such, would enable him to discover the truth of the phenomenon and perhaps of his world. Hence, to deceive oneself is not to keep oneself from explicitly knowing that which one already implicitly knows. Instead, it is to maintain to oneself, as well as to others, that one already knows; it is to refuse to discover that which might undermine that knowledge.

Summary

In recent years the phenomenon of self-deception has attracted considerable interest from a growing number of psychologists as well as philosophers. At least two potentially interrelated questions seem to be responsible for this. They are: (1) what is the nature of self-deception and how does it shed light upon human subjectivity, and (2) how is self-deception related to psychological defensiveness, psychopathology, and anxiety?

Since the answers to these questions presuppose/require a characterization of the essential meanings of being self-deceptive and since a number of theorists, for example, Fingarette, Sartre, and Sackeim and Gur, have already made substantial efforts in this direction, the present paper began with their formulations. While these were found to be insightful as well as provocative, they also seemed to be troubled by several thorny issues, for example, if one assumes that the self-deceiver is actually present, even if unreflectively, to that about which he will deceive himself, then how does it show itself as to be disavowed/refused/avoided and still fail to be explicitly discovered?

It was in an effort to shed light on this issue as well as upon the relations of self-deception to anxiety that the research described in this paper was undertaken. Whereas the formulations of Sackeim and Gur were based upon linguistic analyses and positivistic experimentation, and whereas those of Fingarette and Sartre were based upon reflective analyses of imagined as well as actual experiences of the other being self-deceptive, the general psychological description of being self-deceptive that was offered in this paper emerged out of an empirical-phenomenological study of subjects' firsthand experiences of having engaged in self-deception. It states that:

> The possibility of deceiving oneself arises when three interrelated conditions are co-present: (1) when one is already committed to a particular understanding of some phenomenon of one's world; (2) when certain emerging significations of that phenomenon render that understanding ambiguously uncertain, and (3) when one anxiously lives this ambiguous uncertainty as threatening not only one's commitment to that particular understanding, but also, albeit horizonally, one's commitments to related understandings of other phenomena.
>
> To deceive oneself about the now ambiguously uncertain character of one's particular understanding is to deny, refuse or otherwise negate the signifying nature of one's anxiousness before that ambiguous uncertainty. That is to say, it is to turn away from the possibility of taking up and allowing that anxiousness to inform, if not transform, that understanding. At the same time, it is to rigidly reaffirm the latter, or some variation thereof, as still unambiguously certain.
>
> While the foregoing constitutes a general characterization of the situation and behavior of the self-deceiver, the development of any particular instance of self-deception varies with the interrelations of: (1) the form and source of the emerging significations which have rendered one's already posited understanding ambiguously uncertain, (2) the type of cognizance with which one lives one's anxiousness in the face of this, and (3) the manner in which one denies and/or explains away this ambiguously uncertain understanding, thereby assuaging one's anxiousness as well as rigidly reaffirming one's already posited understanding. Hence, in the de-

> velopment of any particular instance of being self-deceptive, that which has rendered one's already posited understanding ambiguously uncertain may be the emergence of one's own thoughts, recollections, desires, feelings, etc., or the occurrence of another's suggestions, gestures, etc. Further, one may live one's anxiousness in the face of this ambiguous uncertainty without explicitly cognizing it, or one may grasp that anxiousness as a discrete fact but still negate its signifying nature. Finally, one may attempt to intellectually refute or befog the ambiguously uncertain character of one's understanding—one may attack, accuse or otherwise bully the other who has introduced it, or one may flee the situation altogether and immerse oneself elsewhere. However one may attempt to deny and/or explain away one's uncertainty, one seeks to assuage, if not eliminate, one's anxiousness and, at the same time, rigidly reaffirm one's already posited understanding as still unambiguously certain.

In the Clarifications and Exemplications, as well as Implications subsections of the Discussion, I suggested that the possibility of deceiving oneself is founded upon a person's abiding concern with the constituent personal truths or significations of who he has been, is, and/or can become. The fact that these truths or significations are not given in advance, once and for all, but rather are posited as possible in the self-other-world projects of one's life means that they are actually discovered and/or avoided in the unfolding situations thereof. Hence, being self-deceptive was conceptualized as an effort to avoid the discovery and acceptance of those personal truths which would conflict with or undermine that whole constellation of significations and understandings to which one was already committed. It was also grasp as an attempt to reaffirm the continuing viability of that whole constellation. To state the matter succinctly, being self-deceptive was understood as a flight from the anxiously distressing ambiguities of one's life.

Perhaps the most significant, if not controversial, implication of the above-stated characterization of being self-deceptive is that the self-deceiver was seen to be virtually rather than actually present to those personal truths of his world which he refuses to discover and accept. In contrast to the formulations of Fingarette, Sartre, and Sackeim and Gur, I found that although the self-deceiver could have achieved an actual presence to them, he did not. Instead, when faced with the ambiguous uncertainty of his understanding of some phenomenon of his world as well as the intrusive phenomenal manifestations of his anxiousness before that uncertainty, he chose to turn away from the possibility of discovering those truths. That is to say, by treating both the ambiguous uncertainty and the manifestations of his anxiousness as ambivalently present signifiers, and by rigidly reaffirming his already posited understanding, he failed to discover the virtually present truths that were signified by these phenomena. Hence, to be self-deceptive is to sustain an unchanging sense of one's relations to others and to the world; it is to reassert rigidly that one already knows who one has been, is, and/or can become.

Current and Future Projects

It is obvious from the Discussion and Summary that there is much more work to be done. At present I am collecting and analyzing descriptions of situations in which one person, the subject, realized that another was being self-deceptive. I expect that by analyzing these descriptions I will be able to: (1) further clarify the essential meanings of being self-deceptive, and (2) begin to delineate a typology of styles of living out this phenomenon. I also expect, perhaps I should say hope, eventually to speak to the situation of the counselor or psychotherapist, that is, as the one who is present to the other being self-deceptive.

The interrelations of being self-deceptive and being anxious are both intrinsic and complex. In one sense, the ultimate significations of one's anxiousness in the self-deception situation are the personal truths of one's world which one refuses to discover. Yet, it is not these truths per se that is at stake. Rather, it is their impact upon that whole constellation of understandings that one is committed to and that constitutes one's sense of one's world including one's place therein. Hence, although I have already conducted considerable research on the meanings of being anxious (Fischer, 1974), I feel that I need to return to that phenomenon and interrogate it for what it has to reveal about being self-deceptive.

The reader may realize that the psychoanalytic conception of "the unconscious" has not been mentioned, let alone discussed, in this paper. I am aware, however, that my characterization of being self-deceptive, especially my assertion of the virtual character of the significations or truths that are being avoided thereby, has considerable significance for such a concept. Hopefully, I will be able to address the relations of self-deception and "the unconscious."

Finally, I envision a time when I will want to ask: Is being self-deceptive the same as being psychologically defensive? Further, what are the relations of being self-deceptive and being psychopathological, and what does this imply for the activities of the psychotherapist?

* The author wishes to express his appreciation to Fred Richardson for the latter's generous assistance in this work.

References

Canfield, J. W., & Gustafson, D. F. (1962). Self-deception. *Analysis, 23,* 32-36.

Demos, R. (1960). Lying to oneself. *Journal of Philosophy, 57,* 588-595.

Fingarette, H. (1969). *Self-deception.* London: Routledge & Kegan Paul.

Fischer, W. F. (1974). On the phenomenological mode of researching "being-anxious." *Journal of Phenomenological Psychology. 4* (2), 405-423.

Frenkel-Brunswick, E. (1939). Mechanisms of self-deception. *Journal of Social Psychology,* S.P.S.S.I. Bulletin, *10,* 409-420.

Freud, S. (1953-1966). *The standard edition of the complete psychological works of Sigmund Freud* (James Strachey, Trans.). London: Hogarth.

Gur, R. D. & Sackeim, H. A. (1979). Self-deception: A concept in search of a phenomenon. *Journal of Personality and Social Psychology, 37* (2), 147-169.

Hartmann, H. (1964). *Psychoanalysis as a scientific theory: Essays on ego psychology.* New York: International Universities Press.

Hilgard, E. R. (1949). Human motives and the concept of the self. *American Psychologist, 4,* 374-382.

Meehl, P. E., & Hathaway, S. R. (1946). The K factor as a suppressor variable in the Minnesota Multiphasic Personality Inventory. *Journal of Applied Psychology, 30,* 525-564.

Mischel, T. (1974). Understanding neurotic behavior: From "mechanism" to "intentionality." In T. Mischel (Ed.), *Understanding other persons.* Totowa, N.J.: Rowan & Littlefield.

Murphy, G. (1970). Experiments in overcoming self-deception. *Psychophysiology, 6,* 790-799.

———. (1975). *Outgrowing self-deception.* New York: Basic Books.

Penelhum, T. (1966). Pleasure and falsity, In S. Hampshire (Ed.), *Philosophy of mind.* New York: Harper & Row.

Sackeim, H. A., & Gur, R. C. (1978). Self-deception, self-confrontation, and consciousness. In. G. E. Schwartz & D. Shapiro (Eds.), *Consciousness and self-regulation, advances in research* (vol. 2). New York: Plenum Press.

———. (1979). Self-deception, other-deception, and self-reported psychopathology. *Journal of Consulting and Clinical Psychology, 47,* (1), 213-215.

Sartre, J. P. (1953). *Existential psychoanalysis.* Chicago: Gateway.

———. 1956). *Being and nothingness.* New York: Philosophical Library.

Schafer, R. (1976). *A new language for psychoanalysis.* New Haven: Yale University Press.

Siegler, F. A. (1962). Demos on lying to oneself. *Journal of Philosophy, 59,* 469-475.

Solomon, R. C. (1977). *The passions.* New York: Anchor Books.

5/Method and Findings in a Phenomenological Psychological Study of a Complex Life-Event: Being Criminally Victimized

Frederick J. Wertz

DELIMITING THE FIELD AND THE PROBLEMS

THE goal of the present work is to show how a phenomenologically oriented psychology can research a complex everyday event, particularly in terms of its genesis through time. We feel that since the general need for and characteristics of such research have already been well articulated, the following twofold task must now take first priority: (1) to provide results of such an approach which are not merely exemplary but actually manifest a significant accomplishment in a particular problem area where research is needed, and (2) to provide greater concreteness and specificity concerning the methodological procedures involved in such research.

The phenomenon we have chosen to research, namely being criminally victimized, lends a peculiar twist to the present work. Although our research is properly psychological, a field which has contributed much to the study of our subject matter is that of victimology. It is well known among phenomenologists, apart from debates concerning the genuine founding of differentiations among disciplines, that the breakthrough of a rigorous phenomenological perspective in one human science can serve as a guide if not a paradigm for analogous advances in other fields. Therefore without laboring over the rightful ownership of our phenomenon, we hope not only to make a direct contribution to psychology but an indirect one to victimology as well. Before proceeding to our empirical research, let us backtrack and establish our historical context.

Victimology

Although victimology has been in existence for more than thirty years, it has undergone tremendous growth within the last decade. Originally, research involving victims of crimes was directed at gaining knowledge of crime per se,[1] and this led to extensive research on the victim's contribution to crime.[2] We are now at a point where research has broken away from the emphasis on crime and begun to study what is involved in being a victim of crime in and of itself.[3] In this movement, victimology has established itself apart from criminology as a field in its own right.[4] In fact, it has expanded its scope to include all victims (for example, of natural disasters), thus no longer remaining limited to criminal victimizations.[5] Nonetheless, a great majority of the field's research has been dedicated to the study of criminal victimization.

As is common in the sciences of man, particularly when attempting to establish their own respectable integrity as a discipline, victimology has largely taken over quantitative methods from the natural sciences and

1. For discussions of the historical origin of victimology in criminology, see MacNamara and Sullivan (1973) and Anttila (1974-1975). Examples of this sort of research include Ennis (1967) and Biderman (1967), who used surveys of the population to gather data on hidden delinquency. Ennis researched the difference between the number of crimes reported and the number of crimes committed in the same way.

2. There is some disagreement about who was the first to focus on the victim himself. MacNamara (1973) gives Von Hentig credit for pioneering it, but according to Schafer (1968), Mendelsohn claims to be first. Separovic (1974-1975) says Mendelsohn originated the idea and Von Hentig did the first research. Schafer gives names before either. In any case, Mendelsohn (1974-1975) offers types of victims ranging from completely innocent to as guilty as the criminal. Von Hentig (1948) attributes the victim's contribution in crime to his personality and life-style. Much research has been devoted to this, e.g., Nkpa (1974-1975), Curtis (1975), and Arvison (1974-1975). However, this trend has also come under criticism by Anttila (1974-1975) and Silverman (1974-1975), who calls the concept of victim precipitation vague and undefined, demanding more precise distinctions of types of responsibility.

3. To describe this new twist, Anttila (1974-1975) coined the term "victim-centered" research as opposed to "crime-centered" research.

4. Separovic (1974-1975).

5. See the "conclusions of the conference" in Drapkin and Viano (1974-1975), vol. 5. See also Mendelsohn (1974-1975), who has coined the interesting term "victimity" to denote the potentiality in man for being a victim in many circumstances, whose variety he outlines.

applied these to its phenomena. Thus, extensive surveys have been conducted attempting to characterize victims statistically according to traditional variables like age, sex, race, and the like.[6] "Victim-risks," that is, the kinds of behavior which lead to victimization, have been calculated in the same way.[7] The extensive contributions of such studies notwithstanding, we might still raise the question of the quality of the experience of victimization. The quantitative studies can inform us of the figures and probabilities concerning who is getting victimized, how and where it is occurring, but such "external" facts tell us nothing of what it is like to live through victimization.

However, the question of the meaning and qualitative structure of the phenomenon has not been left unraised. Most notably, in the articles compiled by Drapkin and Viano (1974, 1974-1975) in their comprehensive six volumes on victimology such concerns have been addressed. Mendelsohn (1974-1975) poses the question in the most general, open terms, remarking that the victim suffers; he goes on to ask how this suffering is different from the patient, that is, what constitutes the crime victim's suffering. On a more specific level Drapkin and Viano (1974-1975) note that following victimization, a loss of faith in the justice system with correlated alienation and frustration may in some way further the experience of victimization, and they call for study of this process. Often motivating this questioning of experience are the practical objectives of those who deal with victims in social situations. For instance, Maish and Schuler-Springorum (1974-1975) ask whether the victim's perception of the crime is realistic or whether it gives biased evidence in court. Cohn (1974-1975) raises the question of the victim's experience in order to help inform crisis intervention and rehabilitation workers. In general, Horowitz and Amir (1974-1975) and Roy (1974-1975) point out the overall neglect of research on the victim's experience and call for advances in this area.

Although the question has been posed and some answers given by the above authors and others[8], the field remains almost totally lacking in a rigorous, systematic, and comprehensive understanding of the victim's experience.[9] Cohn, in his study of robbery and assault victims, provides facts which pertain to the experience, but they remain isolated and unin-

6. This method is discussed generally according to its purposes and the traditional criteria of reliability and validity by Biderman (1974-1975). Thornberry and Figlio (1972) relate it to race. J. M. MacDonald (1975) relates it to sex. For more examples, see Ennis (1967).

7. For general discussions see Biderman (1974-1975) and Goppinger (1974-1975). For specific studies see MacDonald (1975) regarding having firearms in the house and Curtis (1974) regarding striking the criminal first.

8. For example, Carrington (1975).

tegrated. For instance, he specifies various types of reactions like "rational" (such as getting new locks, no longer keeping money in the house), and "disappointment" (accusing police of ineffectiveness). He draws general conclusions like: age plays no part in the intensity of the reaction, men display anger and shame more than women, and survivors of concentration camps have memories emerge. However, the basic question "what *is* criminal victimization, its parts, their relations, and changes with time?" is still left unanswered. These facts do not cohere to paint the picture of the phenomenon's totality. Similar problems exist despite the rich and often provocative findings of Roy (1974-1975), J. M. MacDonald (1975), and Lapan (1974-1975). Roy reports, on the part of raped women, rage, guilt, shame, worry about the future, and the desire to kill the offender. J. M. MacDonald, in his study of armed robbery victims, reports disbelief, surprise, and fear. Lapan analyzes the experience as portrayed in modern literature and suggests that violence is experienced as senseless, having no rationale or justification as well as calling attention to such themes as dehumanization, alienation, and failure of communication. However, we are still left wondering how all these doubtless perceptive observations of an apparently very complex phenomenon fit together. Is there any order or coherent structure to these isolated facts? Further, which of these facts are essential, and which merely probable or idiosyncratic?

Methodology and Psychology

Horowitz and Amir (1974-1975) attempt to embrace the experience; with the use of interview and questionnaire they uncover the central experience of damage and loss, of being made into an object. Yet they admit they reached a limit in their investigation on account of their not being sure of the purpose of their interviews, in other words, due to a lack of rigorous method of discovery. A thesis of the present paper is that it is precisely this lack of an adequate methodology (and more radically, of course, an adequate approach or philosophical anthropology) which lies at the basis of the failure of research to comprehend the complex unity of this phenomenon in essential terms. Such a methodology would entail not only appropriate methods of data collection and organization but qualitative analytic procedures as well.

One would think that he could turn to psychology for guidance regarding methods which would approach experience systematically in or-

9. Exceptions to this are to be found in literature from the psychiatric community, notably Burgess and Holstrom (1974, 1974-1975) and Symonds (1975).

der to determine its various aspects and their interrelations. After all, contemporary equivocation notwithstanding, psychology has throughout history recognized itself as the science of experience. Indeed some psychologists have addressed the phenomenon of crime victimization[10], but in reviewing this work we find nothing of either the method or results for which we are looking for. In fact, here our questions are not even being asked.

This is not the first instance in which such limitations of psychology have been noticed. Husserl (1970, 1977) has shown that there exists a serious crisis in Western science and particularly the sciences of man which has been a consequence of the adoption of the perspective and methods of natural science without any regard to the proper character of the phenomena under study. The outcome is that human sciences, lacking their own methods, have fallen out of contact with their subject matter, and thus their rightful status as truly rigorous science is in jeopardy. Husserl's insights, besides being extended by later contemporary philosophers, have been appropriated by several social sciences (such as history, sociology, psychology), and with this a new hope has emerged in those fields.

Advances along these lines in psychology have been pioneered by Giorgi and his comments pertaining to the general state of psychology speak directly to the problem we are confronting here in our specific concern about crime victimization. He argues that the psychology conceived as a natural science is fundamentally unable, given its approach, to provide a faithful understanding of human phenomena. In his hope for a faithful disclosure of human life as lived, Giorgi is far from imposing a new value on psychology, for as he points out, throughout its history there have been criticisms of psychology insofar as it approached its subject matter as if it were the same as that of natural science (Giorgi, 1970). Giorgi's contribution lies in his radical reorientation of the approach of psychology in order to make way for a method which can rigorously investigate the qualitative dimensions of human phenomena. Since the general characteristics of a phenomenologically oriented psychology and its convergences and divergences with traditional psychology have been

10. Most of the psychological studies fall into the following three groups: the victim's behaviors which cause a reduction of aggression on the criminal's part (e.g., Griffin & Rogers (1977) and Kanekar & Kolsawalla (1977)), victim's characteristics which effect helping behavior on the part of others (e.g., Skolnick (1977), Soloman & Herman (1977)), and the perception and judgment of victims by others (e.g., Kerr & Kurtz (1977), G. W. MacDonald (1977), and Thorton (1977)). The one psychological work which refers to the experience of the victim as such is Blazicek (1976), who reaches the very interesting conclusion that the victim experiences less dimentionality in space during the victimization than he does in other situations and also less than the criminal (which, however, he leaves as an isolated fact).

extensively enumerated elsewhere,[11] let us proceed by practice and show how these methods can be applied to the phenomenon at hand, namely being criminally victimized.

THE EMPIRICAL RESEARCH[12] [13]

In the following section we will provide not only results but attempt to make clear the way in which our results were arrrived at. It is important to note that we do not propose what we have done as *the* method of a phenomenological psychology. For aside from the fact that it is part of the very meaning of phenomenology not to seize upon a particular method and impose it everywhere but rather to develop appropriate methods precisely in contact with each unique phenomenon, different investigators who we would affirm have developed different methods in accordance with their own preference and personal style of research.[14] Hence the present study manifests merely one instance or variation of phenomenological method in psychology.

The method of analysis in the present research follows the general outlines of the one sketched by Giorgi (1975). We feel that the method of analysis he suggested is particularly interesting, useful, and powerful inasmuch as the steps he elaborates seem to be ones which would in one way or another be present, even if implicit or quickly passed over, in *all* phenomenologically oriented psychological research. We feel what Giorgi has done is to make explicit, order essentially, and thereby formalize the necessary constituents of qualitative analysis so that one can proceed rigorously and systematically, knowing at each step of the way exactly what advance is being made. One limitation of Giorgi's sketch which we will attempt to begin overcoming here is its outline character, that is, its lack of elaboration with a more detailed reflection on procedures. Hence, we see the present work as following from Giorgi's, if not in minute detail at least in essence, and yet making more explicit how this

11. See Giorgi (1971a, 1971b, 1975a) and Lyons (1963).

12. This project was funded by the Public Committee for the Humanities in Pennsylvania, a division of the National Endowment for the Humanities, in 1977. Credit must also be given to Constance T. Fischer, the director of the project, without whose collaboration and support the present work would not have been accomplished.

13. For another account of this research project which includes cases and forms of results which are not discussed here, see Fischer and Wertz (1979).

14. Compare for diversity: Sartre (1948), Van Kaam (1959), Boss (1963), Straus (1966), Colaizzi (1973), Giorgi (1975b), and Von Eckartsberg (1975, 1979).

method has been enacted (carried through). The present work is only a beginning in this respect because the operative, lived procedures of research are constituted by an existential opacity, especially in their early history, which is only gradually and perhaps never completely brought to articulate self-transparency.

The empirical research will be reported on in four sections, each describing a phase of the research and presenting its results. The first phase, data constitution, provides raw, descriptive data, the foundation of qualitative research. The second phase transforms the raw data into individual phenomenal descriptions, that is single examples of our phenomenon. The third phase involves the advent of psychological reflection on each one of these examples and yields an individual (that is, idiographic) psychological structure of each. Finally, analysis moves beyond the individuals to the generally essential, yielding the general (that is, nomothetic) psychological structure of our phenomenon. It will be noted that each phase presupposes and is a transformative refinement of the preceding one in accord with the various goals of research. The offerings of each phase have their own worth and can stand and be utilized independently of the others. The pinnacle of achievement, however, remains the final general structure, insofar as it is an integration of all previous moments of the research.

Data Constitution

A cooperative police department in the greater Pittsburgh area telephoned a representative sample of persons (by type of crime, time since its occurrence, area of township, gender and age of the victim) who reported crimes during the past three years. Of the persons contacted 80% agreed to participate in either telephone or personal interviews with our research team. Together with four doctoral students of psychology[15], we conducted 50 interviews, which were taped and then transcribed. The interviews tapped a broad range of socioeconomic and education levels, home owners and apartment dwellers, blacks and whites. Victim's ages ranged from 18 to early 90s. The sample intentionally excluded completed rapes, attempted murders, and corporate crime; it did include assaults, robbery, burglary, theft, attempted rape, vandalism, and harassment. The goal and result of this phase was 50 interviews in which each interviewee describes a concrete event of being criminally victimized from his own life.

Since the point of this phase was to get as faithful and complete a description of what was lived through by the interviewee as possible, these

15. Robert Bodnar, Mark Johanson, Christopher Mruk, and Michael Schur.

interviews were very open-ended. In general, the victims were asked to describe the crime in full detail (including what was going on before the crime, what it was like to be victimized, and what happened afterwards). Aside from this, questions and comments from the interviewer were restricted to requests for clarification or elaboration and Rogerian-like reflections of what the interviewee had already said.

Since phenomenologically oriented philosophical research attempts to account for *all* data in its comprehension, it would be ideal to include a complete interview, if not indeed all 50, in the present work. This would enable the reader to see and check for himself how rigorous our analysis in fact is. However, since space does not permit this (each interview runs from 8 to 30 pages), we will include an unedited excerpt from one of the interviews. This will be necessary in order to make concretely clear (1) what such raw data are like, and (2) how it may be precisely utilized in psychological research. The following is the first few pages of a 23-page interview with a married, 27-year-old woman, Marlene, who was a victim of assault. Allison, who was also present for parts of the interview and to whom Marlene refers and speaks occasionally, is her 4-year-old daughter.

F.: Please describe the crime that was committed against you first of all.

M.: He didn't succeed. Let's put it that way. But he attempted to put me in a car. Come on Allison.

F.: He attempted to put you—

M.: Yeah. I must have been followed. I was coming down the road late at night. He must have seen I was alone. He followed me to the parking lot and the car looked the same as our neighbor's. So I didn't think nothing of it. I just got right out of the car, right? Which was stupid, but I did it anyway. And I got to the steps and I turned around cause I didn't hear no car doors and I always got a fear over my shoulder. So I turned around and looked and he was at my feet.

F.: OK. You were on foot?

M.: Yeah. I just got out of my car to come up to the apartment building. It was about 3:30.

F.: And this car was following you?

M.: He followed me all the way down the road, but I didn't. (At this point Allison interrupts). Baby's sleeping honey, we'll go over and check on it a bit later. OK? you be quiet. So he was just coming down Leechburg Road behind me. I didn't think nothing cause a lot of cars come down the road. He followed me to the parking lot and he parked at the end of the parking lot and I parked right at the front of building. And I thought it was our neighbors.

F.: Right out here.

M.: Yeah. Right out front. And I figured it was our neighbors 'cause it was the same type of car. So I got out and he must have really flew because I was already on the steps and he was parked at the end of the parking lot and he come and got me from my ankles.

F.: What did he do? He grabbed you by—

M.: He grabbed me like over the shoulders. You know, one of them numbers. You pick you up by your ankles and throw you up over your shoulder?

F.: He did that to you?

M.: He got up that far and it was wintertime and I had a big fur coat on and I guess he couldn't—and I just collapsed out of fear. My legs went, I guess I was dead weight or something and he dropped me. There's a railing out front, and I hung on to that and I just screamed and I kept my legs up and together and he just—I don't know what he was trying to do but he just kept trying to pull me away. I don't know what he was doing. Going up my legs or something.

F.: So he was pulling at ya.

M.: Yeah. To get me away from the railing. He knows I was sitting there—like his car door. You could see his car parked with the door open. He never closed the door. And there was another guy in the car.

F.: So you could see that.

M.: Yeah. I could see that much.

F.: So your first reaction was surprise.

M.: Oh very shocked. I never thought it would happen to me.

F.: How did you understand what he was doing? What was he trying to do? He was trying to get you into the car, you thought.

M.: Oh yeah. Definitely. Definitely into the car. Yeah.

F.: So what did you think were his intentions?

M.: To rape me.

F.: To rape you?

M.: Oh yes.

F.: So you were clear about that? As soon as he grabbed you, you thought, "this guy is trying to rape me."

M.: Oh yes, definitely. What else would he be doing? At that hour of the morning?

F.: Uh huh. OK.

M.: OK. (laugh)

F.: So then what happened?

M.: So I just kept screaming and screaming and screaming, and I got a very big mouth, and my girlfriend heard me in one apartment downstairs and she opened her window. I didn't hear her open her window or nothing, or even say my name, but just 'cause I was screaming so loud, but he heard her and got scared. He finally let me go.

F.: She screamed, ya mean?

M.: No, she just screamed "Marlene, what's the matter?" She thought I was having a fight with my husband or something. So she just started screaming like "Marlene, Marlene what's the matter?"

One will notice that the interview provides us with relevant data, that is, a description of being criminally victimized. But it gives us more than that, including irrelevant data, and moreover even the description of victimization is not yet in readily analyzable form. Specifically, the interview includes such elements as distractions from the task of description and descriptions of matters not constitutive of/or essentially related to victimization. Further, what is said about victimization involves repetitions, skipping around, backtracking, and thus the movement of the description does not coincide precisely with the movement of the lived event. Hence, insofar as we are interested in a description faithfully and comprehensibly reflecting the originally lived event, the achievement of this phase (the interview as such) falls short and calls for further refinement even though it successfully provides an access to the phenomenon.

Constitution of Relevatory Description

The goal and final offering of this phase is well-organized descriptions of the experience of being criminally victimized expressed in the first person language of subjects, one for each interview. Ideally, each description would exclude all irrelevant data in the interview and include all those statements relevatory of being criminally victimized in a way precisely expressive of the original lived experience. This seems simple enough to achieve, and in a sense it is, but following Giorgi more or less, we may specify five different operations which are necessary, whether the researcher is aware he is performing them or not, in order to achieve such a description.

1. The researcher *reads the interview openly*, with no special attitude, in order to familiarize himself with the described experience. At this time the researcher attempts to put himself in the subject's shoes and to live through the experience from the inside so that he is not a mere spectator but achieves a grasp of the meanings the subject has expressed precisely as intended by the subject. The necessity of this operation for qualitative research is obvious.

2. The researcher *demarcates meaning units* in the interview data. This step is largely anticipatory of the coming analysis, which will eventually have to focus on or thematize parts or constituents of the description. This is necessary preparation for a workable analysis, since the whole protocol cannot be apprehended in a single glance. Whether implicitly or explicitly, every researcher differentiates parts of his descriptive data. In this phase and all others involving differentiation of constituents, such parts are never apprehended outside of their context (and indeed their relation to the whole protocol). When done explicitly, this operation also insures that all data are carefully treated and accounted for (thus avoiding possible dangers of sloppiness and/or selective bias). This operation has no one right way and should not be enacted in a technical way; in our experience different researchers have varied in their work at this phase of research, and necessarily so, for meaning units are meaning-unities-for-the-researcher. Each researcher has a preferred way of embracing part/whole relationships which are comfortably comprehensible.

Nonetheless, we would define a unit in general as a part of the description whose phrases require each other to stand as a distinguishable moment. Generally the theme of a unit can be named or differentially identified in a single sentence. For instance, the interview begins, "He didn't succeed. Let's put it that way. But he attempted to put me in a car. Come on, Allison." For us, the first three sentences form a unity which could be put "He attempted to put one in a car but didn't succeed." The comment "Come on, Allison" has a different meaning and therefore would be the second meaning unit for us. This is fairly obvious, but the next paragraph is less so. The subject says, "I must have been followed. I was coming down the road late at night. He must have seen I was alone. He followed me into the parking lot and the car looked the same as our neighbor's, so I didn't think nothing of it." Although this may seem like a unity, since it pertains to one single situation, we note a crucial duality. One group, made up of sentences 2, 4, and 5 could be put, "I was driving down the road at night and was followed into the parking lot by a car which looked like our neighbors and which I thought nothing of." Sentences 1 and 3 express a very different meaning, which arouse only after driving home, that is, through retrospective reconstruction of what "must have really" happened: "He must have seen I was alone and followed me." Therefore, since these have very different temporal coefficients and are rather different kinds of experiences of the same situation, they seem worth differentiating to us.

An instance where various ways of demarcating does not seem crucial is in the following: ". . . he got me from the ankles. . . he grabbed me over the shoulders. . . got me up that far. . . I just collapsed out of fear. . . there's a railing out front and I just hung on." This whole section could be made one unit, which could be named "the struggle with the assaulter," for a researcher who works best with larger wholes. For us of quite a preference for detail, it would make sense to differentiate "the assaultive attack," "the victim's collapse," and "the victim's attempt to hold onto the railing." While we would agree that some ways of demarcating units make more sense than others, we admit the possibility of variations, which might well lead to different comprehensions of the phenomenon. On the other hand, it is not advisable that the researcher spend a great deal of effort brooding over this problem; the point here is only that the researcher organize the description into parts he can work with. Ultimately, the proof of the pudding is in the final results of the research.

We demarcated the first 20 meaning units as follows:

1. He didn't succeed, let's put it that way. But he attempted to get me into the car.
2. Come on Allison.
3. I must have been followed.
4. I was coming down the road late at night.
5. He must have seen I was alone.
6. He followed me into the parking lot and the car looked the same as our neighbor's. So I didn't think nothing of it.
7. I just got right out of the car, right?
8. Which was stupid, but I did it anyway.
9. I got to the steps and turned around because I didn't hear no car doors and I always got a fear over my shoulder.
10. So I turned around and looked and he was at my feet.
11. I just got out of my car to come up to my apartment building. It was about 3:30.
12. He followed me all the way down the road.
13. Baby's sleeping honey, we'll go over and check on it a bit later.
14. So he was just coming down the road behind me. I didn't think nothing cause a lot of cars come down that road. He followed me into the parking lot and I parked right in front of the building. And I thought it was our neighbors cause it was the same type of car. So I got out.
15. He must have really flew because I was already on the steps and he was parked at the end of the parking lot.
16. He came up and got me from the ankles. He grabbed me like over the shoulders. You know, one of them numbers. You pick you up by your ankles and throw you over your shoulder.
17. I just collapsed out of fear. My legs went. I guess I was dead weight or something and he dropped me.
18. There's a railing out front, and I just hung onto that and I just screamed and kept my legs up and together and he just—I don't know what he was trying to do but he just kept trying to pull me away. I don't know what he was doing. Going up my legs or something. . . to get me away from the railing.
19. He knows I was sitting there—like his car door. You could see his car

parked with the open door. He never closed the door. There was another guy in the car. I could see that much.

20. I was very shocked. I never thought it would happen to me.

3. The researcher *judges which constituents are relevant* for the research, that is, which are revelatory of the phenomenon under study. This is probably the most difficult and crucial operation of this phase. In all research, the researcher must discriminate what is going to inform his understanding from what is not. Let us first take an easy case: meaning units number 2 and 13. These do not seem to express anything about criminal victimization but rather manifest the ongoing relationship of a mother to a child who is calling her attention away from the interview. Therefore, at this stage they would be discarded. Equally obvious is the fact that units number 16 to 18 are revelatory of being criminally victimized inasmuch as the subject is describing her struggle with the assault itself. Let us look at a case where relevance is questionable and could conceivable be denied by a researcher. Take number 5 and number 14 in which the subject is not being victimized nor having any experience of victimization. In the present research this was judged as relevant on the grounds (1) it is relevant to victimization as its "before," that is it expresses the temporal ground out of which victimization emerges, and (2) it is relevant precisely as "not victimization," that is, relevant to victimization by contrasting with it, showing us its absence.

Here we see the crux of the issue in this discrimination. In the case of every meaning unit, the researcher's comprehension is challenged to find relevance any way it can, and his choices are based on his specific ability to do so. The burden of proof rests on him. We should mention that it is possible for one researcher to fail to see revelatory possibilities of a given constituent which another researcher would seize upon. Hence in this operation the limits of a given researcher may be revealed. Lest one think that such limits can be eliminated by retaining everything, one should note that the researcher will be called upon in the next phase of research to render explicit what each retained constituent reveals about the phenomenon. Of the first 20 constituents listed above, only number 2 and 13 were judged as not revelatory. Even in the case of these, however, it is conceivable that a given researcher would be able to see, in the relationship of mother and daughter, something relevant to victimization. For example, in the context of other information (which is never to be excluded from this operation) one might see how the relationship expressed in these constituents is "after victimization" and manifests how the subject's life has become through victimization. However, the present researcher could not see any such relevance.

4. The researcher *regroups the relevant constituents* together according to their intertwining meanings and places them in temporal order

such that they accurately express the pattern of the original event. This operation is particularly necessary for interview data, which tends to jump around. For instance, number 4, 6, and 14, though separated in the interview, all express "driving down the road and seeing the following car as the neighbor's and thinking nothing of it," so they must be brought together. Besides bringing statements of related content together, the original temporality must be reconstituted where it is not reflected in the order of meaning units. For instance, number 1, which appears first in the interview must be placed after number 4, 6, and 14, and even after number 16, 17, and 18.

5. Finally, the researcher *discards redundant statements and re-describes* the event from the first person perspective, more or less in the subject's own language. For instance, the description would start with number 4, 6, and 14. They could be nonrepetitively put as:

> I was coming home late at night and had a car behind me. I didn't think much of it because there are a lot of cars coming down that road at that time. It followed me into the parking lot and parked at the end of the lot. I thought it was our neighbor's car because it looked the same. I parked right in front of our building and got out.

The rest of the demarcated units we have been describing are organized as follows (though of course in final form other units in the interview would be integrated with these):

> When I got to the steps, I turned around because I didn't hear car doors and I always got a fear over my shoulder. He was right at my feet—must have really flew. He grabbed me to pick me up by the ankles and throw me over his shoulder. I was very shocked, never thought it would happen to me. He got up that far and it was wintertime and I had a fur coat on so he couldn't—and I just collapsed out of fear. My legs went—I guess I was dead weight and he dropped me. I hung onto the railing and just screamed. I kept my legs together and I didn't know what he was trying to do but he kept going up my legs or something. He was trying to pull me away from the railing. I saw his car parked with the open door, and there was another guy in the car. He attempted to put me in his car, but he didn't succeed. He must have seen I was alone and followed me.

This phase offers individual descriptions of the phenomenon which will serve as the basis for further analysis. This may be considered a preparatory phase in which the psychological interest in the phenomenon has not been made explicit. However, inasmuch as this phase involves understanding, judgments of relevance, and coherent organizing, it draws implicitly on the special interest of the researcher. Since these descriptions are made of the subjects' expressions and would strike subjects as obvious restatements of their own phenomenal experience with no analysis or interpretation, we call these Individual Phenomenal Descriptions. The following is the complete version which arose from the interview we have been using as an example.

INDIVIDUAL PHENOMENAL DESCRIPTION OF BEING CRIMINALLY VICTIMIZED: *MARLENE*

Before this happened I never thought it would. I didn't care; I wasn't afraid. It happens to everybody else. I never thought any of them kind was around here. I'd sit, talk, with men, and think nothing of it. A salesman come, and I'd say, "OK, come in, we'll talk."

The night it happened I was coming home from work where I waitress late and there was a car behind me. I didn't think much of it because there are a lot of cars coming down that road at the time. It followed me into the parking lot and parked at the end of the lot. I thought it was our neighbor's car because it looked the same. I parked right in front of our building and got out.

When I got to the steps I turned around because I didn't hear the car door and I always got a fear over my shoulder. He was right at my feet—must have flew. He grabbed me to pick me up by the ankles and throw me over his shoulder. I was very shocked, never thought this would happen to me—that anyone would sneak up on me. As soon as grabbed me, I thought he was trying to get me into his car to rape me. What else would he be doing at that hour? It was wintertime and I had a fur coat on so he couldn't. My legs went and I just collapsed out of fear. I guess I was dead weight and he dropped me.

There was $80 in my purse. I thought maybe he'd take the money and leave me alone. I tried to talk but nothing would come out, so I threw it at him and he didn't take it. He definitely wanted me—no desire for money at all. I worked all night for that money. It was my paycheck, but at the moment I figured, "Hey, take it. It's better than my life."

So I hung onto the railing and started screaming and screaming. I figured if I screamed he'd get scared or somebody would come out. He kept going up my legs or something. I didn't know what he was trying to do but I just kept my legs together. He was trying to pull me away from the railing, but didn't say anything. He was dirty and raggy but had a nice clean car though. I saw it parked with the door open, and there was another guy in the car.

I figured if he got me in the car, chances are I'd never be seen again, or he'd mess me up so bad there's no sense even living. You imagine the worst at the time. I just kept thinking "my baby's upstairs and I might never see her again. My husband's upstairs and doesn't even know what's happening. He's gonna knife me, and what am I gonna do, resist or not?" The more I thought about it I was gonna fight cause if he gets me in the car, he'll kill me anyway. Even if he had a knife or gun, I'll fight. I was mad. If I had a gun, he'd be dead. At that moment, I hated him.

I just kept screaming loud and my girlfriend in one apartment heard me, opened the window, and started yelling "Marlene, Marlene!" She thought I was having a fight with my husband. Maybe he heard her and got scared, because he finally let me go, jumped down the stairs, ran, and took off. Then I went upstairs.

My girlfriend tried to get the license number but couldn't. When I got upstairs, my husband called the police. I thought maybe the police could pick him up. He has to be a nut. Guys don't do that kind of thing. Or he was drunk. He had been coming from the opposite direction and we both took the same turn so I didn't think he saw me anywhere and followed me. I didn't know him unless he saw me from work, but he didn't follow me from there. He must have seen I was alone and followed me. I didn't know why he left: my girlfriend or my screaming. Thank God for the railing and my neighbor, cause not many of them bother. I was glad he didn't take my purse cause it had my I.D. and telephone number.

The police came. I didn't like talking about it because it brought it all back to me. They wanted to describe him but I couldn't too well because he had his face covered like he didn't want to be identified or he thought I was going to spray something at him. The police weren't sympathetic at all. They look at you like you provoked him: "Did you know him?" Gave me the feeling it's me and not him. "Are you sure you didn't know him?" Made me feel as if I wanted this to happen and I'm not that type! My husband got insulted and said "Hey, she was only coming home." He was really good about it and that helped a lot. He could have been the type of guy to say, "You asked for it." The police gave me the feeling they have more important things to do than go after these guys who attack girls. They said, "OK, yeah, he sounds familiar." Well if he's so familiar, why haven't they done something to pick him up? Why don't they have more patrols? If he succeeded he could have ruined me mentally for the rest of my life, or physically. But they don't seem to care because it'll never happen to them so why worry. They just asked me if I was willing to prosecute and my husband answered for me, "Definitely yes!" They said they'd call and let me know and let me see him out of the books. I would have gone through the whole thing 'cause I can't see guys doing that. He might hurt somebody. I would do it for everybody.

For the whole next week I was sick in bed. My stomach was sick, I lost weight, my head was always hurting, and I couldn't sleep or watch the baby. I'd hear someone fooling in the back and be scared. Every time the phone rang I thought it was him calling me. Or a knock on the door and

I'd go through the wall. I expected the guy to call me or look for me at work. I couldn't go out and thought of quitting work. I like working and the money, but it wasn't worth getting raped. At night I'd wake up crying and screaming; once I beat my husband up (laugh) because I was dreaming of him succeeding, raping me. I just really thought my husband was the guy when I was asleep dreaming and it wasn't. My husband just kept saying, "Marlene, Marlene, you're OK." I didn't want my husband to touch me, and for the first month I didn't let him. I couldn't stand it, hated it, and they guy didn't even do anything—just grabbed my legs. But the thought of being touched made me sick. I remember him touching me and it made my skin crawl. I thought it would ruin my life, my marriage. I was thinking of leaving and going back to live with my parents. But my husband was patient and really understood. He was always there when I needed him. It helped so eventually I got over it. He said, "Hey, I'm not the man!" (laugh). I was taking it out on him.

My husband said he'd come and meet me at work and that changed it. Then I could go back. I didn't want to quit. And he put two bolts on the door. It took a long time but I was surprised by the way he acted. He was the hard type—would never have picked me up at work—but he turned it real soft, like "Don't worry, I'm here." Before he used to stay out all night, and since then he hasn't done it anymore. I could sleep as long as he was there because I felt better, more safe. You need that. If you had to do it all by yourself, you probably couldn't get through it at all, because it helps to cry it out and be a baby about it. You need the comfort, the arms, the affection. I eventually thought, "He's here with me. I don't have to worry."

My parents and friends helped, too. Mom and Dad said, "Now you'll take precautions. You can't let it ruin your life." It could, mentally. I couldn't stand to be alone. My friends would call and come over and keep me company when my husband was out. I wouldn't leave the house. I couldn't even go down and do the wash without thinking he was behind me. I felt better and went when my friends were with me.

For two or three months I never went out past 8:00, dark. If I'm out later I'll call someone to be with me. I was always afraid of the dark and people behind me, and he did both, so after that my fears intensified. I was also afraid they'd get Allison next, when we went out. So I'd hurry up and throw her in the car and lock the door. It was also bad at work. I worked New Year's Eve and saw a guy I swore was him. I went to pieces and couldn't go on working. But then everybody I seen kept looking like him. Everyone with blonde hair I thought was him. I'd keep my eye out. There's lots of guys who will try to jump in bed or something with me. Certain guys give you that funny look. I work in a restaurant and maybe that guy does know me from there, cause we wear uniforms that don't cover too much. It shows a lot of leg. There might be guys who will go to any length to get it after looking at it all night. So I talked to the boss and we're not going to be wearing those uniforms much longer. I used to worry all the time at work.

I was waiting for the police to call back for a long time. I'd have gone to court. I know they put you through a lot but I'd be willing, to save someone else. Maybe a little kid, or even my daughter someday. I kept thinking they'd call me back, but they didn't do nothing or call. It disappointed me 'cause I would have gone through with the whole thing. They said they'd call and they didn't. Well, even if I'd prosecuted, they don't do much. How long do they keep them, a month or two? I don't think the police even bother with these things. They just took the record down: just another one for their files.

It took a long time but eventually I got over it. I've changed a lot though. Before I'd go out for a drink or talk or let a man buy me breakfast, but now I never do. I'm afraid unless I get to know them personally. I dress different, too. I use to like men to notice. Anymore, when a guy compliments me, I don't like it I can't stand it. Right away I think he's gonna attack me. I'm shy now. I don't like attention at all. But I feel more comfortable since I changed my dress.

Now my husband waits in the parking lot for me. I never thought he'd do that before. It couldn't happen with him there so I've stopped worrying. I pity anyone who would try it; he's pretty big. Mom said maybe it was meant to happen—my husband shows a lot more concern for me now. He took me for granted before. It really did change him and he really did appreciate me more after that. It made him think, "What if I lost her?" In a way that's one good thing about it, but I don't think I'd want to go through it just for that, just for the fact of having a husband that cares.

And even if there was a gang of them, I'd see them and not get out of the car. I'd notice because I'm a lot more careful, cautious now. And I carry mace in case my husband isn't around. And I don't keep any identification in my purse any more. I fear men and always wonder: is he one of them? I have to know men well before I'll go out or talk with them. Now I don't let salesmen in. I wouldn't have let you in except that I knew the little boy who was with you. It affected me a lot. I still feel that over my shoulder stuff, and if someone comes up behind me, even a little kid, I jump. I go through the wall.

But he never bothered me since. No phone calls, no nothing. If he'd called and knew my name I'd really be terrified and couldn't go on. But I'm not nearly as afraid as I was. I doubt it would happen again. I only think about it when I talk about it. I forgot it until the police called yesterday. But even yesterday, when the police guy called, I thought, "I don't know about this." When you opened the door, I thought, "Well, I don't know." I'm suspicious of everybody. I wish it never happened. It's just something you're gonna think about for the rest of your life. I'll always remember it and watch myself. I don't think it made me any stronger. It made me smarter, but I don't think stronger.

Psychological Analyses of the Individual (Idiographic)

As we have said, the limits of the Individual Phenomenal Descriptions are that the psychology of the instances of victimization has not been expressed. The telos of the present phase is psychological intelligibility, which involves articulating (1) the immanent significations of each case (including some which have remained hidden from or taken for granted by the subjects themselves), and (2) the structural unity of each case (the interrelations of these immanent meanings). In this phase, the researcher reads each Individual Phenomenal Description and thinks it through psychologically, expressing what he finds in the way he deems most revelatory of the particular case.

The great difficulty of specifying in detail what is involved in the achievement of psychological sense is reflected in the scarcity of the literature on this topic. It seems to us for several reasons that this is the most difficult phase of research to describe. Firstly, the exciting sense of the results or findings absorbs the researcher's full attention at the moment it unfolds, its novelty and "good gestalt" easily outshining the obscure paths which gave way to it. The researcher tends to surge further with his exploration of the phenomenon at hand rather than break his intimate connection with it in order to see how he has achieved this contact. Thus, the researcher's participation naturally effaces itself for the sake of its achievement. Secondly, psychological insight seems to occur as a spontaneous upsurge of a largely intuitive character rather than any following of explicit rules, so that even when its accuracy is obvious, how an insight was arrived at remains a mystery. Further, our reflections upon this peculiar realm have convinced us that this phase of research is both ambiguous and exceedingly complex. To begin with, the researcher both *finds* and *makes* sense at the same time. Psychological insight is both a discovery and a creation. While it can only emerge out of the closest contact with and fidelity to everyday description, it requires a very peculiar posture or attitude as well as the rigorous enactment of multiple active modes of understanding. It is still quite astounding to us how a single, spontaneous, and even simple thrust of comprehension can admit of the many complex distinction which we have made/seen with regard to it.

Strictly within the idiographic level of psychological analysis, we have differentiated 5 components of the researcher's basic stance or attitude toward everyday description and 11 active operations of understanding which have come into play in the present research. Since space does not allow for a detailed elaboration and exemplification of these moments of psychological reflection, we will regretfully limit ourselves here to presenting a brief outline of them and refer the reader elsewhere for the fuller presentation which these procedures require.[16] We do not pretend that our identification of the moments of the researcher's presence in this phase is comprehensive nor even that its approach is the most fruitful one. Rather, we are only beginning to address a severely neglected area in the hope that we will call others to elaborate beyond and correct our findings. We should also mention at this point that we have reservations about our outline being taken as a kind of cookbook, step-by-step rules on "how to do it," and not merely because of its possible flaws but because we question the place and priority of explicit rules in psychological reflection, which at its best seems quite spontaneous. This, of course, does not mean that it is without structure, that psychology has no norms, or that it is not helpful to know what one is doing when attempting to reflect psychologically.

The basic stance or attitude of psychological reflection. We have differentiated several aspects of the researcher's posture as he confronts the phenomenal descriptions. We regret the way that our analytic attitude and the linearity of our prose makes the aspects of the researcher's presence appear separate. These are by no means separate; in fact they not only overlap but deeply imply each other.

1. *Empathic immersement in the world of description.* The researcher uses the description as a point of access to the situations lived by the subject. The researcher places himself in the subject's world and makes it his own in as vital a way as possible.

2. *Slowing down and dwelling.* The researcher mustn't pass over the details of the description as if they are already understood, passing through and beyond each situation as the subject did. Instead, he must slow down and make room for the description in order to dwell upon the situation in all its details.

3. *Magnification and amplification of the situation.* When we stop and linger with something, it secretes its sense and its full significance becomes magnified or amplified. What to the subject was a little thing becomes a big deal to the researcher, who hereby transcends the mundaneity of the subject's situation. The slightest details of the subject's world become large in importance for the researcher.

4. *Suspension of belief and employment of intense interest.* While the researcher originally enters the subject's situation through natural, straightforward empathy, he must also modify this naive absorption. The researcher now takes a step back and wonders what

16. See Wertz (1983).

this way of living the situation is all about. Breaking his original fusion with the subject, he readies himself to reflect, to think interestedly about where he is, how he got there, and what it means to be there. When he thus ceases to believe naively in the situation described by the subject, neither does he disbelieve it. Rather than being at all concerned with the truth or falsehood of the subject's experiences, the researcher takes up an intense interest in their genesis, relations, and overall structure.

5. *The turn from objects to their meanings.* As we said, the psychological researcher is not concerned about reality (or unreality) of the objects or state of affairs described by his subject. He turns his attention from these facts to their meanings (for the subject) and the particular participation in terms of which such meanings arise. This delivers the researcher to the situation precisely *as experienced, as behaved,* or more generally *as meant* by the subject. This is in part what makes the research psychological, namely, a study of man's participation in the immanent significations of lived situations. The psychologist must attend to the exact sense of the situation as the particular mode of the subject's participation regards it.

Various possible activities of psychological reflection. On the basis of the general stance or attitude described above, the researcher may engage in a number of more specialized activities. Again, we must emphasize that these have only been distinguished in analysis; in the research they overlap so much and are so mutually implicative that they constitute an inextricable unity. Ideally, all of these operations, either successively, in combinations, or all in one stroke, would be called into play by every statement in the Individual Phenomenal Description.

1. *Use of an "existential baseline."* Implicit in the researcher's frame of reference are the norms of psychological existence—typical day-to-day life in which the phenomenon under study is not profoundly present or in which other phenomena predominate. This serves as a ground upon which or vis-à-vis the phenomenon under study stands out and is identified, thus revealing itself as a good gestalt, a difference from other phenomena.

2. *Reflection on judgment.* The researcher has already judged the statements in the Individual Phenomenal Description to be revelatory of the phenomenon, so he may now reflect on this judgment by asking "How am I understanding the phenomenon such that this statement reveals it?" or "What does this statement reveal about the phenomenon? How is it relevant?"

3. *Penetration of implicit horizons.* It should be noted that the description itself is not the ultimate object of reflection despite its necessity for reflection; reflection ultimately addresses the situation referred to by the description, more precisely the immanent signifi-

cations that go to make up the subject's lived reality. Once firmly in contact with the subject's world through the description, the researcher can reflect upon things not mentioned in the description but demonstrably present even if highly implicit in the subject's situation.

4. *Making distinctions.* The research differentiates the various moments or components of the structure of the subject's psychological reality. This is achieved by asking each statement what it expresses that is different from the others. The researcher articulates different aspects of the subject's living and their changes. He may differentiate temporal phases, spatial constituents, and other parts of the whole phenomenon.

5. *Seeing relations of constituents.* The researcher addresses to each distinguished constituent, "What has this one to do with that other one, and that one, that one, and so on." Ideally each constituent is related to every other one. Another related question is "What has this to do with the whole; what place does it occupy and what contribution does it make?" Here, the researcher is attuned to coherence, the physiognomy of structure. In thinking through the togetherness and relations (for example, temporal, spatial, social) of constituents, the research sees relative priorities, for instance that some aspects of the phenomenon depend upon or presuppose others in its overall structure.

6. *Thematization of recurrent meanings or motifs.* Closely related to the above procedure, the researcher looks for the unity and consistency of diverse experiences. Spotting recurrent themes is an incipient presence to essential aspects of the case under consideration.

7. *Interrogation of opacity.* In analyzing a protocol, there are always vague areas which perplex the researcher. Sense is often made/found by dwelling with a special persistence in these areas and interrogating in their context.

8. *Imaginative variation and seeing the essence of the case.* One asks all constituents, distinctions, phases, and themes if they could be different or even absent without altering the individual's psychological reality. For instance, a certain event may have occurred at 10:45 a.m. The researcher might imaginally vary this constituent to see if its occurrence at, say 11:00 a.m. or 2:00 p.m. would alter the psychological structure, its meaning. If not, this constituent (for example, the chronological time) is not essential to the psychology of the case. By varying each aspect of the experience, we can ascertain precisely what *must* be involved in order for the peculiar character of the individual's psychological reality to be as it is, thus its essential determinations are grasped.

9. *Languaging.* Throughout this phase, the researcher expresses the sense he is finding/making. Themes, phases, distinctions, rela-

tions are all named, languaged. The goal here is psychologically revelatory description, and thus the results of this phase are no longer expressed strictly in the subject's own language but in that of the researcher, since it is *his* psychological reflection that is being expressed. The transformation of description into psychological language is not a mere translation into or replacement with the abstract, sedimented terms of psychology. What is involved here is original speaking on the part of the researcher, for this phase is psychology in the making. As this speaking originates from the researcher's contact with the case, it is highly personal and specific to the case; the researcher expresses *his* reflection with *his* context of knowledge as it encounters the psychological sense of the case. Often he will take words from everyday discourse, but when he does so in this phase, their meaning becomes special. They are now psychological terms referring strictly to the subject's participation in situations as meant by him.

10. *Verification, modification, and reformulation.* Whenever psychological speaking is involved, there is a distance between what is said and the subject's description, and hence the danger of the researcher losing contact with the subject's lived situation. Therefore the researcher must constantly return to the original description given by the subject in order to verify, modify, or negate his reflective understanding. He implicitly asks "Is everything I say born out?" and "Is everything in the subject's description reflected in my psychology?" He desires as tight a fit as possible and draws on the previous operations to achieve it.

11. *Use of existential-phenomenological concepts to guide reflection.* Actually, this is a secondary and derived operation, since its working is built upon the procedures we have discussed. The researcher might use a general theoretical concept to guide thinking about the case. For instance, he may know that whenever a person experiences a thematic object, its internal and external horizons are implicitly co-given, and this knowledge may lead him to interrogate those horizons in a given instance. Another concept sometimes used by researchers is the "self-world-others" structure, which is believed to be involved in every psychological reality. When a subject describes one of these three general components of the psychological order, the researcher may press his thought to discover how the other two are implicitly given with it. The danger here is not the imposition of concepts which distort the matters at hand (a danger that exists when one uses traditional explanatory concepts). Since existential-phenomenological concepts are developed in light of the phenomena themselves (through the above procedures,), they illuminate in a radically descriptive way and can only help the researcher see what is already there but overlooked. The real danger is that of lazy reflection and its consequent superficiality, whereby

the researcher would only see what these concepts lead him to. Thus the researcher must use them to facilitate true discovery and original thinking without replacing it.

After reflecting upon all the descriptive data of the case, the researcher must pull all his reflections together, eliminate redundancy, and concisely express the psychological structure of the individual case. In doing so, he mentions both the facts of the case and their psychological significance. For the sake of brevity, he need not go over every concrete detail of the case, but must at least show how everything essential to the psychology of the individual arises out of and in turn illuminates that subject's description. The following is the Individual Psychological Structure of the case we have been discussing.

INDIVIDUAL PSYCHOLOGICAL STRUCTURE OF BEING CRIMINALLY VICTIMIZED: *MARLENE*

M.'s victimization involves a complex psychological structure which is composed of several moments or interrelated substructures.

1. *"The before" of victimization.* Prior to victimization, our phenomenon is absent from M.'s thematic field, and its absence is rarely even noted. First let's characterize "the before" negatively: M. does not usually fear, think about, or anticipate being attacked or raped. Rapists, for instance, are virtually absent from her surroundings. Even the rare occasion in which M. is present to rape, it is regarded (whether in thought, imagination, perception of television news, and so on) as something that happens elsewhere to others but *not herself*. To characterize this psychological order positively: the world and men, even strangers, are experienced as safe. There is an implicit, unthematized yet predominant horizon of social harmony, and this allows there to be an openness, at homeness alone in the world with strange men. This world-horizon supports and dialectically allows her to pursue her own ends freely and undistractedly outside her home, in the area where strange men exist, alone. Indeed there she likes being attractive, flirts, talks with unfamiliar men, lets them buy her breakfast, and so on.

This psychological order is lived in the specificity of the moment immediately prior to victimization. M. is involved in the routine task of driving home from work at night. She perceives her surroundings—the road, other, and so on—as familiar, typical, and on the ground of social safety. The car which follows here is interpreted strictly from this order, namely as a familiar, safe, one of the neighbor's cars. The typicality of the situation, in the implicit context of safety, allows M. to proceed freely to her apartment without any distraction, suspicion, or need to interrogate the situation beyond its usual harmonious order.

2. *The virtuality, nascence, and actuality of victimization.* However,

submerged in the midst of the above psychological order is another dialectic which tentatively emerges when M. gets out of her car to walk to her apartment building. It is what she calls a "fear over my shoulder" which she has "always had." Prior to this moment, M.'s fear over her shoulder was not being focally lived. From her saying that she always had it, we assign it the status of a virtuality which is overshadowed by the primary actuality of the "before" order in which there is nothing to be afraid of. But we note that the fear over the shoulder implies victimization. Although, as reported, victimization was absent from the *actuality* of the previous order, it is there as a *virtuality*, unthematized and unspoken of by M.; indeed contrary to all thematic awareness it is a submerged possibility. We could say that this fear over the shoulder had been integrated into the safety of the previous order to the extent that it did not take on a leading role. This is why we called the horizon of safety *predominant*. However M. doesn't hear the door of the other car shut. There emerges a rift in the typical texture of the situation, constituting an indeterminate horizon requiring further interrogation. It is in relation to this tear in the familiar that the fear over the shoulder emerges. M.'s fearful perceptual interrogation of the unfamiliar, which holds the possibility of harm, is her way of living victimization in its nascent form. The empty, fearful anticipation is immediately fulfilled. She looks and sees the man from the car coming close and grabbing here in the vacant lot before the stairs. At this moment the actual order and meaning of victimization is revealed: figural is the other's detrimentality, and ground is M.'s being vulnerably in the hands of the other with her own autonomy lost and the absence of helpful others. The other disrupts M.'s routine project and world by grabbing her and trying to carry her away, strips her of her agency, and is making her prey for his own purposes in the absence of good community. Within this new order she interprets him as intending to rape her. Hence we see how a virtuality blossoms into actuality and in doing so overturns the old psychological order and constitutes a new one.

Let's back up and take another look at what has occurred. Prior to this moment, victimization had the status of a mere unthematized possibility, as such dominated by the more pervasive and overriding horizon of social harmony. In this moment its status changes. In the midst of a rift in the "before" order, victimization becomes a possibility to be thematically interrogated, and then an actuality. However, when this occurs, the "before" order is not completely overturned or left behind. Victimization is lived first by M. in the mode of surprise or shock. It is precisely the previous psychological order, which gave victimization no place, that is shocked. Thus the second moment in the structure of victimization, which culminates in its actuality, both surpasses and conserves the first. On one hand a completely new order emerges, namely victimization, but on the other hand it is not experienced as a full reality. M. is shocked; she can't believe it. She interprets the event within the new horizon of victimization, that is, a rape attempt, but it doesn't make sense. She doesn't know what he's trying to do as his hands go up her legs. Victimization does not emerge fully determinate but in a way is a quasi-reality for M., a strange, shocking one. And we understand why, that is, because it is completely alien to the psychological order she's lived most of her life. Now she is involved in a whole new realm which is essentially contrary to the familiar one which she had assumed to be reality.

Indeed, *not understanding* is part of the very order of victimization. M. has been stripped of her autonomous participation, her ability to define the situation herself, and understanding is part of this. She has been grabbed, become a passive subject, and collapsed on the stairs. Understanding and action, as two sides of her autonomous agency, are lost together. Familiarity, safety, and the autonomy they allow fall away, and M. is delivered against her will and wildest expectation, to a situation which is strange because it was precisely unpredicted and because it is defined by a radical other working against her. In a sense, there is not much to describe in the original moment of victimization; the explosion and destruction of the habitual leaves a kind of void which is only gradually filled in. M. is sure of nothing, can do nothing about it. As we have said, though, we can specify three constituents which do describe the order of victimization: (1) an other's detrimentality—a potential rapist trying to carry M. away and then who knows what, (2) M.'s own vulnerability, impotence, and loss of agency including understanding, and (3) the absence of helpful community. This order is originally elaborated for M. only minimally, since it is contrary in its very meaning not only to everything she has projected for herself in her life but also to her very ability to understand; thus it appears as scary, shocking, strange, and shot through with uncertainty. In the order of victimization, M. is passive, has nothing to say about what is happening. In this sense, from the point of view of the subject, victimization is to a significant extent a negative phenomenon, a destructive ordering.

3. *The struggle against victimization.* As soon as victimization occurs, there is a movement in which a third order is manifest, namely that of a struggle against victimization. This is possible for M. inasmuch as she has not been totally victimized, that is, the other has not destroyed her agency completely. This participation by M. involves the reassertion of her own free status and ability to define the situation for herself, indeed to escape it. This movement occurs on the basis of victimization in that only once M. is already victimized does she struggle against it.

One of the most immediate ways in which M. undertakes this struggle is to attempt to understand the situation more fully. Understanding has the motive of and is a moment of surpassing. We notice that struggling against victimization is M.'s way of living it. She fills in this new situation by elaborating the other's harmful intentions; she figures he's trying to get her into the car to rape her. She looks for others and realizes she's alone. She thinks of giving the other money so he'll leave her alone. Although she is caught in the order of victimization (shock and collapse)—she cannot speak—she does struggle out of it, surpassing her sheer immobility at the hands of the other, by throwing him her purse. This shows a reorganization of M.'s priorities; she is now trying to achieve relative escape through bargaining ("My money is better than my life"). M. is also trying to understand the situation in order to be able to get on top of it. She is implicitly present to a range of possible victimizations and is struggling to achieve the less severe. Here again, we see that the struggle emerges out of the order of victimization, an actuality with many threatening possibilities surrounding it. However, M.'s victimization continues—the situation continues to be defined against her by the other—as he doesn't take her purse. Now she knows he doesn't want money but wants her. As the struggle continues, the positive character of the situation is unfolding.

In M.'s next attempts at struggle, we see the meaning and purpose of this emerging dialectic: to evade victimization and reestablish the pre-victimization order. M. holds onto the rail, an attempt to exert her own free agency and resist being taken over into the hands of a detrimental other. She also screams for help, an attempt to re-call the helpful community which is now absent. She resists the other's implicitly sexual advances by holding her legs together. M. is refusing to be a mere victim. Since the struggle against victimization emerges on the ground of the situation of already being victimized, M. attempts to understand the latter more fully in order to appropriate it in her struggle. She looks around at the cars and the other man in it and begins to imagine the possibilities of victimization. She thinks about him taking her into the car, never being seen again, being messed up bad, never seeing her family again, being cut off from helpful others, being knifed. In each of these variations of the experience we find, at least implicitly, the three constituents of victimization (detrimental other, loss of agency or selfness, absent community). But this elaborate living of victimization is integrated in M.'s struggle to surpass it; hence she thinks about the possibilities of resistance, for example, fighting, going along with it so as not to be hurt more. As being killed moves from an imagined possibility to an anticipated probability, M. decides to fight. This dialectic of struggle, we see, is also one of anger, and M. imagines having a gun and killing the other, escaping victimization by destroying the victimizer in his own turn.

M.'s struggle attempts to reverse the constituents of victimization . Screaming attempts to bring back lost community. Holding onto the rail attempts to keep her agency, her life in her own hands; and fighting, killing attempts to strip the other of his detrimentality. The struggle is triumphant, and in short order the immediate situation of victimization is surpassed. M. hears another come to her aid; thus the restoration of good community. The criminal lets her go and withdraws; thus the disappearance of detrimentality. M. gets up and goes inside; thus her free agency is restored. M.'s efforts have achieved something like a relative reconstitution of her preferred world, the "before" order: freedom, safety, good community. This signifies the termination of the original victimization.

4. *The worlding of M.'s struggle against victimization.* However,

rather than a simple return to the pre-victimization order, we see that M.'s establishment of a preferred situation is only relative. Both victimization and M.'s struggle to surpass it continue to be lived psychologically long after the original situation is overcome, making this phase of the structure by far the most complex and extended in time and space. Why does the order of victimization spread over M.'s whole world even though objectively speaking, she is no longer actually being victimized? The cat is out of the bag so to speak, the cat being potential attack and rape. Just as the emergence of victimization both conserves and surpasses the "before" so does the "recovered" order conserve and surpass victimization. Now that the harmonious social horizon has been destroyed, victimization is a lived reality that cannot be brushed aside. M. now lives in the overarching horizon of victimization. It is part of the very meaning of victimization that it can neither be predicted or controlled, for the initiative is in the hands of the other. And any man is capable of attack and rape. Thus victimization's actuality has receded, but it has come to make up a threatening possibility in the world, one which M. must come to understand and surpass if her life is to return to normal. Hence this moment of the structure manifests the continued living or elaboration and overcoming of victimization in its manifold presence in M.'s world.

Every situation after the original victimization has a bipolar order; what is given is (the continued living of) victimization and what is projected is (the struggle against it for) recovery. We will now look at six different manifestations of this bipolar order: back at home after the attack, the contact with the police, the next week home in bed, M.'s relations with her husband, going back out into the larger world, and waiting for the police, who don't call back.

As we have said, although the crime is "objectively" over, psychologically it is not. The crucial fact immediately after the incident is that the victimizer is still very much present to M.'s experience, namely as "still out there and dangerous." In implicit relation to this, there are several attempts to negate the victimizer as such. M.'s neighbor tries to get the license number of his car. M.'s husband calls the police. The overall project is to "arrest" potential victimization which is now "on the loose," and indeed this is an extension of M.'s original attempt to overcome it. In the neighbor's and husband's acts, helpful community is reestablished, and thus victimization is indeed partially being overcome. M. also participates in a movement toward recovery by exercising her agency through attempts at understanding. Understanding is an attempt to overcome the shock, confusion, and unpredictability constitutive of victimization as it is now still very present for M. During this time, victimization begins to take on positive features (which can then be dealt with). "He has to be a nut. . . or drunk. He'd been coming from the opposite direction and we both took the same turn, so I don't think he saw me anywhere and followed me. I don't know him unless he saw me at work, but he didn't follow me from there. . ." The goal of these thoughts is to defend herself against the outstanding possibility of the victimizer's return. Throughout all this we see that the ambiguity and uncertainty originally constitutive of the incident prevails and continues to motivate a great deal of "figuring." M. has been plunged into this rift in harmonious community with all its unfamiliarity, and she must figure it out and overcome it, for within this realm, as she imagines it, lies the possibility of her own destruction, ultimately being murdered. The struggle is left incomplete in this situation, for the danger cannot be objectified and dealt with once and for all. Figure, imagine, speculate, and infer what she will, the danger lurks beyond M's view, and so her understanding, mastery, and the reconstitution of good sociality thanks to the neighbor and husband remain only partial and relative. Therefore from now on victimization will no longer be a submerged, hidden possibility but will be a dominant theme in M.'s life beyond the original incident.

The police enter the situation, then, in the context of the givenness of outstanding victimization and M.'s hope of ultimate victory over it. Together, they continue to bring the event within familiar, clear understanding, and we recognize this as a movement toward recovery, though only partial, since opacity still persists. However, to M. the police are unsympathetic, and in this sense they frustrate her hope for the reestablishment of good community. Moreover, they themselves, in their way of being with M., constitute an absence of helpful community, thus participating in the order of victimization rather than that of recovery. M. is very sensitive to their way of being with her, and in her perception of them as blaming her we see that she is continuing to live the vulnerability which came to the fore in the victimization. What is at issue for M. here is her sense of helpful community; she wants others to help her. Her husband "takes her side" and thus participates in the meaning of M. being protected by others whereas the police didn't seem to take the event seriously, had more important things to do. While the husband is overcoming the order of victimization (by being for M.'s interests), the police are identified as absent, uncaring others, which is part of the very order of victimization, precisely the one which M. hoped they would overcome. In this sense M. psychologically relives victimization with the police. What makes the police so distant, removed? Remember for M., whose victimization has largely been lived in terms of imagined possibilities rather than the facts the police are concerned with recording, there could not be a more important event than one in which her life is jeopardized, whereas for the police the matter is routine and nothing too bad actually happened. While for the police crime and the criminal are familiar, for M. they are anything but that. M. becomes angry with the police for their inability to eliminate the problem (since it's so familiar to them), thus holding them responsible for the lurking possibility of harm. In this we see how inextricably related the the "detrimental other" constituent is the "absent, unhelpful community" constituent, and how the continuing presence of the later leads M. to continue to live the victimization as a whole. However, the police also present a possibility for recovery, namely that of prosecution, and M. is willing to do everything within her power to do it. The police promise to call and let M. get involved in looking at pictures and reestablishing law and order. In this sense they promise that they will (in the future) be helpful others and M. will (in the future) regain her active agency, which, of course will overcome victimization. Thus the situation with the police is ambiguous. In some senses it is a continued living of victimization, yet at the same time it promises the possibility of recovery in the future. Victimization still has the status of largely not yet overcome.

For the next week, M. continues to live through the order of victimization in a very pervasive way. Sick in bed, her projects and agency are collapsed. She exists as torn away from her everyday tasks; she cannot go to work or watch the baby. M. lives in constant fear, imagining going outside and being attacked, anticipating the rapist calling on the telephone, coming to get her at work. Noises which share some of the meanings of the original victimization such as suddenness, strangeness, intrusiveness, like the telephone, knocks on the door, someone outside, are perceived as "the rapist coming back for me." This is how her world is lived within the pervasive horizon of victimization. We see the constriction or destruction of freedom and agency in the face of the other's potential detrimentality, which constitutes the order of victimization. M. continues for this week to live as a mere victim. The only sense in which surpassing seems to be involved is that by anticipating and imagining the profiles of victimization, she is beginning to bring the realm into view so she can surpass it. At this time, if there is any surpassing, it takes the form of fearful withdrawal/escape. M. stays at home helpless.

Besides reliving victimization in memory, anticipation, perception, and imagination, M. even dreams of being raped, and here we find something interesting. In her dream the rapist turns into her husband and she wakes up fighting him. Indeed, it is not merely in dreaming that her husband's behavior takes on the meaning of victimization. Whenever her husband touches her, it makes her skin crawl. M. lives with her husband in fear and won't allow him to touch her. She's afraid her marriage will be ruined and thinks of going back to her parents. M. is treating her husband as if he were a victimizer, and we must try to understand this. She describes her husband prior to this time as uncaring toward her, "the hard type." This, as well as his being a male with sexual intentions toward her, identifies him psychologically with the criminal. Interestingly, M. is not even the only one to make this perhaps not so strange connection; we remember that the neighbor's first impression of M.'s screams during the attack was that she must be fighting with her husband. It seems for M. that the order of victimization is extended beyond the original situation to those which have some identities of meaning with the original one, and these meanings reevoke the whole order. Prior to victimization, M.'s husband was insensitive, callous, took her for granted, stayed out all night, and so on, but these behaviors were not experienced as thematically fearsome or detestable. These qualities, as we have said, were hidden or overshadowed by the context of social harmony. For instance, sex was safe. After victimization, in the context of social harmfulness and M.'s desire to overcome it, these same behaviors are feared and hated. Indeed, she carries out her struggle with victimization with her husband (for example, fighting him, wanting to keep her distance from him). Rather than living her relation with her husband as an overcoming of victimization, that is, the healing of broken community, safety, freedom, and the like, it is lived as continued victimization. Her husband is identified with two constituents of the victimization order: on one hand, his staying out at night, leaving her alone and vulnerable, his uncaringness, for example, identify him with the absence of helpful community, and on the other his being the "hard type" identifies him with the detrimental other. M.'s first reaction is to withdraw temporarily ("Don't touch me") and to consider permanent withdrawal. Notice that her parents now appeal to her as a refuge precisely because of their meaning of helpful community and their lack of detrimental characteristics. A victim in her own home, M. is helpless and becomes like a baby in need of others' care and help. This is an extension of the previous loss of agency beyond its original situation. She is now "the one who needs the arms, the affection," without which she can't go on. M. is implicitly demanding that her social situation transform itself from one which is perpetuating the pattern of victimization to one in which she is safe, loved, respected, and nurtured back to full participation. Indeed others play a key role in M.'s recovery process. In this situation her husband changes and continually shows himself to have meanings the opposite of victimization—kindness, softness, protection, understanding, encouraging, comforting. He begins to help M. recover by changing the order of their relationship from one of victimization to one in which M.'s own needs and concerns are respected and affirmed. He literally says when she dreams of him raping her or won't let him touch her, "I'm not the guy." Thus he dispells her viewing him as detrimental. But more importantly than saying he's "not the guy," he *behaves* differently; he "turns it soft." He also changes from being absent and unhelpful to present and protecting; he stays home, is "always there when she needs him," meets her at work, puts locks on the doors, and moreover makes M.'s world safe for her. This is a gift, a pleasant surprise for M., which helps her move into an order of life in which she is safe. Without this, she intimates, she "wouldn't have gotten over it," and we can see why: Otherwise she would have continued to live out the fear-anger order of victimization from within the very heart of her world, her own home. Her husband has provided a basic situation of recovery from which M. can branch out to surpass victimization as it still lurks in the larger world.

Many aspects of the larger world have also changed their meaning in light of victimization. For instance, "being alone," as a constituent of the original victimization, now evokes the whole, and so M. avoids it. "Going outside" also reevokes the immediate possibility of victimization and is therefore avoided. M.'s life has been destroyed and continues to exist as such, that is, restricted to and by the profiles of victimization. She imagines the rapist could be out in the hall of her apartment building so she can't even go out to do her laundry except with someone else. Others come to aid, she feels safer, and her expectations of encounter with victimization, in the face of the world's reassertion of the old familiar safety, are frustrated. Hence as the articulations of victimization in the world are, with the help of others, contradicted, their meanings reverse back (that is, anticipated dangers turn to actual safety with caring others). In this way M. moves toward the recovery of agency and transcendence of the meanings of victimization. But this takes time; even when M. begins to go out of the house, she avoids situations with the meanings of the original victimization such as night, dark, aloneness. Fears from the past (for example, of the dark, of people behind her) have reemerged. She continues to elaborate the world of victimization imaginally (for example, "They'll get my daughter if I take her out"). M. struggles to surpass this new world, to prepare and protect herself from it; she goes to the car quickly with her daughter and locks the doors. She also relives the loss of agency in the face of men who look like the victimizer; at work once she "collapsed" when she saw a man she thought was him. M. has become suspicious of men, vigilantly attuned to guys who may be out to get her. She thinks about men and their sexual urges, afraid of these, seeing them now as detrimental to her. She notices guys giving her "that funny look" and worriedly sees herself as attracting these looks with their horizon of possible harm. She reevaluates her life-style and clothing, seeing her own possible role in victimization. This enables her to surpass it; she changes her life-style and clothing so as to protect herself, that is, becoming less flirtatious, wearing longer dresses, carrying mace. Here we see how understanding the victimization can lead to the elimination of its probability. Following the collapse of M.'s old agency (a flirtatious, fearless working woman), a new agency emerges in dialog with the profiles of victimization. This new agency surpasses its previous collapse in victimization as well as attempts to prevent it from happening again. At once M. overcomes and prevents further victimization.

Waiting for the police to call manifests M.'s continuing hope and search for the lost community, an intention to recover the "law and order" which once reigned in her world. She wishes to eliminate the detrimentality of attack and rape from the world, in which it has taken on a focal and pervasive place. M. is willing to play her part, that is, go to court, still strictly as a way of overcoming crime as it has been imaginally elaborated ("to stop him from doing that to others; maybe my daughter or a little kid would be next"). The continued absence of the police's call, leaving their promise unfulfilled, leaves M. isolated, relatively helpless. Since these are constituents of victimization, the police's behavior itself sediments the permanency of victimization in M.'s life. She looses faith in the justice system and elaborates its ineffectiveness in thought ("the police don't do anything about these things," "they wouldn't have put him away for long anyway," "it's just another one for their files"). These new thoughts now play a role in establishing the worldly reality-context of victimization (that is, the absence of helpful others constituent) besides sedimenting M.'s own lived sense of vulnerability.

5. *The new world "after" victimization.* M. lives an "after" of victimization to the extent that it is surpassed and thus no longer predominant

or focal. To this extent she goes back to a normal life with the same basic characteristics we saw in the "before": familiarity and safety of the world, free agency, a horizon of social harmony, and so on. But the "after" is also different from the "before" in that the new matters which get constituted through the living of victimization as well as the new ways in which M. overcomes them are sedimented in the world, integrated within normal life.

M.'s world is now filled with potential rapists and this is assumed to be "the one real world" even though she hasn't always seen it that way. M. believes she is smarter now. However, these profiles of the world no longer dominate her as they once did because she has habitualized avoidances and precautions against this threat, thereby rendering it nonthreatening and of lesser concern. M. is a shy person with men now. She avoids strange men until they are familiar and proven to be harmonious. She is suspicious of strange men and only when her expectations of harm are frustrated is she comfortable. Thus the expectation and avoidance of victimization, as it has been made real in the world, are integrated into the manifold of daily interpersonal relations. M. dresses differently, doesn't like men to notice or compliment her (which means sexual attraction, thus implying the rest of the order of victimization). When she's complimented, she becomes afraid of attack. These changes, while they manifest the presence of victimization, integrate it in a way that overcomes it. They are designed to eliminate the motivations of others to victimize her and thereby leave M. feeling safe. Her new understandings and behaviors restore familiarity and safety to the world, however more ambiguous it is now, so she can proceed toward *her own* ends with ease. We find a similar pattern with other precautionary behaviors designed to negate victimization which are habitualized; for example, M. looks around before getting out of the car, being more careful, cautious. M. usually carries mace with her, thus having strengthened her own agency for struggle to the extent of presumed indominability. She keeps no I.D. in her purse and keeps the doors locked, never letting a strange man in. All these behaviors constitute the integration of the possibility of victimization into a nonvictimized/nonvictimizable existence. Although this pattern is there, however, we have to say that M. still has not completely overcome victimization and put it behind her. She still has a fear over her shoulder and when surprised from behind (which we remember was a constituent of the original event), she goes through the wall. M. is only partially recovered, but not completely returned to normal life.

Others' helping behavior is also sedimented in M.'s daily life, participating along with her own efforts at integrating the order of victimization as surpassed. M.'s husband escorts her or meets her out in the parking lot. He shows more concern; thus his own potentially victimizing characteristics have been changed to be helpful, nurturing ones. M. sees this as a good transformation, one we see having arisen through the movement of overcoming victimization in M.'s world beyond its original showing. M.'s husband now, rather than being a callous, detrimental, abandoning person, is a soft, kind, helpful one, and this is presumed to manifest a lasting transformation of the relationship. Others have been extremely important in M.'s recovery, since she projected her recovery through demanding help. The police faired more poorly in this context, having frustrated M.'s project. It is now a part of M.'s lived reality that the police are at best useless and at worst themselves participate in the order of victimization through their insensitivity and uncaringness. The police are a testimony to the continued presence of victimization for M.

However, besides having overcome victimization through her own efforts and those of others, the world itself has played a part in M.'s return to a normal existence. Situations have not fulfilled M.'s continued and elaborate expectations of victimization. She's never seen the "criminal" again; he never bothered her or even called. If he had, victimization would have deepened and recovery would have been slower and perhaps would have taken a different form (that is, whatever it would have taken to surpass and eliminate his pursuit). But the world has reasserted that M.'s fears are not relevant to a large extent, and thus she has transcended them. Now she doubts it would happen again and in this sense has returned to the pre-victimization stance allowed by this reconstituted horizon of safety and social harmony. M. doesn't think about the victimization much anymore; thus it has been largely made past and returned to submergence in the virtual, dominated once again by the preferred social order. This has been achieved by precautions, helpful others, the world's assertion of safety, and other matters. Yet it is different now because precisely those behaviors which eliminated victimization imply it as an immanent signification. A new world has been born in which victimization exists, and this is all part of a new horizon of reality which is much more full than it was before as well as much more readily thematized in its field of relevance (for example, strange men, being alone at night).

Psychological Analysis of the General (Nomothetic)

The limit of the Individual Psychological Structure is, of course, that it reflects only an individual instance of the phenomenon. The one we have presented, for instance, has much to do with rape. Others have to do with different kinds of assault, robbery, vandalism, and so on. Have we learned or can we learn anything about crime victims in general? It is this issue to which the fourth phase of research speaks. It should be noted that the movement from individuality to generality does not correspond to the movement from everyday description to psychological structure, for the latter has already been achieved with regard to the individual in the last phase. Therefore, the present phase is based on that achievement and works from the beginning within the psychological. That is, it moves from the psychology of individual crime victimizations to the psychology of crime victimization in general. Its goal is what we call the General Psychological Structure. Precisely, this achievement involves understanding diverse individual cases as instances of something more general and articulating that generality of which they are particular instances. The General Psychological Structure is a comprehension of a great diversity of examples.

This movement to generality is founded upon all the attitudes and operations previously discussed and includes them within it. However, our analysis of the researcher's presence during this phase discloses several other aspects beyond those previously mentioned. These procedures are also far from distinct but overlap in a syncretic blend in the moment of research. Again, we will restrict ourselves to a brief sketch here and refer the reader elsewhere for an elaboration and concrete exemplification of these procedures.[17]

1. *Seeing general features of individual structures.* Certain constituent meanings, relations, and so on articulated in the Individual Psychological Structures are already true of all cases even though achieving such generality was not the explicit goal of the individual analysis. This is understandable when we remember that the realm of "immanent meaning" is an ideal one and as such is not strictly attached or limited to the real individual experiences in terms of which it emerges. Therefore it does not necessarily pertain only to one person's private reality. Further, "structure" is a term of knowledge, as such differentiated from the original individual's living from which it is extracted. Therefore an individual psychological structure can as a whole, in principle at least, to pertain to many individuals. On the other hand, of course, even though immanent meanings and the structural knowledge of them transcend individual experiences, this does not imply that they are necessarily true of all, or even many, individuals. The researcher must determine which features of individual structures manifest a general truth and which do not. He may do this by rereading the Individual Psychological Structures and rather than taking the statements as referring to the particular case, taking them as referring to all cases. In doing this, he sees that some statements can be taken as true in the general context and others cannot. Some features almost invariably strike the researcher as equivocal when he attempts to assign them this true-for-all reference, as "maybe general, maybe not" or "maybe general with some qualification or modification." Because the researcher must be critical of his pronouncements of generality based on this operation alone and is filled with questions when he interrogates individual structures for their generality, other possibilities of his presence during this phase must come into play.

2.. *Comparison of individuals.* Rather than uncritically assuming that any statement in an Individual Psychological Structure is true generally, the researcher must actually *find* evidence in all the ones

17. See Wertz (1983).

he has. Thus he compares each individual's psychology to the others and establishes convergences and divergences. The convergences or similarities, when languaged, are general statements which may become a part of the General Psychological Structure of the phenomenon. The divergences manifest typical or idiosyncratic structural features. In this comparison, the researcher often thinks back to the Phenomenal Descriptions in light of the Individual Psychological Structure of another description. In doing so he may discover that features of the latter exist in the other descriptions and/or situations even though they were not previously reflected in the psychological analysis of those individual cases. Indeed, some features may be found to be genuinely common to all even though not being described by all subjects (that is, they may be necessarily implicit.) Thus to be a generally valid insight, it is not necessary that it must have already been made explicit in previous phases but only that it can be found in the other cases upon further reflection. This means that the present procedure is not a mere cross-checking for correspondences of actual statements or anything like a content or factor analytic procedure but is a deeply reflective penetration into Individual Psychological Structures in light of other ones in order to find common features that are sometimes highly implicit.

3. *Imaginative Variation.* To achieve the desired generality, that is, a generality even beyond the actual cases to which our descriptions give access, imaginative variation must again be employed. This time it is used not to gain insight into the essential psychology of an individual case as it was in the last phase but to gain insight into the *generally essential.* Thus the parameters of variation are open further in this phase than in the previous one. One now imagines any and all possible variations of being criminally victimized to see what is invariably necessary for a phenomenon to qualify as an instance of it.

A second and quite related function of this procedure is that it helps the researcher clarify the limits within which he wishes his statements to apply, that is, if he does not want his findings to reflect universality but rather a specified realm of generality. For instance, by imagining a person shot and murdered from behind with no struggle (or even awareness) on his part—no "after" phase, we realized that the struggle against victimization (which includes awareness of it) as well as the "after"—the reliving and surpassing—are not universal constituents of the phenomenon. This led us to specify our findings as pertaining to a less than universal realm of generality we would call "the *living* through or struggle against" criminal victimization, which may not necessarily include a struggle against and after phase of being victimized.

4. *Explicit formulation of generality.* As we have already seen implicitly in the above procedures, the researcher must language the general truths he sees. He must formulate the essential, that is both

> the necessary and sufficient conditions, constituents, and structural relations that constitute his phenomenon in general—all instances of the phenomenon under consideration. He must critically reflect upon his possible statements, "can we have the phenomenon without this?" If the answer, as evident in empirical data and imaginative variation, is "no," then what the statement expresses is necessary to the phenomenon. If "yes," it is unnecessary and must be dropped from his general formulation. The researcher then asks, "if we have *just* this, do we have the *whole* phenomenon?" If "yes," then the formulation is sufficient, and if "no," then it is not sufficient and more must be included so as to reveal the whole.

Now we will present the results of this phase of analysis. One should note that General Psychological Structures may be elaborated in greatly varied detail, depth, and emphasis. One could state the general structure of the struggle with "criminal" victimization in a few sentences:

> On the ground of a usual situation involving a freely enacted task, in a familiar situation with the horizon of social harmony and safety, *S* is shocked by the emergence of victimization—an other detrimental to *S*'s preferred situation has in the absence of helpful community made *S* prey to his own purposes and the vulnerable *S* is relatively powerless to stop this even though it is against his values and will. *S* immediately struggles to overcome his shock by understanding, to eliminate the detrimental other, to restore helpful community, and to regain his lost agency/power and thus return to his preferred situation. Even after this incident is over, *S* continues to live in the horizon of victimization, that is, he relives its constituent meanings in various situations and extends them through recollection, perception, anticipation, imagination, and thinking throughout his world so he may overcome potential victimization as it now lurks in the world at large. Through his own active efforts, help from others and the world's repeated reassertion of safety, victimization is eliminated from the sphere of impending actuality and the horizon of social harmony is restored. By so elaborating and overcoming victimization, that is, by integrating it, *S* shapes a significantly new existence for himself in which victimization is both conserved and surpassed. This new existence is preferred relative to victimization but *not* necessarily relative to that before victimization.

Although we attempted to include everything significant at least by implication, the above statement is very global and lacks detail. We have developed another statement with a bit more detail and somewhat shifted emphasis to show how the expression of the General Psychological Structure may vary.

Being criminally victimized is a disruption of daily routine and a shattering of its taken for granted horizon of social harmony which compels one, despite his resistance, to face his fellow as predator and himself as prey, isolated from any helpful community. This event is originally experienced in the mode of shock and disbelief, appearing to the victim as strange, puzzling, perverse, unfair, and undeserved. As the victim articulates the actuality of this event and elaborates its possible consequence, he struggles with it by looking for ways to escape, counter, undo the violation or find assistance. His efforts to no avail, he lives through his own vulnerability, separateness, and helplessness in the face of the callous, insensitive, anonymous enemy. Whether expressed immediately or not, the victim also lives an inner protest, anger, or rage, and a readiness for retaliation, revenge, counterviolation against the victimizer.

After this original event has occurred the victim continues to encounter its constituent meanings (that is, loss of agency, predatory other, absent community) through a variety of experiences (for example, perception, imagination, anticipation, recollection, even philosophizing) in a variety of situations besides the original crime situation (dealings with the police, justice system, insurance company, and walking in strange neighborhoods). In other words, the victim is pervasively attuned to being victimized and begins to live the meanings of victimization throughout many facets of his world. For example, besides remembering the actual crime and thinking about it, one may be afraid of it happening again in the future; one may be suspicious of all strangers; one may listen attentively to crime on the news; one may doubt his neighbors—why weren't they there to help?" or "could it have been one of them who robbed me?"; one may be afraid to go out alone; one may generalize, "the police are never there when you need them"; one may philosophize "it's a dog-eat-dog world" or "people just don't help each other these days." In this way, one elaborates a whole world of victimization.

Simultaneously and in precise relation to this, there is a movement to overcome victimization as it is being elaborated, that is, to reestablish order, independence, safety, and a helpful community. For instance, one anticipates another burglary, so he puts better locks on the door. Thus one aspect of overcoming victimization is the victim's active efforts by which he establishes understanding, responsibility, and independence. Thinking about crime, the victim may see his own responsibility in the crime (negligence or evocation). Behavioral restrictions (not going out at night) and preventive measures (locking car doors) may be made new habits. The victim may also acknowledge his own potential violence and injustice, thus moving toward an understanding acceptance of this inevitable divergence of human living. By itself, however, the victim's efforts are insufficient, for there are two other necessary aspects of

> full recovery. The second aspect: the world must spontaneously reassert again and again a peaceful sociality, thus rendering "unrealistic" the victim's recurring anticipations of crime. Thirdly, others must actively extend sympathetic helpfulness to the victim, thus establishing relations of mutual affirmation and respect which overcome the victim's alienation and broken, painfully destructive relations with the callousness and insensitivity of others.
>
> These three aspects of overcoming victimization are all necessary yet none are guaranteed. The absence of any one of these can eventuate a deepened victimization, despair, bitterness, and resignation. Yet insofar as these three aspects are fulfilled, the victim may become more responsible, independent, and new relations of reciprocity, as well as a deeper sense of community, may form through the struggle to integrate and overcome victimization.

But even this lacks the full detail and depth we have explored in our analyses. Hence the following statement is the most explicit we have developed to date. This version includes quotations from victims which illustrate the variety of everyday occurrences which are comprehended by our general psychology. The complexity of the phenomenon demanded elaboration under six headings to depict its psycho-logical process: "Before," "The Emergence," "The Configuration of the Struggle Against Victimization," "After," and "A New Order." It should be noted that this does not necessarily correspond with clock/calendar time, since one may continue to live or return to earlier psychological phases while chronological time moves forward. Our phases, of course, refer not to external realities but immanent meanings. We could call these phases substructures, since each is an integral unity besides being a moment of the larger structural process.

THE GENERAL PSYCHOLOGICAL STRUCTURE OF THE STRUGGLE WITH "CRIMINAL" VICTIMIZATION WITH ILLUSTRATIVE QUOTATIONS

Before

Before being victimized, the person is in a *usual situation* (for example, "I was getting into my car to go to work"). The world is familiar, typical. The subject takes for granted that the future he is moving toward will be allowed by others (for example, "On the way home from hockey, we cut through the yard of people who always let us through—it was all right with them"). This unquestioned, implicit yet pervasively overarching sense of good community is involved in his everyday perception and interpretation of events around him and allows him to define his own ends and smoothly proceed toward them without attentiveness to unfamiliar and unexpected possible actions of others. Of course there are parts of the situation which are unclear, but there is no intention to clarify them except in the light of the horizon of safe, harmonious sociality.

> (Burglary) When we got back from our day in the country, I saw the door open and I thought maybe I left it open or neighbor kids had come looking for our kids to play and opened it.
>
> (Purse snatch) I was walking home from the bus after work. Three boys, 14 or 15, passed me and said hello. I shook my head and kept walking. They just went by like they were going to catch a bus. You know, you see kids like that all the time and pay it no mind, just keep going.

Thanks to the horizon of respectful sociality, the subject lives through the situation toward the incarnation of his *own* ends and purposes.

> (Vandalism) The car (which was later turned on its side) was in my own driveway, on my own property and everything. I need my car to get to the doctor, cos I'm sick, and shopping, and I have to take my wife to a faraway hospital in it cos her records are there.

If the other's detrimentality is present at all, it is a very remote possibility which is absent from the person's thematic field on account of being overshadowed by the predominant sense of safety and implicit social affirmation. Thus, the situation prior to victimization shows itself as a relative variation of the subject's preferred state of affairs, that is, involving free agency, safety, cooperation, and smooth actualization of ends.

> (Vandalism) I never had any trouble anywhere I lived. Up till that time I liked it here. I was fixin' the house up, paintin' it. It was a good place to live.
>
> (Prowling/Peeping) We moved here to get away from everything—like stealing, breaking in, minors getting doped. I thought here we'd have a good, safe life.

Such a situation is characteristic of all of ours as we move through our daily affairs. A horizon of safety and social harmony supports our activities, and being victimized is not an actually existent reality facing us. If there is any thought of being victimized at all, it is rather of a quality of "I might be—anyone could be," or more likely, "I know it occurs but it won't happen to me," both consistent with the above-described meaning horizon, as our relaxed, easeful, confident posture testifies even while we ponder victimization. Victimization is thus at most an empty possibility with which we are not concerned in normal, routine daily life prior to its emergence.

The Emergence

Being victimized is the dawning of a new configuration of meaning, and it occurs in lived experience through a developmental process. Unannounced and unexpected, a theme emerges in the situation which progressively shatters the social meaning horizon (harmony) and the engagement it makes possible.

In the beginning of this process, the theme presents itself as strange, unfitting, unfamiliar, perhaps problematic or confusing—all on the ground of the above norm. There is simply a rift in the familiar typical texture of the situation. What makes this theme peculiar is that its opacity, indeterminacy asks to be interrogated, pursued. For instance, a subject sees some children leaving his yard and wants to find out what they were doing there. This is the first hint of the lived fragility of the person's preferred order, that it is not guaranteed even though it has been assumed to be. Thus, he engages in the new theme by focusing his attention on it, which brings the strange or unfamiliar close for the first time. The horizon of social harmony is not yet broken though it may be suspended momentarily. If anything like social detrimentality appears at this point, it does so in the mode of the uncertain, the possible. For example, the subject wonders, "Could those kids have broken something, stolen something, or are they just cutting through?" Through a process of perceptual questioning or suspicion, he realizes thematically another's breach of the taken-for-granted respect.

> (Purse snatch) When they grabbed me, I said "What's this, what's happening, what's going on? What are you kids doing?" Down I went. They didn't say a word. Haven't said a word.

The other's destruction of the subject's preferred order comes to show itself in the mode of actuality. This process can range from a split second, as in this instance, to months. In the next example it takes only a minute, in the following one a few days.

> (Burglary) As I entered the basement door I remembered the door was locked. There was something suspicious going on. I looked around and when I saw the upstairs door was wide open I knew there was a problem, but not what it was. Then I looked in the living room and saw the T.V. was gone, wires hanging disconnected. Then I knew what happened but to be honest I was befuddled. I couldn't believe it.

> (Prowling/Peeping) We found an old chair propped up against the window. I just thought kids dragged it there playing. Then a couple of days later we found a heavy block propped up against the window. Couldn't be kids. So we put a blind on the back window and then it was moved to the side window, and we found cigarettes near my daughter's window. Then I knew it was someone sick-minded, and you never know what a sick-minded person's gonna do.

Through this process of interrogation victimization becomes lived reality, yet as the disbelief expressed in subjects' reports indicates, it is still a relatively empty sort of quasi-reality; it has not entered into full articulation or determinancy at this moment of its birth. This is so because the person's previous world of meaning had been elaborated within the horizon or social harmony, and now that this is destroyed, he is delivered to a strange, unfamiliar, shocking, hardly believable new realm outside the usual norms of lived experience. In other words, just as the harmonious social horizon is conserved in the uncertainty of the original thematization of the situation of victimization ("the open door could be kids playing"), the uncertainty is conserved in the perception of actual detrimentality and destruction in terms of shock, disbelief, confusion ("I couldn't believe we'd been robbed").

> (Vandalism) My wife and I think I hear a noise outside. She got up to look and ran in, said "Your car's turned on its side." I said, "Nah, you've gotta be kidding." I went outside and there it was, laying on its side. I was surprised; I didn't believe it; I didn't know what to do. . . it's so *unusual* to see your car right on its side on my own property where I had a fence up, in my own driveway!
>
> (Purse snatch) All these years I been coming and going and nothing ever happened. Young kids should be in school. I just couldn't believe what they did. That's the truth.

Even when it is recognized as an actuality victimization does not make sense, is not completely understood, and is shot through with uncertainty (for example, "When did he come?", "What are they going to do with me?"). Victimization is originally surprising, alien, and unpredictable, for it is the very tearing away of the familiar world out of the subject's hands. So even when it is clear to the person that his preferred situation is being/has been destroyed by an other, the situation is a kind of void which only gradually gets filled with complete positive sense. He has been torn from his projects and swept up in another's which is contrary to his, thus emptying his world of its usual meaning.

The Configuration of and Struggle with Victimization

The structure of "criminal" victimization has three constituents, which take on their sense within the newly emergent horizon of social detrimentality: (1) the self's agency is lost and one stands helplessly vulnerable, isolated, and immobilized, (2) all helpful community has receded out of reach, and (3) a detrimental other has entered the subject's preferred situation in the mode of destruction.

Lost agency. The victim is immobilized and this new sense unfolds in a posture of passivity. This is necessarily so, since the world he usually acts in terms of has been pulled out from under his feet; immobility is lived bodily as spellblindness and intellectually as confusion. An impotent underdog, the victim is stripped of, or better yet alienated from his own agency in a situation whose purposes, values, and ends are defined by an other to whom he is utterly vulnerable.

> (Assault) As I got to the steps of my house I was grabbed from behind. I just collapsed. He dragged me down the steps to get me in his car and I tried to scream but nothing would come out.
>
> (Burglary) When I saw my house wrecked inside, so many of my things gone, I was dumbfounded. There was nothing I could do about it and I just didn't know what to do next.

Lost community. The helpful, peaceful, cooperative social supports have receded. Friendly others are at a distance, out of the victim's reach.

> (Purse snatch) I was helpless. I started to scream and holler. Ain't nobody hear me—nobody came. I hear dogs barking, that's all. I wanted help to get rid of them. Cars just passed by. Weren't a soul to help. I couldn't get nobody and I couldn't do nothing about it. The whole world was against me.

The detrimental other. In his continuing strangeness, the other is filled in as an unpredictable, crazy, irrational, insensitive, callous, unsympathetic predator—all invasions and eclipses of the person's well-being and participating in the destruction of the preferred situation.

> (Assault) He looked like an animal...a two-headed monster...crazy... like he enjoyed beating me up.
>
> (Burglary) A pathetic person...hardened...calloused...to come in and steal a little kid's piggy bank and their teddy bear. Their toys, that mean a great deal to them, so hurtful.

There is a lot of variation among subjects in terms of how "close to home," how completely, abidingly, and irreparably victimization takes place. Having one's sunglasses taken out of a coat pocket left in a public coat room, having one's house vandalized or burglarized, being subjected to outrageous bodily harm, and having one's family killed are quite different. These variations in the significance of the victimization can be understood as variations in the victimization's closeness to the subject's value priorities and its abidingness in time. With the sunglasses theft, one lives the process we have described above but in terms of something, that is, a part of the preferred order, which doesn't matter that much, isn't so close to the center of existence, and may be forgotten quickly. Victimization strikes one's *sphere of ownness*—we have called it one's preferred order. The question of variations in seriousness and significance is thus: how close to home did the crime strike; how essentially was one's own life affected? In all victimization, it is not indifferent matters which are involved but one's personal world, one's ownmost world, the center of which is oneself and intimately related others. Binswanger has called this region the *Eigenwelt*, often translated "self-world" but literally meaning own-world. Anything can take on this character, but it is its being *mine* which makes it a part of the *Eigenwelt*. When an other destroys something not mine which has nothing to do with me, I do not live through victimization, and this is one limit case for considerations of seriousness. What is the limit, of extreme victimization, in terms of its existential significance? This would seem to be homicide, my being murdered. In this case my *own* world is completely destroyed. Between these two limits we find possessions, home, family, and so on. Further research would be needed to understand these variations in seriousness or profundity of victimization existentially. It is possible that such variations would not be universal for all people, since in each individual case precisely one's *own* relative significances would be at issue. For one person, his wife's happiness might be more central in his *Eigenwelt* than even his own body. For another, his car might be more significant than his wife. Laws concerning the seriousness of crimes and the justice system's work in general are implicitly based on apprehensions of such significance however abstracted from and forgetful of these existential foundations they may be.

The struggle to overcome. In any case, this configuration is originally a simple given for the victim which he has neither prefigured nor chosen, one with gaps, vagueness, and indeterminancy. Thanks, however, to the fact that he is not totally victimized (in other words, dead), he is able to struggle to overcome it, although his triumph is limited precisely insofar as he is victimized. This overcoming first manifests itself in an attempt to articulately understand this confusing situation, which is a partial *recovery of agency*. Understanding is motivated on one hand by the original indeterminacy of the situation and on the other by the person's desire to reestablish himself as a subject (and thus surpass his being a mere object/prey for the other). Understanding overcomes shock and confusion and opens the way for mobility and more differentiated efforts of struggle.

In the midst of this extraordinary situation, the subject elaborates its meaning in a variety of lived experiences (for example, perception, recollection, anticipation). Since the purposes, intentions, and implications of an other are never totally transparent to perception, it is particularly in terms of *imagination* that the subject unfolds the various profiles, possibilities of victimization, and fills in this new realm. The familiar safety has faded away and the victim confronts what is ultimately a life-death situation in which his life is uncertain and very specifically threatened in the hands of the other.

> (Purse snatch) I thought they was gonna snatch my neck off. Anything. Broke my neck. Anything, they could have done.
>
> (Vandalism) I was thinking they would start something else, come back again. Throw rocks at my window and everything else.
>
> (Assault) It crossed my mind I'd be killed. If he got me in the car, chances are I'd never be seen again. They might rape you, or might let you go, or mess you up so bad there's no sense living. . . You imagine the worst at the time.

While this experience tears the victim away from his immediate past and previously projected future, which fade into insignificance, in the newly established context recollection highlights past victimization and anticipation discloses future possibilities of destruction.

> (Prowling/Peeping) I used to trust people but I had a bad thing happen to me—I was raped—and so when this happened, I kept thinking about it and that it could happen again, or to my daughters, and maybe this time I wouldn't be so lucky. I mean, I was beat and bruised, but you could be killed.

In immediate relation to the newly elaborated situation, whether expressed or not, there is a continued inner resistance or opposition on the subject's part. There is an upsurge of protest, rage, and perhaps a readiness for retaliation, counterviolation, or revenge. Indeed by its very definition the situation of victimization runs counter to the victim's preference. So on the basis of the sense made in understanding, the person attempts to get back on top of the situation, negate victimization in its own turn, and reestablish the preferred order. He may do so with regard to any of its three constituents, since by mutual implication overcoming one overturns the whole. A person may escape, run away, or see a weapon and fight the other. He may attempt to bring close helpful others by screaming. All of these behaviors also imply an overturning of the structure of victimization. The example of a woman who tries to offer the other her money instead when she fears rape shows how these efforts at avoiding or overcoming victimization are enacted in light of the increasingly articulate understanding and seek a relatively preferred situation in the face of victimization as understood.

> (Prowling/Peeping) As soon as we realized what was going on, we put a blind up so he couldn't see. We were also afraid he'd come in at night so we put screws in the back window so it couldn't be opened. Then we took the chair he stood on and broke it up for firewood.
>
> (Assault) I wanted to kill the guy right there and then after he attacked me. I didn't think he should get away with something like that. I mean, if people start beating each other up, what would this world be like?

Thus in the immediate situation, the subject manifests an intention to destroy the victimization in its own turn. He is angry, resents the victimizer, and longs for lost community.

After

The "after" of victimization is the situation in which the original incident is lived *as past*. The detrimental other has withdrawn (out of his own choice, the subject's active efforts, or help from others), helpful others have surrounded the subject again. Freedom and agency have been returned. However, this overcoming or making past of victimization is only relative. In many cases, the detrimental other is still "on the loose, out there and dangerous," and even if he is already caught, "there may be others." The ex-victim still feels helpless, betrayed by his community. And a sense of impotence still pervades his agency. Thus the subject does not simply return to the pre-victimization order, but continues to live through victimization, which means that there is still *work to be done* if his preferred order is to be restored. The reliving and overcoming of victimization in the world beyond the original incident constitutes the bipolar psychological order of the situation after victimization. What is the relation of these two poles? Victimization has the status of a given in the face of which overcoming is a projected achievement. Just as the "before" is conserved and surpassed in the emergence of victimization, so is victimization conserved or surpassed in the "after." Thus these two poles are far from separate; these two moments of the "after" are organized in the form of the latter struggling against the former. We will first look at the reliving or continued living of victimization—the first pole—and then look at the surpassing of it—the second pole—even though the two are mutually implicit and simultaneous as we shall see.

Reliving victimization. We find it a fascinating fact that victimization is lived far beyond the confines of the original situation of victimization, both in time and space. This is not too surprising when it involves, for instance, remembering the event and anticipating the return of the particular detrimental other of the original incident, for it is precisely his meaning to be potentially destructive, unpredictable, surprising, out of control, and so on, which means he may strike again and the ex-victim is not yet safe. However, when we speak of reliving, we mean far more than this. All three constituents of victimization are lived through the full spectrum of species of experience (perception, anticipation, recollection, dreams, thoughts) and with regard to a multitude of objects and situations other than those involved in the original incident. We might say that the victim is now attuned to all the meanings of victimization. The key to understanding this is recognizing the fact that the horizon of safety and social harmony constitutive of the previous order has been destroyed, and the world is thus not given in the same way. Now, through time, a pervasive new horizon of experience, namely that of victimization, is existentialized throughout profiles of the world. The world allows this to occur, for the social order has an inherent ambiguity which not only allows but requires assumptions and horizons of interpretation. People as such are unpredictable, out of my control, have intentions which are hidden from me. Since this horizon of victimization is ultimately one which bears on the person's life and death, his well-being, its relevance cannot be ignored. So to the extent that the person had been victimized, his world undergoes a global modification in the direction of victimization, its extensiveness depending upon how completely, how abidingly, how irreparably, and how close to home the person was originally victimized.

> (Assault) For a long time I thought it would ruin everything...my job...my marriage...my daughter...it really did mess me up for a long time.
>
> (Assault) Just a miserable feeling. Something you have hanging on you. You say, "Oh boy, I wish I knew who you were" to every stranger. Always looking at everybody, you think "I don't know, maybe he's one of them." Maybe he was. Makes me suspicious of everybody.
>
> (Burglary) I didn't feel safe—I was really frightened for 6 or 7 months. Before, we heard of robberies but it was like "it doesn't happen to me." After it happened it was constant worry and constant fear.
>
> (Burglary) Some kids are scared of the dark. Our kids are scared of burglars now. They'll see someone who looks gruff and say, "Is he bad, is he a burglar?"

Each subject enters the victimization totality in the larger world through the meanings of victimization which arose specifically in his original situation. What determines whether this or that person, this or that event after victimization will reenliven the victimization totality? This happens by virtue of a lived identity of meaning with the past event. One subject couldn't stand being touched by her husband; the thought of him made her sick. Her husband, as she saw it, was "the hard type," "didn't appreciate her." These meanings identified him with the criminal. A woman who was beaten up by teenagers is afraid (and suspicious) of teenagers, dark alleys, walking alone at night, and so on. Someone who thinks the thieves must have known what was in the house suspects his neighbors and is afraid of being robbed again. Any constituent of meaning in the larger world which is identical to one in the original victimization can evoke the totality, such as a sudden sound, strangers, being left alone, others' insensitivity.

Looking at the vastly varied and mushrooming experience of victimization lived after the crime, we see that it amounts to the branching elaboration of the three meaning constituents of victimization: (1) loss of agency, (2) the absence of helpful, supportive community, and (3) another destructive of the subject's preferred order. These meanings are elaborated in the full spectrum of lived experiences (perception, imagination, recollection, anticipation, dreaming, even philosophizing) and with regard to a great variety of objects and situations (for examples strangers at work, a lonely street at night, interactions with the police, being in court, at home alone).

In the following we see the *loss of agency*—confusion, vulnerability, immobility, helplessness highlighted (with the other two constituents implicitly co-present) in a variety of types of experience of different situations.

> (Assault) I was sick after it. I was in bed for a week. A knock on my door, and I was terrified. I couldn't do anything—watch my daughter, go to work, anything. I never go outside anymore.
>
> (Vandalism) For a period of about 6 months, I stopped fixing my place up—I couldn't go on if it would just be vandalized again. I thought if it kept up I'd leave—I didn't know what to do.
>
> (Assault) My knee, my whole leg swelled up and I couldn't walk. You just hurt and don't understand. No reason. You think but no reason. All of a sudden this happened. Nothing.
>
> (Purse snatch) I kept dreaming I was alone on a dark street with someone approaching. I'd try to run away but my legs wouldn't move. He just kept coming, I was helpless.
>
> (Burglary) You know I started thinking a lot—man is a very vulnerable, helpless creature.

In the following we see the *helpful, supportive community receded out of reach,* absent in the ex-victim's experience.

> (Assault) My dad came home and I wanted to kill the guy who beat me up. My parents acted like they didn't believe me. I felt isolated then cos the people up there didn't help me either and now I felt like my dad was deserting me too.
>
> (Assault) It was just another one to put in their files, but I don't think they did anything. They says, "Oh yeah, he sounds familiar," but if he's so familiar, attacking so many girls, why haven't they done something to stop him?
>
> (Purse snatch) I call the police and it was more than an hour before they got here. By the time they got here those kids could have been in New York.
>
> (Assault) The police said they'd be in touch with me and they never called. They didn't do nothing.
>
> (Burglary) I imagine if I was getting killed outside these neighbors wouldn't lift a finger to help.
>
> (Burglary) Our courts don't do anything to stop all this. The next thing you know, those kids will be right back out on the streets.

The following show the diversified elaboration of the *predatory other* who is detrimental to the ex-victim.

> (Burglary) What's to stop them from doing it again? The whole town knows what I keep in my truck from the newspaper report!
>
> (Assault) I waitressed on New Year's Eve and I seen a guy I could have sworn it was him. I went to pieces. Couldn't work anymore. But then everybody I seen looked like him. I'm suspicious of everybody.
>
> (Burglary) The insurance company robbed me again. We lost $5,000 worth of stuff and they only paid $2,100. Hell, I got robbed twice!
>
> (Purse snatch) I won't go out at night any more because I'm afraid of getting robbed again, or maybe something worse.
>
> (Assault) You know, it's a dog-eat-dog world. People can be pretty mean.

Many things which were unnoticed or taken for granted (such as the neighbor's transience or indifference, strange men, the night) now evoke vulnerability and fear. In light of the new horizon of social detrimentality, the ex-victim's new attunement, the world takes on new meanings. Subjects who continue to relive the victimization totality as their world, each constituent of which implies the devastating whole, sense a complete destruction of their lives impending. Several expressed this as going crazy.

> (Assault) If you don't stop worrying about it you might go crazy from it. Sometimes I think about it. If I'm by myself—you keep it on your mind, keep wondering, get afraid to come down on the street. You just might see anybody, anybody get close to you, you'd be scared, ready to try and hit them or hurt them cos you think they're gonna hurt you. Go crazy. You sure would—cos you'd never know when something's gonna happen, whether people will leave you alone or not.

Every idea secretes an ontology (Merleau-Ponty), and the experiences of victimization lead to a crazy, unpredictable world where others have no care for one's life and constantly stand as threats to it. Some repeated victims, seeing no other way out, have committed suicide, indeed a desperate way finally to take one's life back into one's own hands. The reliving of victimization, whether by further criminal victimization or by everyday situations having identical meaning, amounts to a spreading deterioration of the necessary social supports for the person's life. Now in a more global way, he longs for restored harmony with others that can provide the horizon for a good life.

> (Assault) I just wish everybody would be cool, not, you know, killing one another. Not rob things. The way it used to be. So you don't have to worry about walking down the streets.

Surpassing victimization. Now we return to the process by which the subject surpasses victimization, which occurs simultaneously and in precise relation to the living through and elaboration of victimization in the larger world. It amounts to a reversal of the latter's meanings. Victimization motivates the person to surpass its meanings by virtue of their not being preferred. Every victim's task is to reestablish the world as he prefers it for himself. This involves, for instance, arising out of immobilization and seizing his own agency, out of isolation and into harmonious relations with other, out of danger and into safety. Begun in the original situation, this movement shows ever-greater articulation in relation to the profiles of victimization as they are diversely elaborated afterwards in the world at large. Since the whole world may be transformed by victimization as we have seen, surpassing these meanings may take time, for this surpassing's field of operation is as wide and diversified as the elaboration of victimization. In this process the person takes responsibility for victimization. This process involves three interrelated aspects: active efforts, the world's assertion of predictable safeness, and the other's active helpfulness. Through this process victimization appears as avoidable, preventable, in a word overcomable.

Active efforts. Reliving victimization throughout the world *makes sense.* In an important way, the reliving is already a process of sense-making which, as an achievement of understanding, already overcomes the opacity, indeterminacy, and confusion of victimization. It is an appropriation of new territory. Sense-making (a process which involves triumph of the person's free subjectivity over his previous objectness for the other) dispels the shock, disbelief and confusion, the uncanny irrationality of victimization, bestowing on it increasingly positive features. By thinking about how the misfortune happened, anticipating further occurrences, and so on, the subject moves from being alienated in a strange land to familiar territory which once specificable, becomes handlable in terms of his *own* values and purposes. For instance, after figuring out how the burglar got in, the ex-victim can prevent it. This changes the meaning of the victimization, namely making it something surpassable.

> (Assault) Certain guys where I waitress give you that funny look—we don't wear uniforms that cover too much. Guys look all night and after that maybe some will go to any extent to get it. I realized I was opening myself to it so I talked to the boss and we're not going to wear those uniforms any more.

Sometimes sense-making allows a rather striking transformation in the person such as from fright to a sympathetic posture.

> (Burglary) After all, these are kids who don't want to go to school. I feel sorry for the kids involved. They have a whole life ahead of them and it's a pity if they can't get straightened out.

Following from sense-making, the subject may deliberately avoid situations which carry the indices of (an identity of meaning with) victimization, and he thereby achieves security, safeness, and belonging. Some subjects no longer go out at night. Others move to a new community. Beyond avoidance, an ex-victim may seek or prepare himself for revenge or prosecution, which means destroying the criminal in his own turn.

> (Prowling/Peeping) I brought a gun and I'm gonna have no sympathy for him because he's got none for me. I'm gonna shoot and if I do I don't intend for him to come back. I never want this thing worrying me again.

> (Burglary) I caught a guy who gave me a bad check. I don't care how many people he hosed off. "Guy, you ain't gonna make a living off me. I'm gonna get my money," and I did.

The ex-victim may also take peaceful actions, perhaps educational, with regard to the victimizer, in order to change his victimizing characteristics.

> (Burglary) I stopped in front of his car one day. I told him he had a "pretty nice tape player in there too, don't you? How would you like yours ripped

off?" He parked his car in his own driveway from then on. They're scared of me—they got the message.

(Burglary) I told the one I suspected "I hate to see a kid your age go to jail—if there's anything else missing, you'll go." I hope I put a scare into them so he won't do that again, or something worse. If parents talked to their kids, these things wouldn't happen.

He may also take precautions which insure him against further violations and may habitualize them, thus attempting to prevent the meanings of victimization as he has elaborated it in experience, for example, not leaving the kids home alone, parking the car in the garage, locking the doors, getting an alarm system. The person often acquires possessions which are symbols of his domination over the other, like ferocious dogs and spotlights (that is, his bit, his gaze).

(Assault) I'm a lot more careful now. My husband meets me in the parking lot every night and I pity anyone who tries anything. And I carry mace on me now. I don't put any identification in my purse anymore.

(Burglary) If we didn't know who's at the door and we're not in the mood for company, we used to play dead. Now we answer the door and look out of the peep hole first so nobody will get in when we're there.

(Burglary) Our kids won't go to sleep till all their bikes are locked in the cellar.

Finally, the ex-victim may deliberately seek help from others, which overcomes the isolation and helplessness of victimization.

(Burglary) We don't go anywhere without telling the neighbors to keep an eye out. And they'll call the police if anything looks suspicious. It gives us a greater sense of belonging.

It is in the area of deliberate efforts that there may take place extended responsibility and growth of self by owning up to how the subject's particular lifestyle or negligence contributed to or left him vulnerable to victimization.

(Burglary) Old people look out the window a lot and now I know why. If I'd kept an eye out, it wouldn't have happened. Now I realize people who do are not being nibby, they're protecting their community. Well, we learn by our mistakes.

(Assault) Now I don't flirt with guys or talk to strangers, cos in a way that's askin' for it.

Reassertion of safety. Vis-à-vis the subject's repeated anticipation and imagination of various possibilities of crime, the world repeatedly reasserts a sociality which helps further his life, and this occurs with no deliberation or active effort on his part. The open door turns out not to be left by more robbers but by kids playing. After all, those kids across the street start laughing, seem friendly, and disperse rather than vandalizing the house. The car has been left out and not broken into for months. Thus the anticipations of the victim's totality are frustrated and undermined in the face of an abidingly safe world which is gradually integrated in lived experience and comes to reconstitute the horizon of social harmony. This gift, welcomed and longed for but which the subject has no control over, manifests rationality, order, familiarity, certainty, predictability with regard to others' respect and cooperation. These aspects of the world allow the victim to rest easy and proceed with his life unobstructed. This constituent of overcoming victimization is rarely mentioned by subjects but however subtle or unnoticed, we can see from the psycho-logic of the experience that it is an essential part of recovery from victimization. Perhaps it is the fact that this constituent goes to reconstitute a horizon of safeness that gets taken for granted which makes it only rarely hinted at by subjects.

> (Vandalism) Well, it was about 4, 6, or 8 months that nobody bothered me there, so I started comin' around again, fixing the place up.

Certainly, the absence of this aspect of recovery betrays its necessity.

> (Prowling/Peeping) If it would go for a month without the prowler coming back again I might be able to say "Oh well, it's over." But it keeps happening, so I can't forget it. It's on my mind all the time.

Others' help. Others' active help restores a sense of trust and harmony in the ex-victim's destroyed sociality. This particularly overcomes the constituent meanings of both "helpful others having receded out of reach into indifference" and "the specifically detrimental other." In dialog with helpful others, the person overcomes his isolation, mistrust, anger, resentment, and bitterness and resumes life in good community. The police may participate directly in this aspect of recovery.

> (Burglary) I think it's good that the police are involved so that they can let kids know what possibly could happen to them in the future.
>
> (Burglary) The police came to school and taught our kids how to steer clear of strangers without scaring them.
>
> Burglary) When the police got our stuff back, I was so grateful and surprised. There's some justice in the world after all.

Here "help" involves *sharing values* with the subject and actively trying to establish (rather than destroy or remain indifferent toward) the situation as the subject prefers it. This is especially important in areas which are problems for the ex-victim or which he cannot handle himself. The justice system may also participate in this.

> (Burglary) We were quite pleased when the probation officers saw things as we did—family problems, lack of parental interest, etc. You think the kids are going to be let off but the judge was very thorough. It helped us realize that the authorities' hands are not completely tied. And they cared about the kids. They're getting them therapy. That's a good sign—it's not always like you read—letting criminals off. There's some good people working in the system and that gives me faith.

Notice here that this subject believes in rehabilitation and her faith is restored because the justice system helped carry out her values. Another person might see rehabilitation as worthless, perceive the justice system as in conspiracy with the criminal, and feel further victimized by the system rather than helped to restore a good order. The surrounding community can also play an important part in this aspect of recovery.

> (Burglary) Now, I doubt that anyone could break in and get away with it cos everybody here watches out for everybody else. It's very secure. Our little girl wandered up the street where she's not allowed and a friend of ours saw her, stopped his car and told her to come home. Meanwhile a neighbor called the police. It makes us feel good. People aren't afraid to get involved. They care about each other.
>
> (Assault) We've become a lot closer with our neighbors. We formed a civic club to talk about the crime problem and it's brought us closer together. The neighborhood's safer.
>
> (Vandalism) The insurance company was real nice. Told me to go ahead and fix the car—they'd pay. I didn't know what to do so that helped a lot.

What is crucial is the establishment of close, caring relationships vis-à-vis what is precious and had become precarious. The family plays a key role.

> (Assault) My husband helped a lot. If I had to go through it alone, I wouldn't have made it, cos it helps to cry like a baby and you need the comfort, the arms, the affection. My husband used to be the hard type, but he really turned it soft, like "Don't worry, I'm here." You need somebody to help you through it, somebody to talk to.

In this aspect of recovery, the person's preferences, agency, and moreover life are respected, harmoniously affirmed, even nourished by others, which is the exact opposite of victimization. Others may even sacrifice themselves, go "out of their way" to help, that is, change for the subject's benefit, whereas in victimization his life is sacrificed, changed for the other.

All three aspects of recovery are mutually implicit and thus foster each other. For example, the world's reassertion of safety allows enhanced assumption of agency. In fact, in a given situation, all three aspects of recovery may be mutually intertwined. Take talking, for example. In sympathetic dialog the subject is actively involved, makes a familiar, predictable sense, and the other allows reciprocity and respects his existence in a way that deepens trust. Talking overcomes fear and alienation as it is situated after victimization. Speech heals broken community. Perhaps in light of this we may understand the unusual willingness of contacted victims to participate in our interviews. In their longing for recovery, some even expected someone to come, one subject exclaiming, "And you're the first one to come and talk about this. . . thank you."

Overcoming victimization is an exact reversal of its meanings, a reversal that cannot be taken for granted as to the fact of its occurrence or the character of its occurrence. If the social world doesn't change but continues to be detrimental, or if the subject does nothing about his misfortune, or if others remain indifferent and unavailable, victimization deepens. The world and others, whose being and precise character are not up to the ex-victim alone, are equal partners in his overcoming and forming a newly constituted world. Insofar as the overcoming process is fulfilled in all its aspects, there is a mysterious reconstitution of the taken-for-granted horizon of social harmony, which allows the person to proceed, undistracted and healed, into a future of his own preference. The process of surpassing is always the surpassing of victimization in terms of its unique concreteness. For instance, it involved a near-rape victim's avoiding strange men, wearing longer dresses, being taken care of and protected by her husband. For a burglarly victim, it involved locking the house better, getting neighbors on the lookout, and other measures. As one overcomes the past victimization as well as those other possibilities of victimization one has attuned himself to and elaborated upon, the strange and unexpected detrimentality of others withdraws to a distance and the person feels relieved and at home in the new horizon of social harmony, which silently lets him live again.

A New Order

If victimization testifies to the fragility of the social order, the situation after it has been surpassed asserts its *plasticity*. We find that what has occurred may be nothing less than a psychological transformation which sometimes involves the person's whole existence. This transformation includes the meanings of victimization as they were previously experienced, but precisely in a state of being surpassed. In other words, the new order both conserves and surpasses victimization and does so concretely in several ways.

The original victimization is present for the subject only when spoken about or when something with a similar meaning reminds him of it (like a news shows on crime).

> (Assault) I forgot about it until yesterday when the police called and started talking about it.

In this way the event is conserved in terms of its always being available to memory. Yet is is surpassed in the sense that it is not in the present; it is remembered *as past*, that is, without experiencing the living totality of victimization in the present face-to-face reality. It may be recollected with a sigh of relief, which means it's over. This, however, is relatively superficial when compared to the transformations involving victimization's *implicit* presence in the presentations of the world and in the subject's behavior.

As for the *presentations of the world*, a whole new unexpected realm, whose genesis we have described, has now been brought close, interrogated, made sense of—in short made a part of the person's world. Crime has become familiar. The sense made it sedimented.

> (Burglary) I read the paper, every week it comes out I read all about things that have been ripped off and see how close they are. I'm just hoping I ain't one of the next victims, that's all.
>
> (Assault) This whole thing is so stupid. Just everything. Like the way things are out there. I just think the whole world is stupid. I wish everybody could just be cool.

As a process which builds new relations with the emergent profiles and virtualities of crime, the way the subject behaviorally recovers and maintains safety constitutes a *new and abiding style of life* which, as preventing victimization, implies it in its very surpassing of it.

> (Burglary) If they would have apologized it would be different. I used to be nice but the way I feel now is I don't need the neighbor kids. I don't want to be bothered. When they come around I tell them "out." I just want them to stay away from my home and what I own and that's it; I'll keep them out.
>
> (Assault) I decided to never cut through other people's properties again. Ever since I got beat up, I don't look for trouble like I used to. I try to be friends with everybody. I want to have people on my side, not against me.
>
> (Assault) From then on I said the only way I'd respect a grown-up is if they respected me in return.

Other behaviors imply victimization in terms of their taking precautions against it. The subject manifest *new habits* which reinforce the fortress of his ownness, his preferred order.

> (Burglary) I mark all my stuff now.
>
> (Burglary) Every time I park my car I have a lock on my CB radio and I lock my car when it's sittin' in the driveway, even during the day. I take my radio out of my car and lock it up, where I never used to.
>
> (Prowling/Peeping) I look out the window a lot—just to see what's happening in the neighborhood.

Other such manifestations of a new order are the person's unthinking, *habitualized avoidance* of certain areas or kinds of people and *newly lived restrictions.*

> (Assault) Now I never walk the streets slow at night or answer the security doors in our apartment.
>
> (Burglary) You asked me if it's dissipated from my life. The more I think about it as I'm sittin' here the answer is "no." Cos I still haven't replaced my stereo system and I'll never get another oriental rug, 'cause I'm afraid somebody's gonna steal them.

Things are also acquired which perform the function of preventive behaviors. They become taken for granted maintenance of one's preferred order.

> (Vandalism) Now I've got a dog who barks loud whenever anyone comes near the house, and when he barks I get up and turn on the flood lights I had installed.

Another manifestation of transformation in the new order is that the new social relations which form through the struggle with victimization become integrated into the person's ongoing life, be they for better or worse.

> (Assault) My feelings about the police will always stay with me. They always will. It seems like they're more or less after beer drinkers and dope smokers than they are about the robbers and rapists.
>
> (Robbery) We moved out of that bad neighborhood and now we have people who care around us. One lady walks her dog and makes sure everything looks straight. We're closer to our neighbors now and I doubt anybody could get away with anything here.
>
> (Assault) I feel much more secure. I never thought my husband would be willing to pick me up at work or wait in the parking lot for me when I come home, but now he does. We've become closer.

In the new order, some subjects become more independent, strong, and responsible. Others become more dependent upon others. All these new relations precisely express the person's particular way of surpassing or not surpassing the individual victimization. In any case, new behaviors become sedimented and taken for granted as "really me" (for example, now I'm shy, I wear long skirts and don't flirt with strange men) and the new presentations of the world become the one and only lived reality ("Kids have no respect and now they're taking over"; "The police don't do anything about it but the courts do"). This newly emergent order is preferred over the victim-world as it was originally lived and elaborated, but not preferred without reservation over the pre-victimization order.

> (Assault) My husband is much more concerned about me. I guess he more or less took me for granted before. Now he appreciates me more and that's one good thing that came out of it. But I don't think I'd want to go through it just for that. Just to have your husband care.
>
> (Burglary) We've replaced all the kids' toys but it's still not the same. I don't even know if it was a good idea, 'cause even now they look at the teddy bear and say, "That's the one we got 'cause we were robbed." We try not to emphasize it. But these things happen and it's a sad lesson you have to learn.

Thus the new behavior (like moving to a new neighborhood, locking doors, and so on) is taken as a *necessity* in view of the emergent profiles of the world ("transient communities are dangerous," "people will rip your car off") being *reality.* In looking at how these necessities and realities get established, we have seen that the process is variable and they they are the outcome of a particular dialectic between the subject's personal choice and the social situations as lived in each individual case.

In the new order insofar as surpassing is complete, victimization is largely hidden by the recovery despite its significant psychological presence. That is, the person who surpasses victimization need no longer be aware of it. It is banished from actuality to virtuality. There is an interesting ambiguity concerning the presence and absence of victimization. In one sense it has been put at a distance and made past. It is no longer expected. However, the very behaviors which accomplish this attest to, are present to, the possibility of victimization (such as locking the car, not letting children wander from home, wearing long skirts). These behaviors have the meaning of securing a certain nonvictimized existence which they intend. In view of this we can see how, despite the fact that they imply the pervasive presence of victimization in the world, the person returns existentially to the belief that victimization won't happen to him.

> (Burglary) And you still feel it can't happen to you. Even though it happened to us and we know the statistics and it could happen again, I still think, "Oh, no, it won't ever happen to us."

Each person's way of surpassing secures him so that he does not live through the unpreferred meanings of victimization and can instead return to the undaunted establishment of his own life projects. Victimization is no longer a predominant actual horizon of existence. The belief that it won't happen again testifies to the reestablished horizon of a safe harmonious social order, one which has integrated and handled the phenomenon of victimization. Even the person who asserts, "Now I *do* expect to be victimized," demonstrates the curious ambiguity of victimization's presence and absence in the new order. He refers verbally to victimization (and does so because it has become established as a reality), but he lives as if social affirmation instead were assured, as his relaxed, self-assertive posture shows (for example, as he leaves for vacation, trusting the new burglar-proofing of his home). This existential recession of victimization must occur if the victim is to return to his own life in an undistracted way. Words like implicit, overcome, receded, distant, and hidden begin to point to the character of victimization in the new order.

A Closing Note

Although we have finished our detailed account of method, we would like to mention briefly that the researcher's work is not over with the General Psychological Structure. Indeed there remains a crucial final phase of the research which involves relating the specialized psychological findings to the life-world at large. This last moment of research involves a new kind of thinking whose results are the explicitation of the research as a gift to the life-world. Actually, this has been implicit all along; for instance, the researcher picks a topic which has relevance to everyday human life. Throughout the analyses the implications of the results exert a powerful attraction as a horizon of the work. After the analyses are complete, the researcher must go beyond mere anticipations of these implications and must contextualize his results in this larger arena. Usually it is in the "discussion" section that the meaning and value of the research for concrete personhood and culture are elaborated.

In our study, for instance, we might think through such diverse issues as: What does an increasing crime rate mean for a culture? How do our results bear on the meaning and role of the police and justice system? Do the results have any public policy implications? What practical implications for the "treatment" of victims in crisis centers can we draw? How do our results relate to the studies we cited in victimology and social psychology? What unanswered questions remain and how can they be addressed through further research? In this way the researcher shares the fruits of research with culture at large.

References

Anttila, I. (1974-1975). Victimology, a new territory in criminology. In I. Drapkin & E. Viano (Eds.), *Victimology; A new focus* (vol. 1). Lexington, MA: Lexington.

Arvison, N. H. (1974-1975). Victims of homocide. In I. Drapkin & E. Viano (Eds.), *Victimology: A new focus* (vol. 4). Lexington, MA: Lexington.

Biderman, A. D. (1974-1975). Victimology and victimization surveys. I. Drapkin & E. Viano (Eds.), *Victimology: A new focus* vol. 3). Lexington, MA: Lexington.

Blazicek, D. L. (1976). A social psychological inquiry into effects of criminal victimization by robbery on cognitive dimensionality. *Dissertation abstracts international, 37,* 3932.

Boss, M. (1973) *Psychoanalysis and daseinsanalysis.* New York: Basic.

Burgess, A.W., & Holstrom, L.L. (1974-1975). Rape: The victim and the criminal justice system. In I. Drapkin & E. Viano (Eds.), *Victimology: A new focus* (vol. 3). Lexington, MA: Lexington.

———. (1974). *Rape: Victims of crisis.*

Carrington, E. G. (1975). *The victims.* New York: Arlington House.

Cohn, Y. (1974-1975). Crisis intervention and the victims of robbery. I. Drapkin & E. Viano (Eds.), *Victimology: A new focus* (vol. 2). Lexington, MA: Lexington.

Colaizzi, P. F. (1973). *Reflection and research in psychology.* Dubuque, IA: Kendall/Hunt.

Curtis, L. A. (1974). *Criminal violence.* Lexington, MA: Lexington.

Drapkin, I., & Viano, E. (Eds.). (1974). *Victimology.* Lexington, MA: Lexington.

———. (1974-1975). *Victimology: A new focus* Lexington, MA: Lexington.

Ennis, P. H. (1967). *Criminal victimization in the U.S.* President's commission on law enforcement and administration of justice. Washington, D.C.

Fischer, C. T. & Wertz, F. J. (1979). An empirical phenomenological study of being criminally victimized. In A. Giorgi, R. Knowles, D. Smith, (Eds.), *Duquesne studies in phenomenological psychology* (vol. 3). Pittsburgh, PA: Duquesne University Press.

Giorgi, A. (1970). *Psychology as a human science.* New York: Harper & Row.

———. (1971a). Phenomenology and experimental psychology I. In A. Giorgi, W. Fischer, R. Von Eckartsberg, (Eds.), *Duquesne studies in phenomenological psychology* (vol. 1), Pittsburgh: Duquesne University Press.

———. (1971b). Phenomenology and experimental psychology II. In A. Giorgi, W. Fischer, & R. Von Eckartsberg, (Eds.), *Duquesne studies in phenomenological psychology* (vol. 1). Pittsburgh, PA: Duquesne University Press.

———. (1975b). An application of phenomenological method in psychology. In *Duquesne studies in phenomenological psychology* (vol. 2). Pittsburgh, PA: Duquesne University Press.

Goppinger, H. (1979-1975). Criminal and victimal. In I. Drapkin and E. Viano (Eds.), Victimology: A new focus (vol. 1). Lexington, MA: Lexington.

Griffin, B. Q., & Rogers, R. W. (1977). Reducing interracial aggression: Inhibiting effects of victim's suffering and power to retaliate. *Journal of Psychology, 95,* 152–157.

Horowitz, M., & Amir, M. (1974-1975). The probation officer, the offender, and the victim of the criminal offense. In I. Drapkin and E. Viano (Eds.), Victimology: A new focus (vol. 3). Lexington, MA: Lexington.

Husserl, E. (1977). *Phenomenological psychology.* The Hague: Nijhoff.

———. (1970). *The crisis of European sciences and transcendental phenomenology.* Evanston, IL: Northwestern University Press.

Kanekar, S. & Kolsawalla, M. B. (1977). The nobility of non-violence: Person perception as a function of retaliation to agression. *Journal of social psychology.*

Kerr, N. L., & Kurtz, S. T. (1977). Effects of victim's suffering and respectability on our mock juror judgments. *Representative research in social psychology.*

Lyons, J. (1963). *Psychology and the measure of man.* London: Free Press.

MacDonald, J. M. (1975). *Armed robbery offenders and their victims.* Springfield, IL: Thomas.

MacDonald G. W. (1977). Innocent victim, deserved victim, and martyr: observer's reaction. *Psychological Reports, 41*(2), 511–514.

MacNamara, D. E. J., & Sullivan, J. J. (1973). Making the victim whole: composition, rehabilitation, and compensation. *The Urban Review, 6,*(3).

Maish, H., & Schuler-Springorum, H. (1974-1975). Procedural Victimology and its contribution to victimological knowledge. In I. Drapkin and E. Viano (Eds.), Victimology: A new focus (vol. 3). Lexington, MA: Lexington.

Mendelsohn, B. (1974-1975). Victimology and the technical and social sciences: A call for the establishment of victim clinics. In I. Drapkin and E. Viano (Eds.), Victimology: A new focus (vol. 1). Lexington, MA: Lexington.

Nkpa, N. K. U. (1974-1975). Victims of crime in the Igbo section of Nigeria. In I. Drapkin & E. Viano (Eds.), Victimology: A new focus (vol. 5). Lexington, MA: Lexington.

Roy, K. K. (1974-1975). The feelings and attitudes of the raped women of Bangladesh toward the military personal of Pakistan. In I. Drapkin and E. Viano (Eds.), Victimology: A new focus (vol. 5). Lexington, MA: Lexington.

Sartre, J. P. (1948). *The Emotions.* New York: Citadel.

Schafer, S. (1968). *The victim and his criminal.* Reston, VA: Reston.

Separovic, Z. P. (1974-1975). Victimology: A new approach in the social sciences. In I. Drapkin and E. Fiano (Eds.), Victimology: A new focus (vol. 1). Lexington, MA: Lexington.

Silverman, R. A. (1974-1975). Victim precipitation: An examination of the concept. In I. Drapkin and E. Fiano (Eds.),Victimology: A new focus (vol. 1). Lexington, MA: Lexington.

Skolnick, P. (1977). Helping as a function of time of day, location, and sex of victim. *Journal of social psychology. 102*(1), 61–62.

Soloman, H. & Herman, L. (1977). Status symbols and pro-social behavior: The effect of the victim's car on helping. *Journal of psychology, 97*(2), 271-273.

Straus, E. (1966). *Phenomenological psychology*. New York: Basic Books.

Symonds, M. (1975). Victims of violence: Psychological effects and after effects. *American journal of psychoanalysis*. 75.

Thornberry, T. P., & Figlio, R. M. (1972). Victimization and criminal behavior in a birth cohort. In T. P. Thornberry & Sagarin (Eds.), *Images of crime*.

Van Kaam, A. (1959). Phenomenal analysis: Exemplified in a study of the experience of "really feeling understood." *Journal individual psychology, 15*, 66–72.

Von Eckartsberg, R. (1975). Ecopsychology of motivational theory and research. *Duquesne studies in phenomenological psychology* (vol. 2). Pittsburgh, PA: Duquesne University Press.

———. (1979). *Methods in existential-phenomenological psychology*. Unpublished manuscript, Pittsburgh, PA.

Von Hentig, H. (1948). *The criminal and his victim: Studies in the sociology of crime*. New Haven, CT: Yale University Press.

———. Remarks on the interaction of the perpetrator and victim. *Journal of American Institute of Criminal Law and Criminology*.

Wertz, F. J., (1983). From "everyday" to psychological description: An analysis of the moments of a qualitative data analysis. *Journal of phenomenological psychology, 14*(2).

About the Contributors

CHRISTOPHER M. AANSTOOS received his Ph.D. from Duquesne University. After having previously taught at the Pennsylvania State University at McKeesport, he is currently an assistant professor of psychology on the graduate faculty at West Georgia College. His research interests and publications are in the areas of cognition (especially thinking), and the historical, theoretical, and methodological foundations of psychology. Currently he is preparing a book contrasting the phenomenological and cognitivist approaches to thought.

Address: Psychology Department, West Georgia College, Carrollton, Georgia 30118.

WILLIAM F. FISCHER received his B.A. degree in psychology from the University of Michigan in 1956 and his M.A. and Ph.D. degrees in clinical-child psychology from the University of Connecticut in 1958 and 1961 respectively. In 1965 he joined the faculty at Duquesne as an associate professor of psychology and was promoted to full professor in 1970. Most recently, Fischer has been engaged in research on psychoanalytic theory as revised by Jacques Lacan, in particular Lacan's work on schizophrenia as interpreted by De Waelhens.

Address: Psychology Department, Duquesne University, Pittsburgh, Pennsylvania 15282

AMEDEO P. GIORGI received his Ph.D. from Fordham University. He is currently professor of psychology at Duquesne University and a founder and editor of the *Journal of Phenomenological Psychology.* He is author of *Psychology As A Human Science.*

Address: Psychology Department, Duquesne University, Pittsburgh, Pennsylvania 15282

FREDERICK J. WERTZ received his undergraduate degree from Beloit College and M.A. and his Ph.D. (1981) from Duquesne University. He worked in the Counseling Center and taught psychology at Carnegie-Mellon University. In 1976 he was the associate project director for the research grant "Being Criminally Victimized", funded by the NEH. He is currently teaching at Iona College. Central among his interests are the foundations of psychological science and phenomenological research methods in psychology.

Address: 1105 First Avenue, Apt. 2, New York City, New York 10021.